PRAISE FOR THE BOOK

'*The Winning Culture* encapsulates the lived experience and life lessons of a serving officer in the line of fire – real fire. I wish I had his life and I wish I had written this book. Deep wisdom, presented through outstanding narrative. A great book on leadership and institution-building in a wrapper called culture'
Subroto Bagchi, author, entrepreneur, public servant and co-founder of Mindtree

'Insightful learnings from the Indian Army on how to build a success-driving corporate culture. These takeaways are extremely relevant in the current VUCA environment which is fraught with uncertainties and risks for corporates and their traditional cultural paradigms. An excellent read!'
Rajeev Bakshi, former Chairman of Pepsico India, Cadbury India and Managing Director of Metro Cash & Carry

'General Bali has an expert grasp of organizational culture and the fundamentals of leadership. He masterfully translates military leadership and culture lessons learned into concepts useful for those at the helm of civilian organizations. His book is wonderfully illustrated with gripping real-life examples of Army culture and leadership in action. He couples these vignettes with steps civilian leaders can take to adopt the Army lessons to shape and improve their organizations. The book is hard to put down as it is laced with action. It is, by no means, a typical management tome, but a must-read for anyone seeking to change their organization's culture and improve their own leadership ability'
David S. Baldwin, former Major General of the United States Army

'Having grown up with the discipline and values of the Indian Army, *The Winning Culture* resonated with me on many levels. Maj Gen Neeraj Bali's depth of experience and knowledge shines through each page, making it evident that the wisdom shared comes from a place of genuine leadership and first-hand encounters. His perspective is both unique and universal, making the lessons from the Army relevant and applicable

to varied organizational contexts. Drawing wisdom from our soldiers, the book underscores the importance of risk-taking, loyalty and the potent narratives that can guide our path. As a founder, I can attest to the challenges and rewards that come with cultivating a winning culture. This book provides a roadmap, making it an essential read for leaders and visionaries aiming to craft an enduring legacy'
Radhika Ghai, co-founder of ShopClues, serial entrepreneur and India's first female unicorn founder

'Fighting the insurgency in Kashmir for many years provided Neeraj Bali a tough masterclass in how force, intelligence and human engagement all need to be made to work together to win. In this book, he shows us how we can adapt those lessons for success in our businesses and workplaces'
Shekhar Gupta, Chairman and Editor-in-Chief of *ThePrint*

'Great organizational culture is the biggest competitive advantage a company can have. Through Army and corporate case studies this book offers insights and lessons on building such a culture'
Baba Kalyani, Chairman and Managing Director of Bharat Forge Ltd

'The Indian Army is respected globally for its professionalism and esprit de corps. Through so many inspiring stories, Maj Gen Neeraj Bali tells us the reason the Army fills up every Indian's heart with pride, and why its ethos is very relevant for our corporate sector and what we can learn from it'
Sanjay Kirloskar, Chairman and Managing Director of Kirloskar Brothers Ltd

'Culture is the lifeblood of an organization and courses through its ranks. Neeraj has skilfully drawn comparisons and lessons from the Indian Army's culture to artfully describe how corporate India can learn, imbibe and evolve'
Bijou Kurien, Chairman of Retailers Association of India (RAI)

'Culture is often defined as a way of life, a prime mover of our collective behaviour. The distinctiveness of the Army's robust culture keeps it ever-ready for every contingency and makes victories possible. General Bali has aptly called it 'the winning culture'. This book is replete with real-life stories and personal experiences related to the ethos, values, traditions and leadership in the Army. There are anecdotes and corporate lessons from the Kargil War, counter-insurgency/terror operations in Jammu & Kashmir and the Northeast, and from Veer Naris. It is a must-read for those wishing to learn from the ever-winning culture of the Indian Army'
General V. P. Malik, former Chief of Army Staff

'Most organizations focus their narrative on strategy and leadership. Fully recognizing the role that culture plays in winning organizations, *The Winning Culture* shifts the narrative on organizational culture from the trenches to the frontline. Replete with examples from the Indian Army and corporates, it makes for a culture-building toolkit for CEOs and CXOs. While each chapter is well-researched, 'The Fog That Hangs Forever' is a masterpiece on how culture can enable organizations to win in the most adverse circumstances'
J. Suresh, former Chief Operating Officer and Managing Director of Arvind Fashions Ltd

"Culture is often defined as a way of life. A prime mover of our collective evolution. The distinctiveness of the Army's robust culture keeps it ever ready for every contingency and makes victories possible. General Bakshi aptly calls it 'the winning culture'. This book is replete with real-life stories and personal experiences related to the ethos, values, traditions and leadership in the Army. There are anecdotes and corporate lessons from the Kargil War, counter-insurgency/terror operations in Jammu & Kashmir and the North-East and from Vedic texts. It is a must-read for those wishing to learn from the ever-winning culture of the Indian Army."

General V. P. Malik, former Chief of Army Staff

"Most organizations focus their narrative on strategy and leadership, fully recognizing the role that culture plays in winning organizations. *The Winning Culture* fills the narrative on organizational culture from the trenches to the boardrooms. Replete with examples from the Indian Army and corporates, it makes for a culture-building toolkit for CEOs and CXOs. While each chapter is well-researched, the fact that [illegible] is a [illegible] expert on how culture can enable organizations to win in the most adverse circumstances."

[illegible] Suresh, former Chief Operating Officer and Managing Director of Arvind Fashions Ltd.

THE WINNING CULTURE

Major General Neeraj Bali, Sena Medal (retd), is an Indian Army veteran with extensive operational experience. He notably commanded a Rashtriya Rifles battalion in an anti-terrorist role and served as a security advisor to the Lesotho government in Africa. Maj Gen Bali led an Indian brigade during an Indo–US exercise. An alumnus of the Asia-Pacific Center for Security Studies, USA, he is a teaching faculty at the Institute for Competitive Intelligence, Germany, and the School of Inspirational Leadership, Pune.

After superannuation in 2016, Maj Gen Bali became CEO of the leading engineering company Rodic Consultants Pvt Ltd and managed a rural education society with ninety-two schools and colleges. Currently he is a management advisor to Dynamic Cables Ltd in Jaipur and Notebook. Maj Gen Bali is also a motivational speaker, corporate performance coach and an executive fellow of Woxsen University, Hyderabad.

THE WINNING CULTURE

Lessons from the Indian Army to Transform Your Business

MAJOR GENERAL
NEERAJ BALI

MACMILLAN

First published in India 2023 by Macmillan
an imprint of Pan Macmillan Publishing India Private Limited
707 Kailash Building
26 K. G. Marg, New Delhi 110001
www.panmacmillan.co.in

Pan Macmillan, The Smithson, 6 Briset Street, Farringdon, London EC1M 5NR
Associated companies throughout the world
www.panmacmillan.com

ISBN 978-93-90742-51-6

5 7 9 8 6 4

Typeset in Minion Pro by R. Ajith Kumar, New Delhi
Printed in India by Manipal Technologies Limited, Manipal

FSC www.fsc.org MIX Paper | Supporting responsible forestry FSC® C043100

To my parents Harsh Dev and Sneh Prabha;
My wife Neeti;
Abhishek, Pallavi, Siddharth, Ruchika;
And, above all, Ira: your granddad has many stories to tell yet

CONTENTS

INTRODUCTION

Culture Matters

WHAT MAKES THE COLLECTIVE behaviour of the members of one organization different – often starkly so – from others? The rank and file of some companies may appear doused with an invisible elixir of self-driving motivation, just as much as the leadership at other setups laments their teams' lack of accountability and initiative. There is a palpable buzz of dynamism and innovation in a few while a visible pall of sluggishness shrouds the others.

When we search for answers, most stakeholders tend to ascribe this disparity chiefly to 'money'. The generic explanation is that better-paid employees outperform those receiving lesser compensation. It is a lazy hypothesis because it is largely unexamined.

In the winter of 1999, when I was commanding a Rashtriya Rifles battalion in Kashmir's Kupwara region, Pakistani infiltrators – mostly soldiers disguised as militants – crossed the Line of Control in the Kargil area of Jammu and Kashmir and occupied posts that the Indian Army had vacated for the winter. For decades, both armies had adhered to an unwritten understanding over vacating their respective posts for the harsh winter months. These posts are at heights ranging from 16,000 to 18,000 feet in rugged, barren and cruelly inhospitable terrain. Winter temperatures routinely drop to –48°C. Even occupying these peaks is challenging, and it is inestimably harder to attack up the forbidding slopes.

Pakistan's strategy was breathtakingly audacious: to occupy, with careful stealth, the temporarily vacated bunkers, and thus dominate the solitary artery running from the Kashmir Valley to Leh. The severing of this strategic road would render India's sustenance of the Leh–Ladakh area untenable. It would foment trouble between two nuclear-powered nations. And, ergo, the first whiff of an impending conflagration would attract the world community's focus on – and even intervention into – the Kashmir imbroglio.

The Pakistani thought stemmed from another assumption. The Indian Army would be unable to recapture heights completely bereft of cover, as up-the-hill assaults would be suicidal and prone to failure even before the troops could begin the arduous climb through a hail of bullets. The line of control would thus shift forward for Pakistan.

But the eventual outcome flew in the face of those well-laid plans. The Indian Army units defied those simplistic assumptions, not hesitating to pay a huge human cost to recapture every inch of the ground. Without exception, the officers and soldiers displayed superhuman courage. I mention this fact not to tom-tom a famous victory, but merely to provide an exhibit of concerted heroism so that we can examine the fount of such extraordinary behaviour.

And what was the magnitude of that collective courage? We have an instructive insight from the diary of a thirty-year-old Pakistani officer who was deployed at those heights for seventy-seven days until he 'withdrew' for what *Time* magazine's Asia edition described as 'reasons he wouldn't specify'. He told the magazine that:

> The skirmishes with the Indians started in May. In the early days, we mowed down many of them. Those Indians were crazy. They came like ants. First, you see four, and you kill them. Then there are 10, then 50, then 100 and then 400. Our fingers got tired of shooting at them. We felt sorry for them. Sometimes

> they came in such large numbers we were afraid of using up all our ammunition. There is no instant resupply, so you have to be very careful. We were always worried that we would use up all our ammunition on one attacking Indian party and would have none left when a new group came. But God was always with us. You could see lots of bodies strewn down below or in the gorges.'[1]

Could it be that notwithstanding the meticulously crafted strategy, the Pakistani endeavour failed because it had misread a vital element that drives organizational performance – culture? The Pakistani Army's thought process betrayed a horrendous miscalculation of their Indian counterpart's culture.

This life force called culture is the motif of our theme song throughout the book.

Every organization – company, political party, club, school and college, NGO and government department – has a culture. Indeed, so does every family. It doesn't matter whether that culture has come about as a result of thoughtful reflection and action or has grown like untamed wild grass. Where there is community, there will always be culture. And the quality of that culture will largely sift the wheat from the chaff.

Culture is the prime mover of our collective behaviour. Its silent stream ripples just below the surface – visible here, invisible there – but powerfully guides the behaviour of every group. It is often the sole difference between winning and losing, yet many leaders are oblivious to it beyond trite clichés. Those who are aware that their organizations have 'cultural' infirmities struggle to craft a clear strategy for bringing about lasting change. To be sure, many organizations in the business world are shining examples of distinct and effective cultures. But they are rarities in a sea of cultural mediocrity.

Culture matters.* It matters more than most of us realize in a lifetime. The engine of culture drives human beings, rewarding them with a sense of identity they unremittingly seek. Culture lifts the burden of endless daily doubt and scepticism about the road to be taken. It lends meaning and respectability to our actions. It assures us that we only belong and flourish if we swim in unison, especially when the currents are against us.

The objective of this book is to demonstrate the distinctiveness of the Indian Army's culture that makes daily victories possible. By recounting my experiences in the Army, I try to show how greatly a robust culture contributes to a community or organization's ability to survive and thrive in any situation. However, the lessons and learnings, though meant to be universal, are offered primarily for the business world.

This book's core message is wrapped in true stories and case studies. I have steered clear of tales of gallantry that have already been embellished with the highest awards. Instead, these accounts are of the everyman soldiers of the Army. After all, culture is not represented by the gladiators. It is the script that the ordinary rank and file write every day.

I do not wish to suggest that any organization try replicating the Army's culture. The Army's work environment, organizational structure and goals differ so significantly from the business world that a blindly made copy would be nonsensical. So here is a caveat.

* In the early 2000s, when I was attending a study programme at the Honolulu-based Asia-Pacific Center for Security Studies as a serving colonel, I had opted for an elective on ethnicity and identity politics. Our teacher was a formidable intellectual giant – a distinguished author and educator. Every morning, Dr Robert Wirsing would stroll into the class and, without any explanation or warning, unfailingly shout out two words in a deep baritone: 'Culture matters!' At that point, some of us thought it was an attention-grabbing opening salvo, a wake-up call to focus the class on the fare about to be offered. But as the course progressed, and indeed as I progressed through life, I realized that those two words were pregnant with enormous wisdom. Culture matters. Enormously.

Companies can extract countless lessons for every nuance of leadership and organization-building from the following narrative. They can also learn the framework for effecting change in their culture. The book calls for creating a distinct culture that could set a company on the path of regular wins.

The stories in the book celebrate the Indian Army's culture. Does that imply no flaws in its cultural edifice? Not so. As in the case of every organization, the Army's culture is also imperfect. But one can argue that the Army has far more going for it in the 'credit' column vis-à-vis the infirmities.

During my speaking assignments, the discerning audience has repeatedly sought answers to questions such as: What about the people who join the Army? Are they not more dedicated, patriotic and selfless than people in other walks of life, thus giving the Indian Army a 'cultural advantage' right from the starting line? The truth is that the intake for the Indian Army comes from the very same cities, towns and villages as for other professions. Those who serve in the Army have economic, social or educational backgrounds no different from their countrymen. When a soldier is recruited, he does possess essential character qualities that would mould him into a soldier. Beyond that, he is also like every other citizen – no more patriotic, dedicated or selfless than anyone else.

The truth is that the magic only happens after he joins the Army. The organization pares off the unnecessary attributes and shapes him in its cultural image. The silent subterranean stream called the Army's culture slowly but surely shifts his mindset towards life and work.

The first seven chapters underscore one attribute each that either benefits from a robust culture or feeds it. The last chapter is a primer for creating or transforming culture in other organizations, especially in the corporate sector.

The book presents real-life case studies to prove that the fundamental truth underlying the Army's performance is its culture. To the rest of us outside the Army, it reveals a secret that is hidden in plain sight.

1

STRATEGY FOR BREAKFAST

'Culture outperforms strategy every time, and culture with strategy is unbeatable.'

– QUINT STUDER

I

SOME TWO DECADES AGO, on a bright June morning in north Kashmir's Kupwara district, a small Indian Army convoy was making its way up an unpaved track. A Jonga vehicle was at the helm, with a larger load carrier in its wake, trailing by half a kilometre. The mostly unpaved road was a grey sliver, winding around the slopes of thickly forested dark green hills on one flank and, on the other, brown open fields stretching to a seasonal river.

Militancy in Kashmir had reached a bloody peak in 1997. However, *fidayeen*, or suicide, attacks against Army posts and vehicles that started in 1999 – almost in concert with Pakistan's occupation of the Kargil heights – were still a phenomenon lying in wait.

Unknown to the two officers and four soldiers in the Jonga, a group of Hizbul Mujahideen militants had planted a colossal amount of explosives under the track and were awaiting the passage of the leading vehicle over the precise spot. By itself, the explosive was incapable of prosecuting violence. It was merely inert plastic. But by way of a detonator and underground wires engineered into a receiver box, with a tiny antenna protruding up at some distance, it was transformed into a deadly Improvised Explosive Device (IED) designed for unspeakable destruction. The militants lay ambushed in the forest above, waiting to trigger the IED with a simple handheld radio set. It was common knowledge that Pakistan's ISI was the supplier of these devices.

When the IED burst, the terrifying, ear-splitting boom resonated for miles. People in the adjoining villages rushed out of their homes, fearful that a great calamity had just been unleashed. Those working in the fields froze. No one dared move to the scene of attack.

The blast catapulted the leading Jonga above the line of the surrounding eucalyptus trees, and then, reclaimed by gravity, the vehicle smashed onto the gravelled track. The driver of the trailing truck saw it spin twice, mid-air. Even as they rose skywards, the company commander Major Mohit Whig instinctively put a hand on his co-driver Lieutenant Ravi Loganathan's arm, as if to steady the youngster's nerves.

The crash instantly killed the major and the two soldiers sitting in the rear. It incapacitated Ravi Loganathan and the two remaining soldiers, all bleeding and trapped inside the mangled heap of metal. The Jonga was unrecognizable except for its olive-green paint. The blast made an eight-foot-deep crater.

Anticipating that the militants might approach the site to finish off the survivors and decamp with weapons, Ravi tore through the metal and began spraying the slope with his AK-47. He couldn't see much through the fog in his mind. Due to considerable blood loss, Ravi was battling trauma and increasing weariness, but the moment demanded that he surmount it all.

And surmount he did. Through dwindling consciousness, Ravi kept his resolve intact. An engineer by education and profession, the twenty-five-year-old officer was now in a near-fatal exchange of deadly fire with the militants. He continued to shoot up the slope to ward them off. While he did not hit any, his response had the desired deterrent effect. The militants continued to fire but chose discretion and refrained from approaching the dead and the injured.

I was the commanding officer of the battalion and had visited the two officers' company post that very morning. I had even asked Major Mohit Whig to accompany me in my vehicle. Sensing his hesitation to travel with his CO, I had jovially held out the carrot of my Jonga's music system. He had pointed out that his vehicle had one too. That was the point at which we had parted with a chuckle. An hour later, he was gone forever.

We heard the thunderous boom and learnt of the IED blast over the radio set. The radio operator indicated that there were multiple casualties. Unsure whether there were more explosives along the route, we disembarked and began to run towards the site, our weapons at the ready. Sporadic gunfire echoed in the distance.

On the way, a battalion three-tonne truck passed us. The driver briefly got down and, in a voice quivering with emotion, told me that he was carrying the dead and the injured. They were all there except for Lieutenant Ravi, who had refused the opportunity to be evacuated until he could personally report the incident to the CO.

As we frantically jogged the few kilometres towards the sound of gunfire, an officer running alongside stopped me and pointed out that I had on red-coloured collar tabs that colonels and higher ranks usually sport. The wearing of the tabs – sometimes referred to as the lipstick on the collar – violates the norm of active operations, for it makes the commander an easy target for the enemy snipers. He tersely asked me to remove them. I promised him that I would, but my mind being preoccupied with what had happened, I resumed my anxious jog towards the site of action.

After we covered a kilometre, the soldier running on my left – an Army barber – Lance Naik Roop Lal, asked me: 'Can I have a word with you, sir?'

'Sure,' I replied.

'The advice Major Dev gave you about removing the collar tabs is eminently sound. I completely agree that there is no courage in wearing these into battle when tactical norms prohibit it. What if they shoot you next? There would be utter chaos if that happened.'

I nodded in agreement as Roop Lal paused to catch his breath.

'But sir, my next piece of advice is that you must not remove them today. And not for at least three more months. You must not let the soldiers in the battalion get the wrong impression that a few casualties can shake their CO or the officers.'

What would you say of an organization where such a sterling lesson on leading by example is understood and internalized even at the very lowest rung? How would you rate the strength of a setup where the rank and file believe in their bones that it is the crux of leadership, even if doing so imperils your existence? Where twenty-something-year-olds disregard severely traumatic injuries and blood loss to 'report' matters expeditiously and take action against the enemy without delay?

And can any grand plan or strategy against the opponents marvellously succeed unless the underpinning culture of that organization is so aligned to that very strategy?

The fact of the matter is this: strategies will only succeed where there is a supporting culture. This includes business organizations as well. The converse is also true – a weak strategy may be offset to a degree by a robust culture. Many companies spend days, weeks and months poring over the drafting of strategies that could propel them to substantial gains and wins. But not all of them spend even a fraction of that time and effort to ponder whether a culture needed to support those strategies is in place. The leadership of such companies assumes that no investment is necessary to enquire into the prevailing culture, much less tweak or transform it. After all, the rank and file are there only to obey diktats and somehow deliver. Sophisticated plans are all that's required to help organizations breeze past the post.

As we will see, nothing could be more delusional than ignoring the blanket of culture and assuming that strategy alone can be the prime mover.

II

Arguably, the word that the higher echelons of most organizations obsess over is 'strategy'. We love its lofty sound. It assures us that the leadership is seriously reflecting upon playing a role on the big stage. The reason for this self-seduction is easily understandable. Everyone instinctively knows they can hardly expect to succeed without an overarching vision.

The grand, holistic idea of strategy covers meticulous details of resources, timelines, threats, opportunities and a clear-eyed approach to the summit. It is what welds all the components together for the realization of the larger goal. Strategy is the big picture that allows you to stop fussing with the weeds while trying to grow a forest. It is what the sixteenth-century Japanese soldier-philosopher Miyamoto Musashi described as the ability to 'see distant things as if they were close and to take a distanced view of close things'. Why? Because 'perception is strong and the sight weak', he explained. Therefore, businesses that pore over crafting a strategy before drafting execution plans are right on the money.

But then, not all strategies succeed. Bewilderment arises when strategy runs aground despite all the correct sums about one's resources, material capabilities and competitors' potential. Is there a critical trick such leaders miss that leads to disappointing – even disastrous – outcomes? While looking far ahead, we are sometimes oblivious to a fundamental home truth – a truth called 'culture' that fuels any strategy's success.

If the culture of your team is not aligned with the company's strategy, sooner or later the ship will be dead in the water. The logic of this wisdom is so evident that it is surprising to see so many leadership decisions not seeming to take it into account. I have seen a company harbour an ambitious strategy to 'go international' and compete with multinational corporations. This, even though the rank and file were steeped in a culture of working without processes and following ancient business practices. No one thought these issues would hinder the strategy's success. And a few brave voices that suggested a change were met with scepticism, indistinguishable from derision. If such a strategy so fundamental does not work without preparing the right culture, what hope do more grandiose ones have?

Management guru Peter Drucker famously said 'culture eats strategy for breakfast'.[1] English strategic thinker Max McKeown offered the perfect solution: 'strategy and culture (should) have breakfast together.'*

III

A culture aligned with strategy is the force multiplier that beats the path to the summit of victories. The converse is equally valid.

Many military experts on either side of the LoC believe that the Pakistan Army's strategy to occupy the peaks of Kargil in 1999 was breathtakingly audacious.

Planning for Operation Badr had been in the works since the winter of 1998. The strategy was to prepare and launch both militants

* Hence the chapter's title.

and regular soldiers of the Northern Light Infantry battalions, masquerading as jihadi fighters. These 'militants' were to infiltrate Indian territory and occupy posts on the peaks. An operation of this nature requires meticulously planned logistics. The Pakistan Army spared no effort in developing helipads, improving tracks and stockpiling mountains of ammunition and other supplies, without attracting the attention of Indian surveillance apparatuses. Extensive reconnaissance followed, after which the Pakistanis set up patrol bases.

The theme song of this gargantuan effort was the rewriting of geostrategic realities. East of the Zoji La, the sole artery of surface communication connecting Srinagar–Kargil–Leh would thus be dominated, effectively severing the rest of India's links with that area. In a clear violation of the Shimla Agreement, this stratagem could have altered the alignment of the LoC. But Pakistan was not letting legal niceties weigh it down. It wanted to move the needle firmly in favour of its geostrategic argument. And besides getting hold of peaks, it also planned to capture the strategic village of Turtuk on the Shyok.

Achieving surprise is a significant component of any successful military strategy. Pakistan executed it to near perfection. But no military strategy, no matter how brilliant, can come to fruition without close coordination between the armed forces, the political apparatus and, of course, all military services. Such effort requires a robust culture of transparency, cooperation and information exchange woven into its fabric, leading to an uninhibited support system. Here, the comparison between the two cultures – of the Pakistan and Indian armies – tells its own story.

It is no secret that in Pakistan, the army – and the army alone, not the air force and the navy – calls all the shots. The democratically elected prime ministers serve at the pleasure of the chiefs of army staff, the exact opposite of the reality in India. The Pakistan Army also rides roughshod over the air force and the navy; other uniformed forces receive less attention.*†

Culturally attuned to arrogating the exclusive grasp of 'national interest' to itself, the army evidently chose to hide the plans from its own prime minister. Nawaz Sharif later publicly accepted as much. Admittedly, there is some confusion over this fact, but substantial evidence to the effect that the army top brass felt no need to dovetail the politico-civilian structure into the war effort exists. Leading Pakistani writers and intellectuals, like Nasim Zehra (author of

---

* I witnessed a small slice of this cultural divergence while at the Asia-Pacific Center for Security Studies. Also participating in that programme were three serving Pakistani officers and a bureaucrat. During our conversations, the Pakistani brigadier often raised issues relating to Kashmir and the state of the Indian Army's equation with the political leadership. On one occasion, he mentioned Operation Parakram, the 2001–2002 ten-month-long mobilization of the Army ordered by the Vajpayee government in the wake of the terrorist attack on the parliament. He told me that it astonished him, to date, why the Indian Army did not upbraid its government for the wasteful exercise where not a shot was fired, and yet several lives were lost in accidents along the border. I expressed surprise at his 'naivety' in an even more considerable measure. 'Sir, we in the Army have huge respect for our politicians. They are very wise and, if I may add, clever. Did you expect that having announced the mobilization to the whole world and deliberately giving away the surprise, Mr Vajpayee would have asked us to attack the Pakistan Army lying in wait? It was a ruse that might be repeated many times. There will be no invitation card preceding the attack.' Since I spotted a whiff of scepticism across his brow, I reminded him of how we had handled the attack on East Pakistan in December 1971.

† In another voluntary revelation of the Pakistan Army's unbridled powers, he recounted an incident wherein he had summoned a sitting judge and asked him to withdraw strictures passed against a Junior Commissioned Officer serving in his headquarters. He told me this in a voice ringing with pride. In fact, anyone who knows anything about the Pakistan Army does not even require such anecdotal evidence of its 'predominance' – indistinguishable from unbridled arrogance.

Kargil to the Coup[2]), Ayaz Amir and several others have reached that unmistakable conclusion. Writing five years later in *Dawn* on 23 July 2004, Ayaz Amir repeated what the country already knew: 'But in May [of 1999] came strange rumours of "mujahideen" activity across the Line of Control in Kargil, which was a bit mystifying because the Kashmiri freedom fighters were always thought to be operating inside the Kashmir Valley. What were they doing along the LoC?'[3]

If the public was in the dark, it was in distinguished company for once, for even the heads of the navy and air force knew nothing. Nor, more alarmingly, did most of the corps' commanders have even a whiff of what was afoot across the LoC. There is nothing unwise about keeping an imminent offensive's plans classified from the public at large. But should even the other service chiefs be deliberately blindsided and not considered vital to the war effort?

It was only around 20–22 May that the other service chiefs and the formation commanders were brought into the loop about what had already unfolded. They were informed, in heroic terms no doubt, of the great successes registered in 'filling the gaps' along and across the LoC.

But who else was in the know? As it turned out, a rather limited number of senior commanders: the commander of the northern troops, Major General Javed Hasan, now Commander 10 Corps; Lt Gen Mahmood, later head of the Fauji Fertilizer Company (who says Pakistani generals are not versatile?); Lt Gen Aziz, the DG Military Operations, Lt Gen Tauqir Zia, who later became a cricket czar; and, of course, the Chief himself.

The other grievous error made by the Pakistani planners was misreading the culture of its enemy army. Implicit in the strategy was the assumption that when the summer arrived, the Indian Army would not be in a position to retake the captured mountain tops. Who in their right minds would choose to attack uphill on slopes bereft of cover, with nothing but boulders to give momentary protection from the enemy's firing? Wouldn't that be suicidal to attempt? The reading cost Pakistan a colossal loss of face and, possibly, permanent trauma.

That canvas of turf domination, opaqueness, arrogance and disregard for coordination clashed with the Indian Army's culture which was steeped in very different colours.

On the Indian side, the quality of coordination and seamless communication was of high order. In his seminal work, *Kargil: From Surprise to Victory*, the then Army Chief General V. P. Malik has devoted an entire chapter to coordination.[4] He writes: 'We three service chiefs ... were regularly invited to participate in the Cabinet Committee on Security proceedings. [Thus] the political hierarchy could get to know the views of the armed forces first-hand and, simultaneously, the three chiefs could obtain clear-cut political directives directly from the prime minister.' There was an institutionalized process that prepared the groundwork. And drove the execution of the mission – codenamed Operation Vijay – mounted to retake the heights of Kargil.

And shining another beam of light on the culture of the armed forces, General Malik writes, 'The Indian Army, Navy and the Air Force have inherited a legacy of maintaining a totally apolitical stance ... Unlike many of our neighbouring countries, the Indian Armed Forces have stuck to the concept of loyalty to the constitutionally elected government ... Their oath is to the Constitution of India.'[5]

Once the battle was joined, the Pakistanis displayed another aspect of their culture that would be a complete anathema in the Indian Army – their treatment of the soldiers. They refused to claim their dead. For years, the Pakistan Army disowned the soldiers of the Northern Light Infantry that had perished in this operation. Dead bodies were scattered in many places; without exception, the deceased were given a dignified military burial by the victorious Indian units. The stories of the neglect of their dead – culturally unthinkable for the Indian Army – by the Pakistan Army have been published by its veterans in blogs. In a stirring online account 'Kargil – Tales and Bodies', a Pakistan Army veteran who only identifies himself as Imran, had this to say: 'Not very far from Y Block in DHA Lahore is a graveyard with neatly laid out grave plots on green grassy patches. Here lies buried my friend and course-mate Lieutenant Faisal Zia Ghumman … Not everyone fighting on the desolate heights of Batalik and Chorbat La and Kargil was that fortunate.'

He recounts the different fates of the fallen on either side. '… in Turtuk … A daring dash by a patrol of 11 Rajputana Rifles [of the Indian Army] led by Captain Haneef Uddin was met with stiff resistance. The attack failed with heavy losses, with the daring Captain among the casualties. For some time, both Captains Farhat Haseeb Haider of 7 NLI and Haneef Uddin of 11 RAJRIF shared the same fate, with their bodies lying on the snowy slopes astride Shyok too difficult to be recovered due to treacherous weather conditions and the heavy volume of all arms fire. Captain Haneef's body was recovered at the end of the war and was buried in Delhi with full military honours. Captain Farhat Haseeb Haider lies buried under some unmarked boulder across the divide in a foreign land.'[6] The blog is replete with similar stories and comparisons, including that of Major Abdul Wahab, who was awarded Sitara-e-Jurat for gallantry. 'The officer's body, along with others who fell on Tololing, was never recovered.'*

Only years later, Pakistan published a list of 350 of its soldiers,

* In its 12 July 1999 edition, *Time* magazine published an interview with a Pakistani soldier who had been deployed in Kargil but had made his way back alive. His account gives an astonishing insight into the culture of the Pakistan Army, wherein a soldier can offer a bribe to his officer like someone would do to a feudal master. 'A young soldier from Punjab died in front of me because of altitude sickness. The soldier came from the plains. He fell sick soon after coming up. He offered our commanding officer 200,000 rupees [about $4,000] to let him go down, but the offer was refused. He died four days later. We didn't know his name. I tried to find out, but they refused to tell me.'

mainly from the Northern Light Infantry, in a nondescript section of an official website called Shuhada's (Martyrs') Corner.

Culture will devour even a good strategy for breakfast. The Kargil War was a clash between two militaries, resources, national will and strategies. But it was also a clash between two widely dissimilar cultures.

One army believed that it was larger than the nation and made no effort to take the other wings of the government on board.* The Pakistan Army does not lack courage or devotion to the cause. But equally, its culture, developed over decades of enjoying political power, is also marked by unthinking audacity and arrogance. These are hardly the attributes an organization should flaunt while taking on an opponent. Ultimately, the Pakistani assumption about the lack of the Indian Army's propensity to take casualties proved catastrophic.

And the other army, dyed in the democratic tradition, treated itself as a cog in the giant wheel of the war effort.

In an interview General Malik, the army chief who led the victory in Kargil, unequivocally told me: 'Culture must aim at organizational goal. In our case, it must meet the crux of "fight well and win the battle". And that can only happen if it is resting on the pillars of courage, leadership, esprit de corps (and not just for the living), a belief in the system and adherence to tradition.' It would not be inaccurate to assume that any discussion about culture will elicit many of these expressions repeatedly. In Kargil, riding on the dividends of its culture, the Army unhesitatingly paid the cost. Five hundred and twenty-seven officers and soldiers were killed and 1,363 wounded.

---

* I was always struck by another telling difference back at the Asia-Pacific Center for Security Studies. The Indian officers introduced themselves as a Colonel so-and-so from India in class every day. By contrast, the officers from the Pakistan Army invariably rose to say 'Colonel so-and-so from the Pakistan Army'!

But the Indian Army took Kargil back.

What defines the culture of your organization? Does it work as a powerful engine to accelerate strategies up the mountain of success? Or does it substantially drag the progress, pushing every step into an enervating mire?

IV

The genesis of the Kargil War – and indeed at the heart of the warped relationship between India and Pakistan – is the dispute over the status of Jammu and Kashmir. Since the late 1980s, Pakistan has fomented insurgency in the state, pushing thousands of militants to create instability and bloodshedding.

As any military expert knows, counter-insurgency is among the most brutal fighting campaigns. It is slow, painstaking and messy. The great Lawrence of Arabia likened it to eating soup with a fork. The war on militants is complex because it is fought on a borderless battlefield inhabited by civilians.* It is an asymmetrical contest where the 'weak' play by an entirely different set of rules. The militant is hardly recognizable because he does not wear a uniform, live in a camp, travel in distinctive vehicles, or have to follow laws that prohibit extortion and killings; instead, he moves in small groups and stays in civilian houses.

In asymmetrical warfare, the weak will win the match-up unless the 'stronger player' can exhibit staying power and adaptability to the new paradigm. That script has unfolded in Vietnam, Northern Ireland, Afghanistan and during many other conflicts. In the business world, it unfolds daily between established entities and the unorganized marketplace, peppered with entrepreneurs working out

* Militants remained militants until the 9/11 attacks. After that, the world began referring to them as terrorists.

of garages and other makeshift locations. And on the globalization scene, asymmetry is what loaded the dice against the West – the less advanced countries follow their own set of 'rules' concerning labour and environmental concerns, etc. – thus beating the West's cost of manufacturing.

How has the Army fared under this constant bleeding for decades? How well has it sustained its motivation through a seemingly never-ending war? What has enabled the soldier to consistently display resilience and fortitude in the face of human cost and repeated criticism from the uninformed?

It will be instructive to put this phenomenon under a lens and see how individuals have regularly acted to meet organizational objectives in Jammu and Kashmir – and other counter-insurgency operations. What sustains ordinary soldiers? Could it be that monetary rewards or medals lie at the heart of this collective motivation, and that the Army's culture plays only a subsidiary – even minor – role?

Spoiler alert: like all other anecdotes in this book, what follows is not a 'Param Vir Chakra' story. Rather, it represents how the rank and file respond and how the ordinary do the extraordinary, almost every day, owing to a hardy organizational culture.

Jubin Mathew was a shade over seventeen years when he entered the portals of the National Defence Academy to train for a commission in the Indian Army. The tall, slightly built young man came from Trivandrum. Four years of rigorous training later, he was commissioned into the Bihar Regiment – a regiment of the infantry whose troops primarily hail from the states of Bihar and Jharkhand. As is the custom in the army, unlike the troops, the officers of infantry regiments can be drawn from any state.

Five years later, at the age of twenty-six, Jubin was promoted to Acting Major and handed over the command of a 100-soldier company in the Manasbal area of Jammu and Kashmir. Militancy was raging through the state.

On a spring day in 1997, when the Valley is arguably at its most resplendent, Jubin's battalion got a tip-off about the presence of three militants in a village near Soura. Two of these militants were foreigners, their descriptions typically matching those of Pakistanis or Afghans. Since no one knew their precise location, the unit cordoned off three adjoining villages at night, and the troops waited for dawn to commence the search.

Unbeknown to them, the militants were outside the cordon. After the familiar sounds of the *azaan* wafted through the area and the sun began to rise, they made their move. A soldier spotted them scampering through the fields. Challenged, the militants fired a volley at the troops and, in the heat of the moment, erroneously scooted back into the cordon, disappearing in the village's narrow streets packed with houses.

Jubin's company began to search the village, cordoning off streets and cautiously moving towards the suspected area. One of the militants noticed this movement and fired. The bullet hit a soldier – a Non-Commissioned Officer (NCO) – in the shoulder. Now that the cordon had narrowed down the location of the militants, the troops rapidly surrounded the house from which the shot was fired. Jubin's men made several offers to the militants for peaceful surrender. So tight was the cordon around the target house that the soldiers making the surrender offer could directly exchange words with the militants. But no surrender transpired.

Jubin had taken cover behind a tiny hut where the house owner had stored *shali*, or husk. The troops decided to end the standoff as the day progressed, lest it drag towards nightfall. The pinpoint location of the militants inside the house was still unclear. Instead of ordering a soldier to scout for more information, Jubin took it upon himself to stick his head out to see if he could locate the enemy's movement. At that precise moment, a militant looking in that very direction, shot Jubin in the head.

During the operations, troops wear bulletproof jackets and headbands called *patkas*. These mostly shield the soldiers from being killed by a bullet, but the impact does injure the wearer. The bullets hit Jubin on his patka, instantly smashing his spectacles. Several splinters managed to pierce the armour and lodged themselves into a side of his forehead, penetrating deep enough to reach the bone. But Jubin had survived the battery.

After the medicos quickly administered first aid on the spot, they moved to evacuate Jubin. But he refused. He wanted to stay and continue leading his men. 'It was just a graze,' he told me later, his tone light and playful. 'All I was concerned about was the black eye I had got – as if I had lost a boxing bout.' He was underplaying the trauma and injury from being shot at such close proximity.

The operation went on until the troops had killed all three militants. Mission achieved, the unit doctor insisted that Jubin be evacuated to the Base Hospital at Srinagar for a thorough examination. They travelled in a Gypsy that Jubin drove.

Twenty-two years later, some of the shrapnel is still embedded in a bone in his head. As a consequence, his hearing has also been impaired.

But then, after his surgery, Jubin refused to accept the official order to go home on sick leave for recuperation and instead returned to the battalion. Several years later, when I asked him why he had violated that order and put his well-being at such risk, he quietly replied that he was concerned about the shortage of officers in his battalion.

'No one had asked me to rejoin and, of course, no one could ever have. But there is always a deficiency of officers in the unit and, being an officer, I thought it was my responsibility to bolster the troops' strength.'

The story has several lessons for practitioners of 'leadership' – leading from the front and, by example, complete devotion to the organizational goals and more. What moves ordinary individuals to act in this way? What binds them to an organization's core values so that their lives are subservient to the big idea – the strategy? While these are fascinating quandaries to explore, the answer to winning organizations is crystal clear.

It is culture. A force so silently compelling that individuals like Jubin willingly let duty supersede their self-interest. And victories are assured only when that culture works in tandem with the organization's strategies and plans.

But we are not done with Jubin Mathew yet.

Four months after he had refused the order to proceed on sick leave and returned to be a part of the ongoing battles, Jubin's battalion received another piece of actionable intelligence. A source informed them that at least a couple of militants, armed to the teeth, were present in a village near the townships of Manasbal and Ganderbal.

Jubin's troops surrounded the area inside the village where the militants had been spotted. The Acting Major took cover behind an adjoining house. Close to this location, was a small hut that shared a wall with the cattle outhouse. Jubin's deputy, a young lieutenant, entered that hut with a small team. Unknown to the young lieutenant, one militant was hiding in the cowshed. Only a thin mud wall separated the officer and the militant.

Both officers explored the possibility of lobbing a grenade into the target house. The lieutenant decided to smash a hole in the cowshed wall for a better view. The moment he cracked the wall, the militant fired from barely a metre away, killing the young officer. A soldier from his team stepped up to retrieve the officer and took the next burst of bullets. He, too, died on the spot.

Hearing the gunfire, Jubin cautiously stepped into that house, hoping to save the entrapped team. Instead, he caught two bullets – one in his shoulder and one on the forehead, smack in the middle of both eyes. The kinetic force of the bullets threw him backwards, but once again, his life was barely saved by the bulletproof patka. (The injuries would result in other medical complications, though.)

As most commanding officers do, Colonel (later Brigadier) Pradeep Rathee was also a part of the operations. He moved forward with another small team that included a soldier who, in Army parlance, was the CO's 'buddy'. The buddy was the next to go – shot dead. It was then that Jubin noticed that he, too, was bleeding. Nevertheless, he decided to try dragging away the soldier's body under threat of fire.

There were two other fatal casualties in this firefight.

In the end, after the militants were killed, Jubin was evacuated to the Base Hospital in Srinagar. His hearing had suffered permanent damage – the bullet hitting against the patka had affected nerve fibres in one of his ears.*

He did not receive any medals for these two operations, a point I make only to reinforce that a robust organizational culture generates its own momentum, not always hostage to the quid pro quo of awards and rewards.

What explains such focus on achieving organizational goals that individuals are willing to die rather than abandon the mission's pursuit? It isn't that fuzzy thing called patriotism because having served for nearly four decades, I can say without ambiguity that I have never heard that word being bandied about by anyone in the Army.

So is it intense training? Training does play a role in the efficacy of any setup. And it indeed shores up the strength of a culture. But it is equally evident that no amount of training can prepare any group to lay down lives so readily.

The presence of a culture wherein most individuals are implicitly aligned to the overall strategy is what takes an organization to the finish line. Such a culture provides a momentum that transcends other motivations, including pecuniary gains. Few in the business world recognize this powerful phenomenon. The corporate has

* When Jubin was in the military hospital for the second time, I wrote him a short note: 'Very proud of you, Jubin – but don't lose your head.'

collectively made up its mind that people work for money and money alone. It is a lazy approach that seeks to absolve responsibility to motivate teams. After all, what can the rider do if money alone makes the mare go?

To be sure, money does play a role. But it is never the sole contributor. Look around, and you will see many 'well-meaning' organizations struggling with enervating inner dynamics, continually seeking answers for better performance, even though their monetary compensation to the employees compares favourably with that of other companies. A culture that only relies on money as the prime motivator surrenders the locus of control to the cheque book.

But if you recognize that human beings work for many reasons beyond a pay cheque, you will fashion your organization's culture accordingly. Soldiers in the Army get a salary – but their extraordinary motivation is despite the absence of year-end appraisals and bonuses. They – and all of us in the world – work for many other reasons. To create an identity. For acknowledgement. To fulfil a desire for power and growth. To seek love and appreciation when our lives may be too barren. And possibly an amalgam of so many other inner needs. Creating a culture that takes all of this into account – and not just money – is really where our focus needs to be.

V

A resounding majority of the students of contemporary military history would concur that in 1987 the Indian Army walked blindfolded into Sri Lanka. The Indian leadership, acting on the counsel of the security establishment, had convinced itself that the Liberation Tigers of Tamil Eelam (LTTE) would tamely follow their diktat and roll over. All that was needed was to send a few troops for 'peacekeeping', a euphemism for overseeing peaceful surrender. And with this 'flag march' approach, we would usher in long-lasting peace. Or so went our strategic fantasy.

But hope is not a synonym for strategy. Indeed, it is hard to fathom what strategy we might have had since the prognosis was based on fuzziness bordering on delusion.

Or are we being too harsh in hindsight?

On 4 August 1987, 100,000 Sri Lankan Tamils gathered on the grounds of a temple in Jaffna to listen to their thirty-three-year-old militant leader, Velupillai Prabhakaran. In the previous month, the Indian government had brokered an agreement to end the bloody internecine conflict between the Sinhalese-dominated government and the minority Tamil community. The Indian prime minister Rajiv Gandhi and President J. R. Jayawardene of Sri Lanka had inked this agreement. The signatories presumed that the LTTE, the powerful guerrilla force led by Prabhakaran, would now disengage from its deadly operations against the Sri Lanka Army. Notably, Prabhakaran was not even a signatory to the accord. The LTTE supremo had arrived at this juncture with palpable disinclination. The idea of disarming his cadres was anathema to him.

That morning, speaking softly from a handwritten speech, he signalled that the LTTE would lay down its weapons because 'we have no choice but to toe the line of the Indian government. There will be an armed confrontation with the Indian Army if we don't. We don't want that. India is a powerful country, and we cannot do anything to stop it.'[7] His equivocation was manifestly clear. And evidently, what he said was not the crux of his thoughts. Those who listened carefully to the concluding call would have come to a vastly different understanding of what was about to unfold.

'It does not mean we have given up our dream for Eelam.'

It is worth noting that Prabhakaran did not say when the weapons would be surrendered. The Sri Lanka Army chief, General Cyril Ranatunga, assured the audience that the arms surrender would begin the same afternoon. But after his speech, Prabhakaran drove away in a black van, escorted by a phalanx of fighters armed with AK-47 and M-16 rifles. The LTTE would renege on the promise to disarm in the following months.

With this as the backdrop, the basis of the strategy of deploying troops with the singular aim of peacekeeping was hardly prescient. In a subsequent chapter, I will tell the story of the first battalions that landed in Jaffna, and how a flawed strategy had led to the misreading of the situation and the subsequent inadequate preparation. The consequences were enormous; in the first fortnight itself over 300 soldiers had perished, and 1,100 were maimed. Eventually, the campaign cost the Indian Army 1,200 fatal and another 3,000 wounded casualties.

Operation Pawan – the codename of Indian Peace Keeping Force's operation to take control of Jaffna – was not the Indian Army's finest hour for a tangible victory. But it is equally valid that the sheer bravery and commitment of the troops compensated for the infirmities in strategy. There was no distress withdrawal – far from it. Riding on its culture of implicit obedience, an appetite for professionalism despite privation and placing the unit's honour above anything else, the rank and file of the Army stood and fought. It overcame stiff odds with pluck and held its own.

In 1986, Sukhwinder Sahota was twenty-two years old when he joined a Madras regiment battalion as Second Lieutenant. He was already dyed in the olive green colour; his father had recently retired as a subedar, and Sukhwinder himself had studied at the Military School Belgaum for nine years. He was a sportsman who would lead the Services hockey team that year.

In July 1987, just as India and Sri Lanka inked that ill-fated accord, Sukhwinder's battalion was inducted into Sri Lanka with an amphibious landing at Kankesanthurai jetty, north of Jaffna. That was a period of lull – and being lulled. It was common knowledge that India had trained and armed the LTTE cadre.* And some of

* In an exclusive interview to V. K. Shashikumar of Mediagrove, LTTE leader Kumaran Pathmanathan ('KP'), who is now in Sri Lankan custody, said that India started training the Tamil rebels in the early 1980s around the time peace talks started floundering. They 'were called Thimpu talks [as they

its leaders, including Velupillai Prabhakaran and Gopalaswamy Mahendraraja, alias Mahattaya, routinely visited the battalion's makeshift Officers' Mess.

The charade of bonhomie fell apart when LTTE cadres stepped up operations after refusing to lay down weapons. They shot down a soldier from the Madras battalion. The soldier died in Sukhwinder's arms, which stiffened his resolve to operate aggressively against the LTTE.

Sukhwinder was the commander of the Commando Platoon, a team of the fittest and best-trained soldiers entrusted with independent missions. He rapidly acquired the reputation of being a firebrand leader, fearlessly venturing out with the platoon to hunt for the quarry and strengthen the intelligence network. The opponents, too, were tough, favouring death by cyanide over being captured. The frequent operations by the Commando Platoon began to restrict the freedom of the LTTE militants and cause attrition. It enraged the local LTTE leadership. One day, the CO, Colonel G. S. Sidhu, summoned Sukhwinder and informed him that apparently the militants had placed a bounty on his head.

---

took place in Bhutan]. But the talks failed. Around that time the Indian government gave [military] training to Tamil youths. So we [LTTE] had a base in Tamil Nadu. We had a [military] base in India. All the four Tamil [militant] groups, very strong groups, were trained and armed by India. Like I told you, that was the Cold War period and the international environment was such.' ('Indira Gandhi helped train Tamil rebels, and reaped whirlwind,' *Firstpost*, 23 May 2011.)

'At that juncture, Prime Minister Indira Gandhi decided to offer military training to the cadre of different Tamil militant groups ... The camps were held from 1984 in various parts of the country, including Tamil Nadu, Karnataka and Uttar Pradesh, to train the militants in the use of modern arms. The camps were under the control of the Central agencies. However, the Union government claimed that they were meant to train the militants in self-defence. The largest LTTE camp was located at Kumbarapatti in Kolathur.' ('The largest LTTE training camp was located at Kolathur', *Hindu*, 28 August 2014.)

'I suggest you take leave and go home till things cool off.'

Sukhwinder replied, 'Sir, in that case, please send the entire Commando Platoon on leave. I am not prepared to protect myself any more than them.'

On 19 December 1988, Sukhwinder Sahota (now Acting Captain) left the company base for another foray, searching for the militants. Fifteen kilometres away, where the road traversed thick forest through a tiny inhabitation of twenty houses, the LTTE lay in a deadly ambush. The militants were behind a wall along the road that the convoy had to take.

When they entered the area, militants rained automatic fire on all the vehicles. Several long bursts riddled Sukhwinder's Mitsubishi vehicle. The driver was killed instantly, and the out-of-control vehicle flipped over. Sukhwinder and another soldier, Kunjumon – his 'buddy' – crawled out of the overturned vehicle and stayed hunched behind its frame, still the target of continuous deadly fire.

Within the first few moments of the firefight, Sukhwinder had been shot in several parts of the body. He was losing blood and drifting in and out of consciousness. Even though there was a din all around, Sukhwinder appeared to have lost his hearing, and even his vision seemed to have been impaired. Anticipating that the militants were bound to finally approach the vehicle to finish them off and take away their weapons, the Acting Captain murmured instructions to his buddy: 'Kunjumon Tambi, whenever you hear the LTTE approach, nudge me into consciousness.' Even in that parlous state, he was aware that if the LTTE made it to his 'dead' body, it would be all over for his team, and they would probably cut his head off for public display.

A few minutes later, he felt frantic prodding. Kunjumon was desperately signalling that the LTTE cadres were bearing down upon them. Sukhwinder swung his loaded carbine and emptied an entire magazine of twenty-eight rounds at hazy outlines. Then he fell back into his coma.

All nine militants who had laid the ambush were killed that day. Five of them ran into the Quick Reaction Team rushing to the site. The Commando Platoon had already neutralized the rest. Sukhwinder had killed at least one.

When the QRT tried to lift Sukhwinder Sahota into a vehicle, they were horrified – in the process of picking him up, one of the soldiers's fingers had slid into his skull and what appeared to be grey matter began to spill out. Sukhwinder had received eleven bullet injuries – five in the legs, two in the torso and four in his head. One bullet had stopped a millimetre short of puncturing his heart. The soldiers 'stuffed things back' into his head, bandaged and rushed him to the base.

The doctors were stunned that he was still alive. And they knew that only a miracle would keep him breathing even for a few hours.

The Army flew Sukhwinder to the Meenambakkam airport in Chennai, where a team of doctors took charge. But before he could be transported to the hospital, they realized that if he was to have even a glimmer of a chance, he must move to Pune instead. The injuries were too severe to be treated at the Chennai hospital. Immediately, the aircraft took off for Pune with doctors on board.

As the aircraft rose to the skies, the doctors estimated that, in the best-case scenario, if Sukhwinder survived the flight and immediate operation, he would be a vegetable for the rest of his life. And even that would be miraculous.

Thirty-four years after the day Sukhwinder's bullet-ridden frame was brought to Command Hospital, Pune, I sat across him to recapture his thoughts for this book. The recovery has forced him to lead a life of caution. For fear of suddenly exciting the shrapnel still lodged inside his head into an unwanted motion, in all these decades he hasn't been permitted to taste chillies or do any kind of aerobic exercise whatsoever. But the fact that he had driven alone for several hundred kilometres to speak to me should tell you that he is fitter than many at fifty-eight.

'The doctors were right about there being zero chances of my survival. But they were not aware of my determination,' he said with a hearty chuckle.

Four days into frenetic efforts to save him, the doctors were no more hopeful than when they had first set their eyes on him. His blood pressure was immobile at 240/130, and his pulse was hovering at 38. 'I would have been given up for dead in any other setting,' Sukhwinder said. 'But they were Army doctors, and they would not let go.'

His 'Tambi', who shared his blood group, stood by his bed and watched him round the clock. The battalion had sent two other soldiers with the same blood group, just in case he needed replenishment. A nurse was always at hand, awaiting the moment he would emerge from his coma.

Numerous pieces of shrapnel lodged in his head had made surgeries complex and risky. The doctors called experts abroad to make sure they would do everything right. Eventually, the surgeons decided that a few fragments of the bullets would have to be left unextracted; the alternative was too fraught with dangerous possibilities.

After seven days, when he finally drifted out of unconsciousness, Sahota could not see or hear. It appeared that he had lost these two senses. The doctors decided to keep him on anaesthesia to send him back to sleep for better chances of recovery. But so acute was the pain that he woke up in no time.

'Maybe the pain triggered something or untangled my nerves, and when I came to my senses, I could see and hear again.' Another chuckle.

And what was his first reaction? Those standing around saw him grope around the bed, searching for his weapon.

A few weeks into recovery, Sukhwinder began to plead to rejoin the battalion in Sri Lanka. 'I could not bear to let the battalion down and wanted to unite with my men as fast as possible.' The incredulous hospital CO could not believe his ears. But the requests were relentless.

'Later, I had to take voluntary retirement from the Army. The doctors pronounced my state as "sixty per cent disability". But I would have joined in a heartbeat if the Army had ever recalled me, especially to serve when the unit fought in Kargil.'

Now a businessman in Maharashtra, Captain Sahota has visited the battalion several times. 'No one who served with me is now serving in the battalion. But when I go, the officers and soldiers still lift me up on their shoulders.'

That is what it looks like when culture trumps strategy.

The written and unwritten history of Operation Pawan is awash with tales of similar sacrifices and privations. These are not tales of gladiatorial actions but of 'ordinary' officers and soldiers who fought because that is what was expected of them. These stories explain why the Army fought doggedly despite being saddled with a deeply flawed game plan. No matter how broken the tools of strategy were, the workmen made up for it with sheer determination and a focus on achieving the mission. These attributes are permanent refrains in the musical score of the Army's culture.

Could it be that we place disproportionate emphasis on crafting strategies and not enough on the culture that will make the achievement of goals possible? That certainly appears to be the case with many companies. But as the history of the conflict in Sri Lanka – and arguably in Siachen – instructs us, a robust culture supports thoughtful strategies and can even mitigate imperfect ones.

VI

On 13 April 1984, India captured the 76.4-kilometre Siachen glacier on the Saltoro ridge, a bleak and glaciated wedge between the territory occupied by Pakistan and China. The operation, codenamed Operation Meghdoot, aimed to pre-empt Pakistan's push to occupy it. It was a race to the top and ignited a conflict that neither side had predicted. This can be perceived as an instructive tale of how operations can spiral out far beyond the initial intent of the opposing armies.

Before 1984, Pakistan used to permit foreign mountaineers to explore the area; India would send its climbers to ensure that nothing mischievous was afoot. Gradually, the civilian mountaineering expeditions changed into army patrols. India sensed that Pakistan planned to induct military forces to capture the Saltoro ridge. Thus began Operation Meghdoot, and the ongoing artillery war on the glaciated terrain – at heights of up to 21,000 feet – has claimed over 800 Indian lives, mainly due to the inhospitable weather.

Does Siachen have overwhelming strategic importance in the first place? The jury of military thinkers is out on the subject and on any day, you will find an equal number of well-reasoned arguments for and against it. Having clambered up the glacier thirty-eight years ago, both sides have argued that the area has immense strategic importance. Sceptics question that claim. The Indian strategy can now be summed up in two words: defend it.

How do organizations act on a strategy that is bereft of discernible meaning and rationale other than that 'it has to be done'? What impelled the rank and file to show stunning heroism for thirty-eight years because nothing less would get 'it' done?

Avalanches are not a rare occurrence on the glacier. The one that hit the area of Tiger Saddle at midnight in May 1989 buried a parachute tent in which a JCO and eight soldiers of a battalion of the Brigade of Guards regiment were asleep. Before anybody could stir, over twenty feet of snow had enveloped them.

Two fortuitous factors saved the team from instant death. The hut had been sealed carefully and even under the enormous weight of snow, it retained an oxygen bubble. Two other team members who had been deployed at a nearby observation post for surveillance rushed down the slope and began to dig furiously. In the pitch-dark night and with oxygen scarce in the environment, it took them a few arduous hours to extricate everyone. By the time they ripped up the hut, the rescued soldiers were in varying degrees of hypoxemia – confused, incapacitated and in severe shock. Gradually, most of the soldiers began to stand up and move, but two of them continued to be inert, unable even to speak or sit up.

There is no good time for an avalanche, but this one had come at a particularly harrowing moment, at the end of a fortnight of inclement weather with zero visibility, high winds and constant snowfall. Temperatures had dropped below 50°C. Urine streams froze into sticks of ice. No supplies had been forthcoming. Movement on foot and airlifts by helicopter were impossible. Inhabitants of the now demolished parachute hut had already begun to run out of food. They had survived on besan rotis, salt, tea leaves and sugar for the past couple of days. Their sole connection with the rest of the world, the ANPRC 25 radio set, was on its last legs; the battery was rapidly draining. The radio operator was forever warming it up on the stove to keep up correspondence with the Company HQ at Sia La.

Unable to move, the party remained out in the open for two nights. No one could stay still; within half an hour snow would accumulate and threaten to bury anyone sitting down. Exhausted, one of the soldiers dozed off and had to be dug out of several feet of fresh snow that had piled up above his head. The soldiers did not use shovels for fear of injuring him; they used their bare hands to remove the snow.

The weather did not let up for the next two nights and the party had no choice but to remain in the open. While the two 'frozen' boys were showing no signs of recovery, the health of the others was deteriorating fast. The commander Naib Subedar Ram Chander decided that it was time the party risked everything and began to find its way to the Company HQ. Ordinarily, movement in those conditions would be against all teaching. Still, the need for survival had decimated the choices.

Ram Chander decided to stay with the two immobilized soldiers, as he was the team leader. He retained another soldier for assistance and marched off the rest. One of the soldiers, Havildar S. N. Thakur, recalls how everyone in the team had protested against the idea of the JCO staying behind and putting himself at risk, but he pulled rank for the privilege of looking after the stragglers. 'We knew what he was doing,' Havildar Thakur reminisces. 'We were taught in our battalion that leaders never leave the injured or the dead on the battlefield.'

As we will see in subsequent chapters, never leaving anyone behind is one of the Army's credos, a part of its cultural DNA.

'Watch for the footmarks,' the Junior Commissioned Officer counselled the departing group. 'Step into the one matching the direction of the toes. If you make a mistake, you will end up in Pakistan.' Tied to each other by a rope, the party began its less-than-hopeful trudge.

They foot-slogged all day and night. Snow had obliterated the route markers. Their throats were parched to a point where they could not speak or produce any saliva. All communication was in whispers and gestures. Their urine first turned yellow and then red before drying up altogether. They started picking up a few grams of fresh snow to suck on.

Finally, the weather cleared, and the sun's glimmer filtered through. They saw a snow scooter out to deliver logistical supplies and waved it down. The Company HQ was not too far.

Hav Thakur remembers the moment. 'Eventually, we had no energy left to move and began to crawl.'

The HQ requisitioned Cheetah helicopters for the evacuation. The entire team needed immediate medical care. All survivors had to be flown down from the 23,000-foot altitude to the base camp at 12,000 feet. Like everyone else, Thakur's foot had swollen to the point that a meat cleaver had to be used to cut up the boots and prise open the socks. After first aid, the helicopter ride began.

'I was so exhausted that I just wanted to lie down. But the space inside the Cheetah helicopter was cramped. And I was worried that I might press some wrong button by stretching out and crash the helicopter! The co-pilot saw my discomfiture, reached out and cradled my head. He then made me lie down. 'I was huddled, but it felt heavenly to finally stretch my weary limbs for a bit,' Thakur recalls.

The CO and many others had lined up to receive them at the base camp. Moved to the Advance Dressing Station, they were fed soup and milk as they still couldn't ingest solid foods. An Mi-8 helicopter flew them to Thosie and an An-32 aircraft to Chandigarh. Trained medical assistants accompanied them. Surgeons immediately operated on Thakur for severe injuries. Both his legs were amputated below the knee. All the others met similar fates. The two soldiers who could not move perished before the rescue team could reach them. So did the JCO Naib Subedar Ram Chander and his assistant, who had volunteered to stay back.

When this episode occurred, Lt Gen Prakash Menon had been a young Major in the battalion. Twenty-four years later, he got a surprise call from Thakur.

'Saab, I learnt that you had become a general. Very happy to hear that.'

After Menon had thanked him and asked how he was doing in his house in Bhagalpur, Thakur made a request.

'Please help my son enrol in the army.'

Menon reminded him that the army's recruitment process did not allow recommendations. But he would do what he could. Sadly, Thakur's son died in a motorcycle accident before he could realize his dream.

Menon says that Havildar Thakur calls him every year, especially on Holi. 'I am a south Indian, but since the troops of my battalion were from Bihar, Holi is our favourite festival – and he knew it. The way he says Jai Hind on the phone makes my hair stand; he puts so much emotion into it.' Once, when Menon was posted in Delhi, Thakur called him with a request. He had heard that a Madras regiment soldier – someone he did not even know – had been rescued from an avalanche in the northern glacier. He wanted Menon to go to the hospital and look him up.

'Why did you want your son to join the army? After all, you lost a great deal of your life – and won no medals either,' General Menon remembers asking Thakur.

Of course I knew the answer even before I heard him. That is the answer we are likely to hear from most army men, including those who have retired or were boarded out of service after being wounded or have lost their kin in the army.

Thakur told General Menon, 'Sir, there is no better life than in the army. Within weeks of joining the recruit training, you develop a sense of pride that fills you with *jazba* and *josh*. You feel that the first family you have is your battalion. Even today, the battalion invites me to the annual Raising Day functions. The last time I attended one was at Amritsar. The CO had sent three soldiers who lived in a nearby village on leave to accompany me. With their help, I went in a wheelchair. When I reached the venue of the functions, all senior veterans – officers, JCOs and OR – were there. They spent so much time sitting next to us – asking about our welfare, eating and drinking with us … where else would have I found this *izzat*? We were seen off with affection, and the unit gave us gifts and memorabilia. I became younger by years, sir.'

Peter Drucker was right. Culture does eat strategy for breakfast. When we draw up a strategy for our organizations, we must paint the details on the canvas of the prevailing culture. If the culture of a company appears inadequate to support its strategy – of diversification, going international, pivoting to a new clientele, seeking a merger or acquisition, making a bold move, turning into a public enterprise and so on – the leadership must take steps to transform or reinforce its deficient elements first. It is a painstaking process that requires time and effort.

For the success of any strategy, culture can be the critical defining element. It can elevate the team's performance to such levels that even the feebleness of the original gameplan may be rendered largely inconsequential.

2

WHY ARE OFFICERS DYING?

'You don't lead by pointing and telling people someplace to go. You lead by going to that place and making a case.'

– KEN KESEY

I

SOME NAMES CAN NEVER shake off their association with controversy and drama. If you take a roadtrip from Delhi to Jammu, forty kilometres before you reach the state's winter capital, straddling National Highway 44 is a nondescript district town that has made more than a few marks in recent history.

Samba – then an even sleepier village-town – shot to national prominence in 1979 when news broke of a festering spy scandal. Allegedly, Pakistan's military intelligence had cultivated two Indian Army soldiers serving in a brigade headquarters in Samba. At less than fifteen kilometres from the international border, Samba's proximity was the key attraction for the Pakistani plotters. The handlers tasked the moles with reporting the Army's dispositions along the western border. Army inquiries into the espionage hinted at a startling revelation: by casual association, the two 'spies' had drawn 168 unsuspecting serving officers and soldiers into their dragnet. However, after two decades of investigation, the duo's claims proved to be a piece of poorly scripted fiction. Indeed, in an affidavit, one of the culprits exonerated the rest of the 'suspects' of any involvement. But, by then, the place was imprinted on the collective consciousness of anyone interested in military matters.*

In the years since that failed 'espionage', the military cantonment on the outskirts of Samba has been the object of Pakistani terrorists' attention in more than one instance. In the high noon of militancy in the 1990s and early 2000s, the intense pressure of the Indian Army along the Pir Panjal range of mountains in the north forced Pakistani intelligence machinery to look elsewhere for infiltration by terrorists. There has been a tacit and time-honoured agreement between the two countries that while both continue to regard the Line of Control as an unsettled boundary, there is no such ambiguity about the international border. The latter is off-limits for transgression. But over the years, Pakistan has hardly demonstrated any propensity to conform to such niceties. The geographic reality is also that the crisscrossing rivulets and streams that embellish the area provide cover to surreptitious intruders. The border near Samba thus became one of the preferred 'gateways' for pushing in terrorists.

In May 2008, two terrorists sneaked into the military station, creating a hostage situation. A day-long battle later, both were killed after the operation had consumed the lives of two soldiers and a journalist. In a repeat instance, in September 2013, Pakistan-sponsored terrorists created another terror situation at Samba.†

---

* However, we need to absolve Samba on another count of notoriety by association – the origin of the character Sambha, Gabbar Singh's famous sidekick, played by the actor Mac Mohan in the blockbuster movie *Sholay*, had nothing to do with this hamlet!

† These were not the only attacks on Samba army installations. In 2015 and 2018, terrorists attempted strikes but were felled by security forces. In the

It all began in the wee hours when three terrorists, armed to the teeth and dressed in Army uniforms, commandeered an autorickshaw from a village, barely a kilometre from the international border. They ordered the driver to take them to Samba. Unable to locate the military camp, they first struck a police station, killing three police officers. Then they took control of another vehicle – a Tempo – and reached Hiranagar, a military outpost some six kilometres from the main town.

In the initial phase of any militant attack, intelligence is always sketchy, and the available inputs may not be credible. This informational vacuum takes time to fill. Commanders must therefore make sense of chaos from the fragments at their immediate disposal.

The morning events that started with the hijacked three-wheeler and moved to the police station had been fast-paced and shrouded in fuzziness. 16 Cavalry, a regiment of the armoured corps located at Hiranagar, did not receive any coherent alert about the impending attack. The terrorists disembarked at the cantonment gates and unleashed indiscriminate firing on the sentry.

The volley of fire took the sentry by complete surprise, and he was shot on sight. Now the entry of the militants was unopposed. Just past the gate was a two-storey building that housed a makeshift officers' mess. They proceeded to storm it. At that time of the day, there was only a *masalchi* (utensil cleaner) present in the mess, busy washing utensils to ready the place for breakfast. He received the next burst of fire with fatal consequences. The terrorists then went on a room-to-room search, lobbing grenades before they entered, a clear indication of their military training.

It was the period when the unit had dispersed after the morning physical training parade. The CO, Colonel Avin Uthaiya, a second-generation Army officer, had taken his shoes off and settled at his desk in his house to review official mail. He heard blasts and AK-47

---

latter instance, the BSF discovered an eighty-metre-long trans-border tunnel that had been dug to facilitate infiltration.

fire and instantly deduced that the regiment was under some sort of attack. Barefoot, he rushed out in his morning parade clothes: a camouflage shirt and trousers. His family stayed behind, oblivious to what was unfolding just 200 metres away.

As Uthaiya ran towards the din, he saw a unit vehicle that had been readied as an armed escort for a convoy. He grabbed the weapon from the driver and shouted instructions for activating the Quick Reaction Team. He then rushed towards the gate and found the sentry bleeding to death. Realizing that the action scene had shifted to the officers' mess, the CO turned to enter that building.

There is much more to this story. But already, a question leaps out from the first few minutes of the unfolding saga – what impels the most senior officer of an organization to throw his life in peril, without even waiting for backup? What engenders such ownership in an individual that he instinctively steps up to protect the people he leads? We come across countless Army stories where leaders readily move into harm's way to protect the rank and file – an instinctive demonstration of what it is to lead by example. It can be argued that no cultural attribute contributes more to the Army's effectiveness than the propensity of its commanders to lead from the front – and always set an example, no matter how costly the sacrifice or privation.

A volley of bullets halted the colonel's progress. When he was moving towards the mess complex, a terrorist appeared at the door and shot him in the arm and chest. Avin instantly lost most of his elbow. During the rest of his endeavours, he could barely grasp a weapon.

Tanks are the primary weapon of armoured corps units but are seldom brought into play unless it is a full-fledged mechanized battle. During peace station tenures, tanks leave the garage only for firing practices or training purposes. Fortuitously, 16 Cavalry had recently returned from a field firing exercise, and the tanks were out for a 'gun-cleaning parade'. While some soldiers were busy cleaning the tanks, the rest of the regiment had moved to the barracks at the end of the morning physical training.

Grievously wounded and in severe pain, the CO first struggled to hoist himself over a boundary wall and take cover. But he immediately realized he could hardly influence the unfolding 'battle' from a defiladed position. He made a second excruciatingly painful effort to climb back. As he barely scampered over the wall, Avin noticed that his arm was hanging by a sliver, and the gunshots had blown away bone and tissue. Cradling his shattered arm with the good one, he hurried to where the tanks were parked.

The regiment's second-in-command, Lt Col Bikramjeet Singh, was Colonel Uthaiya's neighbour. He had seen his commanding officer rushing towards the sound of firing and blasts. He too quickly grabbed a weapon from another stand-by vehicle and ran towards the growing pandemonium. His buddy followed him.* By then, the Quick Reaction Team too had started moving in, and Bikramjeet passed rapid instructions to rush and protect the married quarters where officers and other ranks lived. The duo then moved towards the officers' mess to engage the terrorists who by now were on the top floor and had the apparent advantage of dominating the area.

Over the next few minutes, Bikramjeet and his buddy perished in the firefight.

Meanwhile, Col Uthaiya had reached the tanks. Two concerns were playing on his mind – the proximity of the married quarters and the ammunition dump to the scene of action made these areas vulnerable. On his instructions, the soldiers lifted and lowered him into a tank. Commandeering that tank, the CO asked the driver to move it towards the mess building. He then instructed that the officers' mess be rammed using the full weight of the armoured vehicle.

---

* Jawans who assist officers in maintaining turnout were initially known as 'orderlies'. Subsequently, the title was shifted to '*sahayaks*'. Now these assistants are called 'buddies' to denote the special relationship an officer shares with the soldier assisting him.

The tank smashed into the mess wall, quickly reversed and struck again. Then it came to a standstill, the engine still running. The driver noticed that his commanding officer appeared to have passed out due to blood loss. He reversed his tank with a mighty roar and moved back towards the headquarters.

But within minutes, Col Uthaiya regained consciousness and asked the driver where they were. The driver informed the colonel that he had moved the tank to a safe area to evacuate the CO for medical attention. But the CO had other ideas. Avin ordered the driver to move the tank back to the mess area and resume bludgeoning the building. During the second round of that assault, Col Uthaiya fainted again.

This unconventional manoeuvre unnerved the terrorists; their Pakistani masters had never handed them a playbook that described retaliation by armoured vehicles. Unable to take the mayhem elsewhere, the militants crouched inside the building, allowing the unit to gain valuable time. Three more tanks arrived, all commanded by young officers who were not about to be left out of the action. The new entrants signalled for the CO's tank to be driven to safety and took position a mere ten metres away from the terrorists, now holed up on the first floor of the building. The Quick Reaction Team had sealed off all escape routes. The encirclement was getting stronger as all soldiers on miscellaneous duties, such as distributing food to sentries, receiving soldiers returning from leave and working in the garages, also rushed to the armoury and grabbed weapons. More and more soldiers had inserted themselves into the cordon without needing formal orders.

Teams from the neighbouring Sikh Regiment battalion also arrived, as did a group of the Special Forces.* Another infantry team secured the nearby Army Public School, obviating an attack on another potential target.

* Erstwhile name: the Para Commandoes.

At this point, the tanks faced the building, their engines running, guns loaded with lethal ammunition but could not fire because a piquant situation had developed. The leading tank had a newlywed officer whose wife was also on the first floor of the mess, trapped in a guest room. The young lady hid, fearing a horrendous outcome. Her fears were well founded – the terrorists were holed up right outside her room. Thankfully, thus far, they were not aware of her presence.

The dilemma of the troops encircling the building was unnervingly plain – how to eliminate the militants and simultaneously rescue the civilian. The petrified woman managed a brief mobile call with her husband, wherein she conveyed her extreme trepidation through urgent whispers.

The column's commander from the neighbouring Sikh Regiment battalion (whose troops too had arrived without being requisitioned) managed to shout to her. 'Push out the cooler from your window!' he instructed. The contraption landed with a loud thud, masked by the rest of the din.

The Sikh soldiers took their turbans off and fashioned a rope with them. A volunteer, Havildar Baljeet Singh, climbed up to the first-floor window. When he tried to enter, his AK-47 rifle got stuck in the window frame. The moment demanded immediate action. Baljeet got rid of his weapon and signalled the lady to come to the window. That must have been a horrifying scene for her – an unturbanned man with a flowing beard, summoning her frantically might not have looked like an Army soldier in that heart-stopping moment. She froze. Baljeet knew that it was not a moment for gentle explanations and parleys. He stepped in, swung her over his shoulders and rappelled down on the makeshift rope made of turbans. A silent cheer went up as he moved her to safety.

The soldiers witnessed the rescue, and the officers gave an immediate all-clear signal to the tanks. With his wife out of harm's way, the young officer fired a deadly 125mm high-explosive round into the building. The first floor was damaged from the impact. The next round pierced the house and exploded on the rear retaining wall. After that, a decision was taken not to fire the main gun; it could have been unsafe for the troops in the cordon.

The firing of the tanks was the defining moment in the morning's frenzied operations. The unexpectedly powerful retaliation seemed to have paralyzed the terrorists and pinned them down; their next move unclear. Would they storm out, all guns blazing? Would they await the darkness?

The Special Forces team deliberated on the next course of action. The only entry into the building was the one that Havildar Baljeet had heroically used to retrieve the lady. But surely, using the same route would be quite hazardous, even foolhardy.

Still, it was no time to demur or take counsel of one's fears. The Special Forces team entered the building through the same first-floor window the Sikh Regiment soldier had used. They killed the remaining two of the three heavily armed terrorists. A sniper, Maj Pankaj of the Sikh Regiment, had earlier picked one out with the help of an aviation corps helicopter pressed into the action.

The dead terrorists were in their twenties. Besides the arsenal, they had carried handcuffs to create a 'Boko Haram' hostage situation and a blaze of publicity.

Four army personnel, four policemen and two civilians had also died that morning. It took hours of thorough search to clear the damaged building of booby traps. The Army finally called off the operation at dusk.

As early as 8 a.m., a TV grab showed a soldier of the regiment under attack, carrying a casualty on his shoulders. The soldier was flagging down a car for help. Also visible in the same shot was a tank moving along the fence.

The corps commander, Lt Gen Praveen Bakshi, was shocked that a live operation was being telecast not only for the rest of the world to see but was also to the handlers of the terrorists, potentially providing them vital information. It brought back memories of Operation Parakram: the then defence minister George Fernandes had spoken angrily of a similar spectacle of minefields along the border filmed by a well-known journalist. Lt Gen Bakshi rang up the Inspector General of Police and asked him to stop the absurdity. In five minutes, the police cleared the entire area of print and electronic media reporters.

But that is not all that had caught Lt Gen Bakshi's eye. He enquired about the brave soldier who, even while under fire, had been seen rescuing a fallen comrade. That was an action worthy of recognition.

The staff officers later informed him that the rescuer in question was a 'repeat offender', an ex-non-commissioned officer whom a court martial had recently tried for an offence, ordering his discharge from service. The court's judgment was under final review by the Army's legal branch before being sent for by the endorsement of the army commander at Chandimandir.

Lt Gen Bakshi told me he had strongly felt the man had more than atoned for his misdemeanour with a display of such selfless courage. 'Wasn't that the acme of soldiering?' he said. He firmly took it up with the army commander to consider a lenient view during the judicial review. The latter agreed. The Army reversed the court's orders of the soldier's discharge from service. The rationale was crystal clear: by going beyond the call of duty during operations, you stand a chance to redeem yourself.

There is more.

A helicopter had been requisitioned to transport the mortal remains of Lt Col Bikramjeet to his hometown, Chandigarh. The entire leadership of the Army in the area, led by the corps commander Lt Gen Bakshi, lined up at the helipad in Mamun to pay their last respects. But soon after, another piece of worrisome information arrived: the helicopter had lost radio contact. Everyone feared the worst.

At 5:30 p.m., with darkness only an hour away, the waiting brass learnt that the helicopter had landed en route, awaiting sanction for Lt Col Bikramjeet's wife to accompany the remains.*

'I found this incredulous,' Lt Gen Bakshi recounted to me. 'I was on the verge of giving the go-ahead, which was way beyond my charter, when I received a call from Headquarter Western command at Chandimandir that the Ministry of Defence sanction was not forthcoming. I strongly objected. I couldn't imagine asking the widow of a martyr to disembark. Within minutes came the response: the helicopter would carry her, sanction or not, consequences be damned. We paid our last respects to Lt Col Bikramjeet Singh; the exhausted crew refused to be replaced and, instead, donned their night-flying goggles and took off for Chandigarh.'

The three fallen soldiers hailed from Tamil Nadu, Rajasthan and Kerala. The staff was making arrangements for moving their remains by commercial flights. While details were buttoned up, Lt Gen Bakshi travelled to Pathankot to meet the injured. 'En route to the military hospital, I received a call from the Army commander in Udhampur, Lt Gen Hooda. He advised me that sending the balance of the three fatal casualties by military aircraft was far preferable because the bureaucratic procedures of the civil airport and airlines could be excruciatingly long, even humiliating.

Lt Gen Bakshi agreed. 'I decided to cut across all channels and called up the SASO WAC, Air Marshal B. S. Dhanoa (later Chief of Air Staff). I requested military aircraft to transport the remains to the three states. He responded positively and confirmed in thirty minutes that the requisite aircraft had been diverted and would be in position by 7 a.m. in Jammu. I must mention that the chief minister of Jammu and Kashmir, Omar Abdullah, insisted on coming to Samba at night to commend the troops and was there the next morning to pay his respects to the fallen.'

---

* Civilian travel by service helicopters requires an ink-signed copy of approval from the defence minister. Only the spouses of the Chief of the Army Staff and the Army Commanders are exempt from this requirement.

When Lt Gen Bakshi reached the military hospital in Pathankot, he learnt that Col Avin Uthaiya was in the operating room. His wife Kavyaa was sitting at the entrance to the operation theatre. Lt Gen Bakshi walked in, not knowing what to expect. The surgery had just been completed, the doctor conveyed that the bullet had done severe damage, but his condition did not appear to be life-threatening.

'His wife was overcome with relief and went back to doing what only the wife of a commanding officer can do. Leaving her husband's side, she marched off to meet the families of the other casualties. Her husband was in safe hands and, as the first lady of the unit, she wanted to look after the others.'

Later, Col Uthaiya told Lt Gen Bakshi that when he saw the seniormost officer by his bedside, he had felt assured that he would pull through.

Lt Gen Bakshi recalled, 'I asked him what propelled him to go back and charge the terrorists for a second time. His simple answer was, "I had been hit, and I knew that, in all likelihood, I would die. But I had to prevent the terrorists from reaching the jawan's married quarters. So, I wanted to create a diversion."'*

As he sat by Col Uthaiya's bed, holding his hand, Lt Gen Bakshi could see him swimming in and out of consciousness. 'Only once did he show some awareness of the situation. He pressed my hand and said something I can never forget.'

'Sir, did we get them?' Col Uthaiya asked, his voice a weak murmur.

When I nodded in affirmation, he smiled and again drifted out of consciousness.

* Among others, Lt Col Bikramjeet Singh was awarded a Shaurya Chakra, while Col Avin Uthaiya, Maj Pankaj Kumar and Hav Baljeet Singh were all decorated with the Sena Medal for gallantry.

II

It needs no exceptional analytical skills to internalize the full force of this culture's uniqueness.

It is one that propels the head of an organization – the commanding officer in this case – to rush down, even barefoot, to take personal charge of the situation when his people appear to be in grave peril.

This culture instinctively makes him ignore bullets that have blown off his elbow and that may soon dismember his arm. It makes him put aside his unimaginable pain and insist on staying the course to lead even through a cycle of repeated fainting.

That same culture makes a Sikh Regiment soldier, with zero affiliation to the unit under attack, scale a wall to drop himself unarmed onto a floor brimming with terrorists, to rescue a lady with whom he has not even the remotest connection. Also consider the non-commissioned officer, recently disgraced, who buried whatever rancour he may have carried and hoisted a fallen comrade onto his soldiers to safety and for medical attention. Or the young officers who, in a couple of years since they ceased being civilians, now believe that they are to lead from the front quite literally. The second-in-command who does not wait for the reinforcements and throws himself into the battle. The helicopter pilots who will defy rules and darkness to carry the mortal remains of a fellow soldier. The senior officers – in this case, the corps commander Lt Gen Praveen Bakshi – who will go to any lengths to be with the injured, even holding their hands. Even Kavyaa, the wife of the commanding officer, who, upon assurance of her husband's stable condition, follows her unwritten mandate of taking care of other families because they too are family to her in the most real sense. The CO himself, who, upon regaining consciousness, does not instinctively check to ensure he still has both elbows but simply asks, 'Did we get them?'.

The magical ingredient that makes all this possible is the quality of 'leading from the front' and 'leading by example' – two phrases that can be used interchangeably in most contexts. The Army cultivates it from the day a soldier enters its fold. It encourages and rewards its practice. It drums into everyone that taking responsibility and stepping up are the basics, rather than glorious acts.

Every detail of the story above, including the words of the injured CO, is accurate – as is the case with all other accounts in this book. If they sound far more heroic than what one sees on the celluloid screen, it is because they are.

I will even go so far as to say that if there is one, just one, leadership quality that distinguishes leaders from the rest, it is this: good leaders lead by example. They are in the midst of the action. They are visible, not perpetually hidden behind a frosted glass door. They are seen not merely on plaques or in coffee table books but also among the troops and the workers. The followers must know in their bones that their leader is more competent, works harder and takes more significant risks than them. He cares for and will protect them. At the very least, he will share, in equal measure, their suffering and the pain of every defeat. That is easily the theme that recurs in almost every Army story.

Leaders who lead from the front and are visible in the vortex of action achieve that one thing all of us desperately want from our organizations. We want to feel safe – both physically and psychologically.

A CEO, a manager or department head who stays with the team as it grapples with a difficult assignment or is having a challenging day. The plant or production head who is on the spot to ensure that the last set of orders is safely loaded onto the delivery vehicles. The principal who is simply present in close proximity, while their staff and students are working late into the night to prepare for a college function. Even monarchs would perch on top of an elephant in the middle of a swirling battle so that the soldiers could see that they were on the scene rather than in the safety of their tent. The head of a major bank who chooses to visit the remotest of branches, not merely to audit performance but be present among the lowest-ranking team members, is building morale through visibility and fellowship. These examples are no different from that of a CO in close proximity during a firefight with militants.

Good leaders do not interfere and micro-manage; that would render the exercise far less useful. Instead, they reassure and even calm frayed nerves. They are present for any last-minute guidance, but more importantly, as an unmistakable signal that they care.

III

The presence of commanders in the middle of the action has a calming and inspiring effect. That is an essential nuance of leading from the front. Capt Nirbhay Sharma learnt this lesson on the East Pakistan battlefield during the 1971 war.

Tangail is a district around 100 kilometres east of Dhaka. The Indian Army's 2 Parachute Regiment was tasked to capture Poongli bridge on the Jamuna, thus severing the Pakistani brigade's only link to Mymensingh. This was to make a stand against the fall of the capital city.

On 11 December 1971, the battalion boarded two C-119 transport planes at Dum Dum and Kalaikunda and was para-dropped in broad daylight over a widespread area. After regaining command and control, the paratroopers moved swiftly to their destination, the Poongli bridge. The plan had thus far worked like clockwork and the troops captured the bridge well before the retreating Pakistani soldiers could reach it. Later at night, the Pakistani brigade reached the bridge to an unexpected and fiery welcome.

But even for the well-trained paratroopers, uncertainty loomed. Dropped in an alien and hostile land, even they felt the lack of situational clarity that isolation can generate. The paratroopers were strung from the bridge along the river and scattered over four kilometres. Communication was patchy, often due to the need to preserve information security by maintaining 'radio silence'. Most soldiers did not have an up-to-date sense of the unfolding scenario. The emerging situation hardly cleared up through the night. The 'fog of war' did not lift even when dawn broke.

Nerves were clearly racked on all sides – the withdrawing Pakistanis could counter-attack, the Mukti Bahini cadres were raring to go and unfamiliarity of the location all added to the stress. In this situation of mounting uncertainty, the soldiers were prone to engage anything that moved with lethal fire.

There was also a stampede of civilians in all directions. Many were wading through fields to retreat from the scene. Still others were attempting to approach the river to welcome the liberators. The situation was ripe for possible collateral damage as civilians could get caught in the unremitting crossfire. That could result in a tactical error turning into a high-profile mistake of strategic proportions.

Concerned that there might be unintended casualties, the CO Lt Col Kulwant Singh Pannu repeatedly asked his young adjutant to 'ask everyone to stop firing'. But the troops were spread across the riverbank and, for security reasons, radio communication had to be used sparingly. At last, the adjutant despatched a few soldiers to convey the CO's 'personal message'. When the troops learnt that he was near and in complete control of the situation, the firing subsided. 'But I realized that day,' Capt (later Lt Gen) Nirbhay Sharma said, 'how vital it is for leaders to be present and visible.' It reassures the troops that the leadership is around to give directions and to hold their hands if things go south. It may not be necessary for leaders – particularly in the corporate setting and large companies – to be 'visible' or 'near' in the literal sense. In some situations, it may even cramp the style of the subordinates. But through personalized communication, regular visits and gestures that go beyond the transactional, leaders can effectively convey a sense of being present. The effort must be genuine, or it will not matter. Of course, nothing can replace the physical presence of the leader, especially when the team is faced with a crisis or challenge.

Lt Gen Sharma recounts another moment from his regiment's history where the same lesson was highlighted. In 1948, in Jammu & Kashmir, the 3 Parachute Regiment troops were advancing from Rajauri to relieve Poonch from the threat of marauding Pakistani raiders. The column was facing sporadic and largely desultory opposition on the way. But near Galuti, sections of the battalions lost contact with each other at one point, and a potentially chaotic situation developed. It was a pitch-dark night, and it appeared that there might be a loss of control over the situation.

The CO Col Dharam Singh decided the troops would rally if they could see where he was – the moment demanded visibility. Going against the basic operational tenets of staying concealed from the enemy, he climbed a large boulder and lit a cigarette – something no one else in the battalion could have dared to do.

Decades later, Nirbhay Sharma, then a major general in command of a Rashtriya Rifles force in north Kashmir, was able to put the lesson of 'being visible' into action.

In the 1990s, there were no quiet days for the Army in Kashmir. The evening a portion of Pattan began to burn was another moment when a tactical matter could have easily flared up into a politically strategic problem.

Pattan is a small town in the Baramulla district. The highway from Kupwara to Srinagar winds through it and, at one point, passes through a tunnel with houses on either side. The geography presents an ideal location for an ambush. The militants have exploited such spots on more than a few occasions to fire at Army convoys. The idea is to not just cause damage to the Army but to create an inflammatory situation that could trigger collateral damage among civilians when the troops unleash retaliatory fire. The Army is conscious of this stratagem, and troops have, therefore, almost invariably been restrained in their response.

That evening, Maj Gen Sharma received information that a firefight was ongoing in the town and a locality had caught fire. The militants had managed to kidnap and kill a soldier. The soldier was on a regular patrol through the town and was briefly dissociated from his compatriots to visit a shop. That is when he was ambushed, dragged inside the shop and murdered.

On noticing the his absence, the rest of the patrol had tactically retraced their steps, only to be greeted by a volley from the militants' AK-47 rifles. A house was set ablaze in the process. Towns and villages in Kashmir are thickly inhabited; once a fire starts, a large number of houses can burn down, unless the situation is rapidly controlled.

Gen Sharma knew that protocol or norms did not warrant his presence near the scene. Indeed, other commanders in the chain would step in. An officer of his rank is not required to put himself in harm's way unless there are compelling reasons. But he was equally aware that a number of the permanent incumbents were on leave or away, which could add to the flux of the moment. Brutality against one's compatriots can understandably charge emotions. And the cocktail of anger, danger and uncertainty can result in operational situations with undesirable outcomes.

The General drove up to the town in a cavalcade, went on to the centre of the town and stopped next to a police station. Two shops were already ablaze, and the air was thick with the exchange of gunfire. Suddenly the troops saw their highest-ranking officer in their midst. It added a sense of reassurance to the moment.

Why would a senior Army officer risk his life by jumping into the fray most recognizably? Why would he place himself in a dangerously chaotic situation where he would be directly responsible for the consequences of every decision that junior leaders take in the chain? 'I sensed that when troops see me, they will feel calmer, and the situation may become a tad easier to handle,' he later told me. 'And what of the risk you put yourself in,' I asked? Gen Sharma shrugged in response.

Easier it did become. The firing ceased, order was restored, and the blaze was put out.

IV

So, let us turn to the curious title of this chapter – why are officers dying?

On 18 February 2019, an *India Today* headline told us that in J&K, an Army major was among four soldiers killed in an encounter in Pulwama.[1] On 17 June the same year, it reported another skirmish with the militants. The headline read, 'Army Major killed, another officer and two jawans injured in Kashmir encounter.'[2] There is, however, nothing unique about these headlines. Every loss of this nature is horrendous. It devastates the families and the soldiers' units. Hardly a week passes without reports of an officer or two and a few soldiers having perished, even if the pieces may be somewhat hard to locate in our newspapers.

Since 1989, when the conflagration erupted in the Valley and later spread across Pir Panjal into Rajouri, Poonch and Suarnakot on one side and Doda-Kishtwar on the other, the Army has regularly suffered casualties. Even the frequency of such losses is no longer noteworthy. But the surprising subtext is the almost unfailing presence of an officer or two among the mix of casualties. The ratio of officers to Other Rank – the JCOs, NCOs and soldiers – in a fighting unit hardly suggests that so many officers should be in harm's way. Indeed, a far more significant proportion of officers are killed or injured than what the logic of the ratios indicates. So, what is at play here?

In the first decade of the millennium, I found myself working with a mandate to assist in coordinating all anti-terrorist operations in the Kashmir Valley. These three years had come on the heels of a previous three-year stint of commanding a Rashtriya Rifles battalion – units raised solely to fight militancy. It turned out to be a remarkable period of education; professionally, I was exposed to the 'strategy' end of the business of fighting insurgency and could thus join many dots that had eluded me during my experience as a ground soldier.

Every week I was required to brief a three-star general on the state of counter-insurgency operations in the Valley. I decided that these briefings must rise above the bare bones of statistics which, though fascinating, were a repetition of the unlimited data that the commanders receive daily, sometimes even hourly. How could I lift this a notch or two on the usefulness scale?

I decided to analyse one aspect of operations each week and present the findings during the briefings. I selected the incidence of casualties in operations as one of the first subjects to explore. Could the data lead us to answers for reducing attrition? My team had to dive deep for answers since operations have several moving parts and myriad factors can result in casualties. We scrutinized every conceivable angle, not just the officer casualties. The analysis threw up several conclusions. And among those conclusions was the answer to the question posed in the title of this chapter. That revelation was at once revealing and unsurprising.

As the branch dealing with counter-terrorist operations, we had a humongous amount of meticulously maintained historical data on many operational aspects, including casualties. We went to work to find an answer to the question of officer mishaps. The absence of a conclusion from the data was also treated as a conclusion. During this exercise, I suspected we might be unable to interpolate the data to reach a concrete and discernible answer. I was wrong.

We looked at the data from every conceivable angle. Which type of operations caused the most casualties? Was it 'cordon and search', 'ambush' or 'pin-point raids'? Did the bulk of these occur during the day or night? Which terrain was the deadliest – jungles, mountains, built-up areas or plains? During which part of the operation were these casualties most frequently incurred? What about the servicemen's length of service, level of experience, rank and even mode of entry into the Army? How many of these officers and soldiers had received the pre-induction orientation and training at the Battle School – an organization set up for this precise objective?

At the end of this exercise, we saw clear daylight on some of the issues. Others remained elusive and ambiguous. But on the core question, we had clarity.

A typical anti-terrorist operation, say, in a thickly built village, starts with some information about the presence of the militants. The precise location is often unknown, and the search becomes vital to the effort. Since troops are moving into an area figuratively blindfolded, it is arguably one of the most perilous stages of the operation.

After a cordon has been drawn around the suspected narrow winding *mohallas* (streets) – or in some cases, the entire village – the search party led by an officer approaches the perceived target. Movement through constricted spaces with no cover from the fire drawn from any window or rooftop can be hazardous – but it is unavoidable. The tactical playbook legislates that a few best-trained soldiers – called scouts – move right in front, going from cover to cover, watching each other's back. Arguably, this is the riskiest part of most operations.

The command element – the officer's party – is to be located within the remaining column – sufficiently ahead to be able to react to any evolving situation. But in no case is it required to be at the head of the column – exposing the commanders to first shots would hardly make tactical sense for the mission. The idea is that as information from the scouts percolates back via radio or even word of mouth, the commander – who is forward enough to be close to the likely eruption of action and central enough to control the party

– will construct a picture from the developing scenario, make rapid decisions and pass appropriate orders to the team.

But as we the analysts had already suspected, a different script was being followed in reality. On numerous occasions, the young officers insisted on leading from the front – *literally*! Officers, especially young lieutenants and captains, instinctively feel that they must not put the soldiers in greater jeopardy than their own selves. The culture of the Army makes them feel protective towards the men they command – no matter that the officer may be several years younger than his team members.

I had seen this first-hand as a CO; when danger loomed, officers defied classical training and caution to be physically ahead. And now, I was discovering this was a paradigm, not an outlier. Officers keen to lead by example and from the front silently consign the tactical teachings to the backburner, even as they suffer casualties.

In 2021, I checked the ratio of casualties incurred by officers to all other ranks in the conflict-ridden Valley of Kashmir. The total strength of the Army in the Kashmir region comprises 700-plus officers and approximately 44,000 other ranks, a ratio of 1:60. The actual numbers reflect a vastly different equation. One officer loses his life for every fourteen soldiers that perish in operations. The story of non-fatal casualties – that could easily have been fatal but for providence and the wayward aim of the militants – is even more instructive. There is an officer among every eleven wounded soldiers.

A similar picture emerges when we cast our attention on the previous operations. Statistics tell us that the ratios of officers to men of other ranks killed in the 1965 and 1971 wars with Pakistan were 1:9.3 and 1:9.8 respectively. It was higher – 1:7.5 in Sri Lanka. The Kargil conflict ratio is equally skewed.

Is this a good thing? I cannot unequivocally say it is. But does it cast a precise beam of understanding as to why wave after wave of Indian Army soldiers was willing to face certain death while attacking the bare slopes of Kargil because the officers were with them every step of the bloody journey? One of the prime reasons for implicit obedience in the Army is because the soldiers respect the officers – and that is not a mere treacle-like statement. It is the bedrock of the Army's culture.

V

My civilian friends often – and understandably – ascribe the phenomenon of 'leading from the front' to superior training or even patriotism. The latter is, of course, no more than well-meant sentimentality. Army officers are no more or less patriotic than anyone else, and truth be told, words like 'patriotism' are seldom heard in any discourse within the Army. These are certainly not any part of the socialization. On the other hand, training is intrinsic to cultural development. As will be delineated in a subsequent chapter, training forms a critical cement that holds the structure of culture together. But culture is a sum of many parts, not just training alone. And the totality of that culture drives officers and soldiers to lead by example and consistently from the vanguard.

Twenty-one-year-old Padmapani Acharya had joined his Rajputana Rifles battalion from the Indian Military Academy. The son of an Air Force officer, he was considered 'chirpy and naughty' by his colleagues, always ready to act 'without too much reflection'. Some said he often did not mind jettisoning tact while speaking his mind.

The battalion was deployed along the Line of Control in the Kupwara sector. The posts dotted high-altitude mountains at 12,500 feet. In those days, the area was prone to infiltration, and the battalion had the onerous task of vigil over highly challenging terrain. Heavy snow and inclement weather added to the difficulty of patrolling the area.

In the early 1990s, the battalion tasked young Acharya to lead a two-day patrol. The party had ten soldiers. They were to plod through relentless snowfall, worsened by stormy winds, to detect if enemy infiltrators were using these bleak circumstances to slide into Kashmir and cause mayhem. The presence of such patrols is aimed at deterring these kinds of enterprises. The patrolling party was self-contained for forty-eight hours.

As they embarked on the mission, Acharya realized that weather and fresh snow had made the task even more hazardous than usual. Visibility was minimal, and the chances of going astray were more likely. His first decision was to put himself at the head of the column, the rest of the troops now following him in single file.

A day into the gruelling march, the weather deteriorated even more, and the nightmare of the patrolling party losing its orientation became a reality. In the growing blizzard, half of the patrol separated from the others at one point and was untraceable. Acharya and the remaining squad began to retrace their steps. But the snow had obliterated their footsteps, and it was near impossible to realign with the original approach. But he continued to move back and reached the only landmark they had crossed that was still visible: a looming cliff.

Amidst these trying moments, the radio set decided to die. Acharya could no longer communicate with anyone in the world. And, naturally, there was no way he could now requisition a helicopter either.

Back in the battalion headquarter, once the Commanding Officer realized that an ominous radio silence had descended, he decided to launch another patrol to rescue the first. The brigade commander briefly questioned the wisdom of pushing more soldiers into hazards, but the CO was crystal clear. He said, 'No matter the cost, we won't leave even one soldier behind.'

After a day's effort, Acharya reunited with his original team members that had fallen back. Conditions made progress impossible, but he was unwilling to abort the mission. At night, there was a real danger that the snowfall could bury all the patrol party members, so Acharya made soldiers sit in pairs, facing and continually 'slapping' each other to stay awake. In the morning, in sub-zero temperatures, he took off a piece of his clothing and set it on fire, hoping it would attract the notice of a search party.

And it did.

On the seventh day after its deployment, the second patrol launched by the unit located Acharya's band of soldiers, now completely sleep-deprived and enervated to their chilled bones but still alive and, surprisingly, with their morale intact.

Acharya was a freshly minted lieutenant. He hadn't the decades of training that makes people professional. Yet, as a leader, he did the right things. Officers of 2 Rajputana Rifles are proud that the battalion has never lost a battle in nearly two centuries. The battalion's culture had already rubbed off on Acharya. He actively led and kept his men alive. His example undoubtedly catalyzed his men to persevere.

There are no medals for such exploits because, in operational areas, these are not uncommon. The display of the core attribute of this style of leadership only earned Acharya the privilege of exercising it repeatedly. And he did. Years later in Kargil, in 1999, he heroically led his company to capture Point 4590. He perished during that attack and was decorated with the Maha Vir Chakra.*

When the time came, Acharya's younger brother also joined the Army – in fact the very same regiment.

When the then CO of the battalion Col (later General) Parnaik was recounting the story of the patrol, my own experience in Arunachal Pradesh (back then it was called Northeast Frontier Agency or NEFA), came flooding back into my mind.

I was a newly commissioned second lieutenant. The battalion ordered me to lead a patrol, from the unit's location to a tiny hamlet

* More on this in chapter 6.

called Tidding. The 'route' was a dotted line on an ancient map, going through thick foliage over several ridges. By all accounts, we were among the first to explore that route. The purpose of the patrol was to check the feasibility of using this approach during operations.

I left with ten soldiers, the most senior being a lance naik. We were self-contained for two days, the expected period for the expedition's completion.

But the duration turned out to be a gross underestimation. It began to pour almost an hour after our departure, and there was no let-up for days after that. The foliage turned out to be far more formidable than we had imagined. We had to hack through near-impenetrable undergrowth and trees using *dah*s (a long sword-like knife with a gently curving blade) and our bare hands. The promise of a 'track' proved to be a false one. The footpath on the map, represented by a dotted line, was just that – a dotted line. Rains, landslides and foliage growth had obliterated it possibly years ago.

Our difficulties compounded rapidly. The washer of the stove fell off, rendering cooking impossible. In any case, with water pouring from the heavens, that effort would probably have come to nought. The radio set, an ANPRC-25, stopped working, and we were now incommunicado as far as the unit was concerned.

The moment we entered the forests and began our climb, swarms of leeches greeted us. They would crawl up our legs or drop onto our bodies from the foliage above and attach themselves to any exposed body part to suck our blood. It is tough to pull leeches off. These creatures were so rampant that we eventually gave up trying to yank them off and would instead wait for them to get their fill of blood and drop off on their own. My overalls developed a tear and, to my horror, I found that several leeches had silently crawled in and started feasting on my legs. At one point, I looked at my deputy, Lance Naik Vijay Singh, and pointed out that there was a leech attached to his cheek! 'I know, sir, but I am too fed up of getting rid of them. Let it suck my blood and fall off.' Over the next few days,

I had nearly 200 leech marks all over my body – and so did the members of my patrol.

After we realized that using the map to navigate our way to Tidding was proving useless, I decided to become the pointsman and use my common sense to maintain direction.

But the climbs and descents over slippery earth and through a never-ending wall of foliage proved more arduous than we had imagined. We had to fell trees to create footbridges over raging mountain streams, now swollen and angry after the relentless rain, and crossed over these logs by tying ourselves to each other.

For food, we ate dry rations. To sleep at the end of each day, we would create a bivouac of banana leaves and huddle together as water sloshed around us. We were perpetually wet to the bone. The spectre of elephants deciding to pay a nocturnal visit and stamp on our leafy huts haunted our nights.

Every night, I would assure the team that we were on the right path; every morning, I would buck them up with the pledge that we would reach the goal by the end of the day. The soldiers were becoming increasingly weary. But what struck me even then was that they believed in what their young greenhorn leader was promising. We finally made it to Tidding after four days, debilitated and battered by sleeplessness and blood loss.

When I look back on the patrol, I am surprised at the energy and optimism I was able to summon to rally the men. Where did I find it? I am sure that the culture of leading from the front instilled in the National Defence Academy, the Indian Military Academy and, of course, my own unit – 4th battalion of the Bihar regiment, had seeped in deep enough for me to feel entirely accountable for the mission's achievement and the wellbeing of the soldiers in my command. It was as if I was on autopilot, bereft of any doubt about what I was required to do. The thought of aborting the patrol never once crossed my mind. And there was no whimper of such a suggestion from anyone in the patrol. They hardly knew me, yet believed in me, and I had instinctively felt compelled to honour that belief by pushing myself far more than my physique would normally allow.

I was only twenty years old. But the culture of the Army was already working its magic on me.

I could not have articulated leadership principles with any cogency then, but I can make a few points after decades and the gift of hindsight. Leaders must take more significant risks than the people they command. The feeling of safety, both physical and physiological, is a critical requirement to motivate individuals and teams but is among the least understood by most so-called leaders. Employees in an organization yearn for the safety of their jobs, the assurance of growth, fair play and support during a crisis. They root for the leaders who can provide them with that blanket of security. And what would such a leader look like?

Such a leader has to be more competent and dedicated than the people whose loyalty he seeks. He must care for them authentically. The word 'authentically' bears repeating. Sadly, a great deal of corporate behaviour is transactional – relationships only last the length of a project or a tenure. This has come to be accepted as the norm. Therefore, everyone can clearly tell that their connection with the leader is only need-based. It might work for managers. But the failure to recognize that the relational – not transactional – will foster genuine leader–follower bonds flies in the face of the most basic tenets of leadership.

The 'by-example' leader must be visible, especially when the chips are down. It is valid for leaders at all rungs of the hierarchy. If the business development team struggles late into the night to prepare a critical tender bid, a good leader would be present – not to interfere or micro-manage, but to send the clearest subliminal message of solidarity. When a company hits a rough patch or in the event of an extraordinary crisis like a pandemic, the best leaders are visible through physical presence – to the extent possible – personalized communication and virtual video calls.

The problem of visibility is somewhat complicated when the organization is large. We will address that conundrum in chapter 3. But no matter the size of the enterprise, a mere name on the frosted glass door or a picture in the annual report will not cut it. All leaders must be seen as often as is humanly possible. And when that is not possible, regular communication – not impersonal emails or letters, but more personalized efforts and even symbolic gestures – must continue to reassure the rank and file of their presence. This has to be an effort born of authenticity, not a mere fulfilment of a bureaucratic 'engagement plan'.

Leaders who lead by example have another responsibility. They must always exude calmness and keep their heads, especially, in Rudyard Kipling's immortal words, 'when all about you are losing theirs and blaming it on you'.* If the leader appears calm under adversity, he sends ripples of that serenity all around him. Unfortunately, the converse is also true.

VI

Sam Manekshaw once narrated an interesting experience in his inimitable witty manner. During the Second World War, Manekshaw served with a battalion of Sikh troops – 4th Battalion of the 12 Frontier Force (formerly 54th Sikh), in Burma.

During a conference, the name of one of his company soldiers – the burly, six-foot-four-inch-tall Sohan Singh – came up for promotion. But Manekshaw refused to recommend his name. The reason? Sohan Singh had been promoted several times earlier and had to be demoted each time due to indiscipline.

Later that day, Manekshaw returned to his makeshift

* Rudyard Kipling's poem 'If' compulsorily adorns the wall of each cadet's cabin in the National Defence Academy and has undoubtedly shaped a fragment of countless officers' consciousness in the Indian Army.

accommodation in the jungle. An extremely worried senior JCO of the company, Subedar Balwant Singh approached Manekshaw and informed him that they had arrested Sohan Singh earlier that evening. The soldier had openly announced that he would shoot and kill Manekshaw that night.

So Manekshaw ordered that Sohan Singh be formally marched up to him. Singh's official weapon, a pistol, had been taken away from him as a precaution. A charge was read out. Manekshaw asked Singh if he had committed an offence. A shamefaced Sohan pleaded that he had made a mistake. Manekshaw then proceeded to load a pistol and handed it over to Sohan. 'Are you brave enough to shoot me? If you are, go ahead,' Manekshaw said.

A sheepish Sohan repeated that his utterance had been a momentary lapse of reason. Sam gave him a playful slap and asked him to be on his way.

But apparently, the storm had not yet subsided. The company soldiers looked worried when Manekshaw returned from the officers' mess after dinner. Subedar Balwant Singh was pacing up and down. 'Saab, Sohan will surely shoot you tonight,' the subedar warned. After he had been let off, Sohan had gone around repeating the threat to several soldiers. He was determined to carry it out.

Manekshaw asked for Sohan to be brought back.

To everyone's puzzlement, he ordered Singh, 'Tonight you will be my sentry outside my hut. And tomorrow morning you will bring me a mug of hot tea and another mug of hot water for me to shave. Now get going!'

At dawn, right on time, Sohan brought him the two mugs of hot water. And, to use Manekshaw's own words, followed him 'like a lamb for the rest of the war'.

When Manekshaw would recount this story, he would say with his usual candour, 'Ladies and gentlemen, if you think I wasn't frightened, you are mistaken. I was terrified. But if I hadn't done that and instead put Sohan Singh behind bars, everybody would have said – see, our leader is scared.'[3]

'Everyone is frightened. It is one thing to be frightened and quite another to show fear. When your knees are knocking, your teeth are chattering, and you are about to make your own geography, the real leader emerges. If once you show fear in front of the men you command, it doesn't matter whether they are soldiers or clerks or labour or students – you should quit.' You can replace the word 'frightened' with any synonym, and the wisdom will still ring true.

Sam Manekshaw is of course a legend. Still, in many ways, he represents the quintessential Indian soldier to whom leading by example was far more critical than even the peril that the action may have caused to his life.

Incidentally, this was in 1942, and Manekshaw's troops were among the force guarding a bridge over the Sittaung river. In a battle with the Japanese, Manekshaw was hit nine times with bullets in his belly and lungs. Such was his courage – and the imminence of his death – that the British military commander pinned a military cross on a semi-conscious Manekshaw. But the latter did not fade away, and finally made it on a stretcher to a hospital after thirty-six hours. Confusion possibly reigned in this ad hoc facility and, after some effort, Manekshaw's orderly Sher Singh managed to summon an Australian doctor and pointed out the multiple bullet wounds to him.

Eager to keep Manekshaw conscious by engaging in small talk, the doctor asked him what had happened to him. He said, 'A bloody mule kicked me.' The doctor broke into a hearty laugh, 'I see you have a sense of humour. You might be worth saving!'

VII

People don't follow you for what you say. They follow you for what you do. Once they begin to think for themselves sufficiently, even our children are inclined to follow only our example and question our pronouncements. If that is true for our flesh and blood, how can we ever expect our team members to buy our wares unless supported by our deeds? And yet we do!

Countless MDs, CEOs, Heads of Departments and other 'leaders' have proclaimed from the pulpit, 'We are a family. You can always come to me if you ever face a problem.' And they invariably fail to notice the barely concealed scepticism rippling just beneath the expressions of the employees. What is more, they never seem to recognize that rarely a 'family member' will ever approach them. To believe that people will follow you because you say clever or even rousing things, is an act of self-deception and naivety. The loftiness of words from lecterns dissipates with the alacrity of snow on a hot furnace when actions do not back it. If only good advertising could sell potentially flawed products, marketing – not production and quality control – would reign supreme. And we would believe every word that all the politicians say!

The idea of active leadership is hardly new. Yet it is a matter of some bewilderment that while the principle is intuitive to the collective leadership within the Army, it is far less favoured in the rest of the world. The corporate relies on hierarchy, protocol, process and monetary inducements to create followership. But none of this kindles instinctive followership.

Perhaps it is best understood in the words of Edmond Chandler who, writing in 1919 in the *Sepoy*, said that 'the Gurkha does not love his officer because he is a Sahib, but because he is *his* Sahib, and the officer has to prove that he is *his* Sahib first … A strange officer … is not adopted into the Pantheon at once. He has to qualify … but once accepted, he is served with fidelity and devotion that are human and dog-like at the same time.'[4]

This style of leadership requires competence and courage. The courage to be wrong, to lose face and more and, in the case of the Army, to risk one's life and limb. But is courage an inherited bonanza available in ample measure in some and denied to the rest of us?

How can it be that soldiers are imbued with reservoirs of courage to lead by example from which they can draw at short notice?

While it is a fact that the Army's recruitment and selection system aims, among other things, to identify the presence of courage in someone's character, its display is primarily cultivated. Army men are taught to 'act brave' because there is no one who is not scared during a battle. Even the first blast of an AK-47 going off in close vicinity can shake one's nerves. But the culture of acting brave, hugely supplemented by the desire to uphold the unit's izzat, drives leaders across the chasm of fear.

And how do we create a culture of leading from the front, and indeed, any other attribute? We will turn to that in the final chapter. We will also find answers to how that culture may sustain a sense of selflessness, even a tiger-like fearlessness.

To lead by example and from the front are optional – provided one is happy to embrace mediocrity and refuse to rise above transactional behaviour. If, however, a leader wants to scale greater heights, then there is just one attribute that he needs to pick from the colossal menu card of leadership to-dos – lead by example.

3

THE STRENGTH OF THE CHAIN

'No one can whistle a symphony. It takes a whole orchestra to play it.'

– H. E. LUCCOCK

I

THE STRENGTH OF THE weakest link determines the sturdiness of a chain. Indeed, every link matters. A culture that fosters teamwork and understands the secrets of collective motivation mitigates the presence of weaker links. It gives the chain the tenacity to withstand extraordinary stress.

And yet, when you speak to many MDs and CEOs, they lament that their organizations lack teamwork. People work in silos and refuse to cooperate. Even within teams, coordination and exchange of information are not always the norm. We all want motivated teams, high on initiative and cooperation – but managements often seem short on ideas of how exactly to bring that about. A few erroneously believe it is a problem for human resources to solve through policy statements and workshops. Why is building teams that work in harmony such a challenge?

The fault does not lie in the stars. This infirmity lies in our inability to develop an enabling culture where the leadership consistently rewards teamwork and proactive action. And wherein, equally, any resistance to these desirable practices is appropriately penalized. It needs conscious and thoughtful effort to create such an environment. Mere shibboleths and speeches will flounder expeditiously.

The secret sauce for forging teamwork and motivation has many ingredients. But the least known of these may be an awareness that each team member has of the scale of his or her individual contribution to the enterprise's success and accomplishment of goals. It is achieved when everyone understands their actual role – not just the job description or task at hand. The criticality of such an understanding is not simply a theoretical postulate. It must be an intrinsic part of the onboarding process – and then systematically and periodically refreshed in everyone's consciousness. Do the receptionist and the security guard understand that they help raise the company's image and are, therefore, vital players in the branding effort? Does the salesman know that he is not merely a hawker of products but an ambassador of the company whose conduct could spur repeat orders and whose inquisitiveness can build the company's competitive intelligence database? Is the supervisor aware that properly loading finished products onto the delivery vehicles can contribute to fewer customer complaints, and thus he is a part of the quality assurance team?

Every employee contributes to a company's revenue or profitability – sometimes both. But does the leadership make enough effort to ensure every team member appreciates their role?

In the late 1990s, as CO of a Rashtriya Rifles battalion in Kashmir, I accompanied a company on an operation to search for militants on the higher reaches of a mountain ridge. We were away for two days. It was already dinnertime when we finally trooped down to the company base – with nothing to show for our efforts. The company commander and his subaltern suggested I join them for dinner instead of travelling another hour to the battalion headquarters. I agreed.

But before we sat down for our meal, we decided to visit the cookhouse – the *langar* – and look at the food served to the soldiers. The fare was ordinary – rice, rotis, dal, vegetables and salad. I summoned the soldier who was in charge of the kitchen. Since the company had returned after two days of a gruelling outing, should he not have ensured a better than regular fare?

'This week the Army supply did not provide chicken nor eggs,' the langar commander replied.

I asked the company commander to hand over adequate money to the soldier so that he would troop down to the nearest village and return with some eggs available for sale. This might cause a slight delay, but the company would be able to enjoy a nicer dinner.

The next day, I returned to the company for a debriefing. At the end of the debrief, I asked the langar commander a simple question, 'What is your role?'

'To supervise the preparation of food, sir.'

I pressed him. So, would it not matter if the food was tasty and hygienic instead of stale and poorly cooked?

The langar commander sensed a trap. 'No, sir, my role is to supervise the preparation of tasty and hygienic food.' I could see his mind's wheels beginning to turn. We were already making progress in understanding his fundamental role.

And why would that matter, I asked. After all, irrespective of the food quality, the langar commander's pay would remain the same. After all, the Army does not award bonuses or have any appraisal system aimed at financial rewards at the end of the year.

'Sir, when the food is tasty, it positively affects the company's morale.'

But why should a langar commander be concerned with morale and motivation?

'Because, sir, when I give them excellent food and their morale goes up, they go out and kill terrorists.'

'And that, son, is your role. You are helping the company eliminate terrorists. Indeed, you are helping raise the izzat of the battalion. That is your role – not the mere supervision of food preparation.'

Teamwork begins to kindle when the management finds ways to make every employee believe that he plays a role far more significant than what is in the bare bones of his job description. And in Army units, where this knowledge becomes a part of the culture and is carried forward in the shape of traditions, the result is often astonishing, even moving.

II

The morning the motorcycle-borne terrorists fired multiple shots from point-blank range at two soldiers, I was a few kilometres away. The year was 1992, and the insurgency stoked by the United Liberation Front of Asom, or ULFA, was pockmarking a few areas of the state. As a part of the force to quell it, our brigade had been inducted from the high mountains of neighbouring Arunachal Pradesh. We were now deployed in the district town of Mangaldai in Assam. I was the staff officer for operations – the most crucial job a young major could hold.

The three battalions reporting to the brigade were spread out in a counter-insurgency grid. A battalion of the Rajput Regiment was at Tangla, a tiny hamlet some thirty kilometres from Mangaldai. A solitary black-tarred ribbon wound through nondescript villages and connected our brigade headquarters with the battalion. The road sliced through paddy fields on either side, running on a raised platform throughout its length – a mirror image of most rural roads in the state.

Every morning, a two-soldier motorcycle team of Despatch Riders would drive from Tangla to Mangaldai to deliver and receive official mail. While one of the soldiers drove, the other rode pillion, cradling a carbine in his lap for their protection. This was daily routine, and the hours rarely varied, which can be a mistake when insurgent attacks are likely. The area was largely peaceful, which might have reduced the Army's incentive to vary timings and schedules. In any case, there was no option of taking another route.

That morning, I was outside our tented accommodation in Mangaldai when I heard a commotion. A civilian truck, laden with labourers, halted and informed me that an injured soldier was in the back. Sepoy Ashok Singh, the pillion, had been shot multiple times by motorcycle-riding assailants, who had fired at him from behind and continued the volley as they rode past. The Army motorcycle crashed, but Ashok Singh had fired back even after he had fallen. Unfortunately, the bullets had missed the fleeing militants.

There was no time to lose. The truck was headed to a hospital. After a quick first-aid treatment, I ordered a group of soldiers to accompany the wounded, and instructed the driver to proceed post-haste.

In that moment of trauma, it did not immediately strike me that there had to be a second soldier in the team. What had happened to him? I imagined the worst.

Before we could launch a search, a Willy's jeep drove up, chock-a-bloc with locals. The second soldier, Lance Naik Gopal Tewari, was nestled in the middle, bleeding from several gunshot wounds. We moved him to a tent and lay him on the floor. While a doctor attended to his injuries, I questioned him about the incident. Another soldier offered him a glass of water. Waving him away, Tewari said, 'I have only been shot. I am not about to die. Wait, let me complete my report first.'

He was evacuated, and both the wounded lived to serve the rest of their tenures.

But a couple of questions niggled me. Why did the two wounded soldiers not arrive in the same truck, which meant Tewari had lost precious time? And why were there no fired cases (or cartridges) of the Army ammunition found on the scene? After all, the soldiers had reported emptying their magazines while firing at the fleeing terrorists.

Two weeks later, both questions were answered.

It is Army regulation that after firing practice on the range, all fired cases must be accounted for and deposited. The accounting of these cartridges is taken very seriously. Any loss of training ammunition attracts a court of inquiry. The rationale is to obviate pilferage or loss. Units are sensitive to these stipulations, and it is a matter of the unit's pride not to incur the loss of a single fired case.

The rule, however, does not apply to 'service ammunition' used in wars and operations. It should have been evident that fired cases of ammunition expended in the heat of battle are not required to be deposited.

Lance Naik Gopal Tewari was a little less than crystal clear on the nuances of these orders. When the firing ceased, he said, the two wounded soldiers had time to take stock of their injuries. As the trauma subsided a notch, he realized that being the more senior of the two, he was, by default, the commander on the scene. It instantly became his self-assigned responsibility to not only report the incident in person so that a manhunt could be launched, but he was also accountable – or so he surmised – for collecting the fired cases. Lance Naik took the call and evacuated the junior soldier first while he busied himself with searching and counting the fired cases – even as he tended to his wounds. Shot and bleeding, he had been crawling around to pick up the cartridges, lest his battalion get a bad name.

For an organization to take audacious risks, it needs an ecosystem composed of many Lance Naik Gopal Tewaris. It requires a culture that makes you conscious of your duty as a 'senior' without a ceremonious appointment or an elaborate succession plan. Similar stories can and have played out in hundreds of other instances in the Army. Its culture impels individuals to transcend their welfare and focus on the organization – the Army. It is not a taught regimen or born out of fear of punishment. It could hardly have been a punishable offence for Tewari to rush himself to the hospital in a vehicle that was so readily available. His placing a higher priority on searching for fired cartridges of course had nothing to do with fear of official retribution; in these circumstances, to ascribe it to the thought of a reprimand is a nonsensical notion.

Instead, Lance Naik's action had to do with a culture that strengthens the body and sinews of the Army; allowing its members the leverage of taking risks. That culture, reinforced by traditions, norms and processes, instils in individuals the belief that their credible performance enables the entire organization to succeed.

III

South of Shopian town in Kashmir, straddling a local road, is the village of Memender. Over the years of insurgency, Memender had developed a reputation for being home to more than a few residents who supported the idea of militancy. Naturally, militants favoured the village for stopovers. When troops from the nearest Army base at Balpora moved out for operations, geography dictated that they pass through Shopian. And when the column entered the town, an early warning would invariably reach Memender.

Winters in the area can be punishing, even towards the end of February. The winter of 2019 was no different.

Sandeep Chaudhary, the superintendent of police at Shopian, received a tip-off that he promptly passed on to Col Shaitan Singh, the CO of the local Rashtriya Rifles battalion. Two militants were holed up in Memender, and at least one of them was a Pakistani national. That night, the troops moved on foot, taking circuitous routes to avoid passing through the town.

The sky was clear. The temperature had dipped to –4°C. The village was nestled in dense orchards, robbed of its foliage by the biting cold. In the moonlight, the setting was not only eerie but also dangerous – it exposed the troops to lookouts from within the village.

Maj Ankit Yadav led the first company, which silently settled into a cordon around the suspected area. Maj Nilaav Surendra, a paratrooper, beefed up the cordon with his company. The CO, too, joined in with a small team.

Three large houses stood at the village's periphery, defiladed from observation by tall, tin walls. The source had pointed out that the terrorist duo was likely to be in one of these buildings.

Perhaps the barking of the dogs gave away the Army's presence – the terrorists woke up with a start. Darkness is a better friend to the surreptitious than sunlight; a little past midnight, the terrorists decided to sneak through the encirclement. The first move was a crawl in a small drain beneath the boundary wall. Naik Jitendra Chauhan and Paratrooper Nicky Lalbiakdika heard a rustle, almost too close for comfort. They held their nerve, aimed and fired into the dark. The two militants scampered back.

'There was complete uncertainty at this point', Major Surendra told me later. 'When the AKs went off, we had no clue who had fired at whom. It was a while before we could make sense of this chaos.'

Two teams decided to move up to search the houses – Maj Surendra, Maj Yadav, Hav Pawan, Paratrooper Vinay, Hav Sandeep and Paratrooper Sumeet. To say that a search is the most delicate and hazardous part of such an operation would be an understatement. In the deep darkness, search parties are blinded, quite literally. They must also be mindful of not causing collateral damage and thus move slowly and deliberately. While soldiers cannot fire at the first thing that moves without ascertaining its identity, the terrorist is not similarly constrained. This gives the latter a deadly advantage in the first few seconds, often making the difference between life and death for the leading soldiers.

One of the parties managed to reach the house owner, who silently pointed out that the militants were in the backyard. The party decided to pull back to a more tactical position. But the militants were in a frantic hurry; they scaled the tin wall and dropped out. Noticing figures in the dark, they began to fire at random.

Subedar Gajender was the closest to this volley of fire. He stayed calm and returned the compliment with his weapon. Perhaps that is what drove the militants into the safety of a nearby *nullah* (stream). And this is how they seemed to have reached the proverbial cul-de-sac.

Unable to see anything, the officers decided to keep the nullah under surveillance and commence the search in the morning. The troops in the cordon waited in sub-zero temperatures, eyes peeled at the nullah.

As dawn broke, two 'buddy pairs' crawled forward – Maj Surendra with Hav Sandip and Maj Ankit Yadav with Hav Pawan. The militants lobbed a grenade when these teams were barely ten metres from the nullah. Fortuitously, there were no casualties. The teams threw a couple of grenades of their own and inched closer. Suddenly, a terrorist – later identified as a Pakistani – rushed out and released a burst of fire. Nilaav and Pawan were almost in the direct line of attack but miraculously came out unscathed. Both of them shot and felled their assailant. The two were about to reach the rim of the nullah when the second terrorist emerged and met the same fate as his confederate.

The story is another remarkable example of young officers leading from the front. But that is not the most distinguishing feature of the tale. I discovered that nugget when I reached out to Maj Surendra to fill in the gaps in my research – I had obtained the initial account from official sources. That brief case study largely credited Nilaav for the operation's success. I pulled up the research document on the virtual call. When I read it out, the major was quick to object.

'This is not accurate, sir. Your outline is factually correct but does not mention every member of my team that participated and did so well. Who is to say whether this achievement belongs to any one individual?' He insisted on my including all the names in the story. To me, the officer's insistence on sharing credit with his team spoke as much about teamwork as the details of the operation itself.

In a culture where credit for and recognition of contribution are shared collectively, winning is far easier than in one where each member is working for themselves, and only individual success matters. Such a culture only materializes when teamwork and sharing credit are intrinsically rewarding. Payoffs govern human behaviour. And those payoffs are often psychological and social. The Army fosters this by virtue of being rooted in tradition and norms that place the battalion, company, or platoon's izzat above material gains.

In the business world, the focus is often mainly on transactional wins. Unless the organization's processes and SOPs reflect rewards and reprimands vis-à-vis teamwork, it may not be possible to create such an environment. Many professionals praise their teams as a form. But making less-than-sincere proclamations from the podium is not the same as genuinely sharing credit. Leaders must single out team players and ensure their words to such employees reflect gratitude and high praise. When cooperation, coordination and credit-sharing become rewarding, every link in the chain acts in concert.

IV

In January 2004, a potentially perilous decision confronted twenty-six-year-old Army doctor Capt Devika.

Devika had graduated from the Armed Forces Medical College. After a year's internship at Command Hospital, Kolkata, she was on her first duty tour in Pattan, near J&K's Baramulla. At the time, she had been married for four months.

The area had the unenviable reputation for being a terrorist hub. Devika's charter included looking after the sick and the injured, but she also routinely visited villages and treated civilians in Army-sponsored medical camps.

On this crisp winter evening, an IED, built into a transistor radio laid by the terrorists, burst amidst a patrolling party of soldiers. There were several injuries, one of them critical; a soldier had borne the full impact of the blast on his abdomen and chest, and shrapnel had cut up his face.

A phone call alerted Devika, who was already in the medical inspection room when a dozen casualties streamed in. A couple of soldiers had fractures, others superficial injuries. One injured soldier had deep wounds in the legs and could not sit, even though his vitals were normal. The most concerning case was that of the soldier who was bleeding profusely from severe abdominal injuries. He had enormous difficulty breathing without a respirator; it was suspected that he had broken several ribs. His stomach needed to be stitched up to prevent his intestines from spilling out.

Devika had only one other working hand in this facility. But another Army nursing assistant, after hearing about the blast, left the barracks in a rush and came forward to help. Together, they administered painkillers, bandaged the wounds and sutured the cuts.

While this frenetic activity was ongoing, the General Officer Commanding of the division, Maj Gen Raj Mehta, arrived with a few staff officers. He recalls that he saw Capt Devika Gupta with her hands encased in bloodied white gloves right up to her shoulders' stitching skilfully to stop the intense bleeding.

This party of visitors started moving about, checking on the state of each soldier and questioning the medics. The young Capt Devika felt that the well-meant interference was slowing down the treatment. She summoned all her courage and ordered everyone to exit and wait outside. 'I will brief you only after the situation has stabilized,' she told the GOC.

Devika requested an ambulance to evacuate the critically wounded soldier to Srinagar. The GOC had a different thought. Given the dangers that might lurk on the two-and-a-half-hour-long journey, he wanted the doctor and the compromised soldier to travel in a bullet- and mine-proof Casspir vehicle. For protection, an armed Quick Reaction Team vehicle would, of course, accompany the Casspir. That was the standard operating procedure for movement at night.

Devika firmly refused. The patient needed to travel lying down. He had to be given an Ambu bag for breathing and intravenous drips to stabilize his condition. The Casspir would be decidedly safer, but what use was their safety if the patient was lost? She insisted on travelling in a far less protected ambulance with the soldier.

In simple parlance, Devika was 'disobeying' a general. Maj Gen Raj Mehta later recounted the moment: 'With all my men waiting for my reaction at being "dressed down" by this girl with three years' service to my thirty-six, I did the only thing any officer and gentleman would have done in a war zone. I saluted her.'

The journey did not start well. Barely a few kilometres later, the Quick Reaction Team vehicle broke down as the small convoy was crossing Baramulla. Now the ambulance had to wait for the replacement vehicle to arrive.

Again, Devika put her foot down because the soldier's condition was deteriorating by the minute. It was not the time to take counsel of one's fears. She ordered the ambulance to move on without protection, violating stipulated practice and self-preservation norms.

The soldier made it to Srinagar and went on to make a recovery. The next day, terrorists shot dead a BSF doctor, who was moving in a similar ambulance vehicle.

'I suppose I would have been a different person had I not been in the Army,' Devika told me. 'Around me, I had seen everyone take risks, get involved in dangerous work. I had seen that people always looked after their teams. I considered the wounded soldiers as members of my extended team. At that moment, I was full of energy, and my confidence peaked. The Army environment is so different.'

Devika was one of the newest links in the chain. Of course she drew from the reservoir of character to rise above herself when the chips were down. But the 'environment' also made her do what she did. It made her see the vital interest of the 'team' as even more important than her life.

That environment is called 'culture'.

Every link matters. An effective way to prevent weak links – ones that are so bereft of character qualities that they are unlikely to fit in – from populating the organization, is to focus on the intake quality. The selection process for induction is crucial to building the right culture.

One of the many areas where the Army's distinct culture is most apparent is its sophisticated approach in selecting its officers and soldiers. It has a precise datum of acceptance to ensure leadership quality and uniformity of the organization's character. The Army pores over the candidate's knowledge and skills, but eventually, these two are subservient to the third piece it investigates – personality. Or character. In corporate parlance, it could be called the 'attitude' of the aspirant.

The Army believes that skill set and knowledge, two attributes placed above all else by the rest of the world, can be imparted. But can the inner core of a man or woman joining a company be sufficiently moulded?

To be fair, we may not be comparing grenades with grenades here. The Army's selection process is about the entry level, whereas new entrants can seep into the system at any level in the corporate world. All the same, the defining difference is the relegation of character qualities to a tier below acquirable attributes in the world of business, vis-à-vis the approach of the Army.

As per the Army's belief, you can only plunge below the surface to assess someone's personality when you adopt a three-pronged approach: *mansa* (thought), *vacha* (speech) and *karmana* (action). A search for the point of convergence of the three will throw up the correct answer. These are the three gateways through which every candidate must pass through.

The Services Selection Board – the step after a candidate has qualified on the written test – establishes the meeting point between mansa, vacha and karmana to decide whether the prospective officer would have what it takes. An inclination to make a life-long commitment. It deploys a triad of experts – a psychologist to map the mind, a Ground Test Officer (GTO) who puts the candidates through simple hoops to assess their actions and an interviewing officer who mines the candidate's words during their extensive interaction.

To qualify, a person must receive nods of approval from all three. And the three assessors are not permitted to consult one another before putting pen to paper.

Many intangibles make up a 'personality', while opinions on what constitutes any intangible can vary. Who can say what initiative precisely means? Or courage for that matter? To reduce fuzziness to the bare minimum, the Army provides its recruiters with as precise definitions as possible.*

---

* For example, 'initiative' is the ability to originate and sustain action. It has four aspects: the ability to take the first step and to act first, usually in a new or subsequently emerging situation, in the right direction and maintain it. 'Courage' is the ability to appreciate and take purposive risks willingly. It includes the ability to meet acknowledged danger, the spirit of adventure, an enterprising spirit and a willingness or desire to dare a risk or a hazard and the capacity to keep oneself composed in adverse situations, enabling one to be steady in facing and handling such situations.

If the focus on attitudinal factors and character trumps all other parameters, the organization will benefit in the long run. Selecting the right people who can align themselves with the company's goals has obvious merit. But the problem is two-fold. Most companies do not have a systematic methodology to go deep beneath the superficial and look for a candidate's core traits.* Even several rounds of interviews mostly end up confirming factual data. In any case, the approach in many companies is intrinsically short-term: fulfilment of vacancies, ensuring the hired person has adequate experience, the requisite educational qualification and background, is willing to accept remuneration fitting the HR budget, etc. All these are important markers to study. But nothing is nearly as critical as the person's character or attitude.

Hiring the right people is akin to scattering healthy seeds that will add to the company's culture. As Ralph Waldo Emerson pointed out, 'The sower may mistake and sow his peas crookedly; the peas make no mistake, but come up and show his line.'[1]

V

Three months before Nilaav Surendra's team displayed its heroics, not too far from that scene of action in a village called Hipura Batagund, another bloody tryst with militants had gone down.

A Rashtriya Rifles battalion, mainly comprised of soldiers from the Jat Regiment and Artillery, had notched up a big success in November of 2018, felling four terrorists. Radio intercepts had hinted that a band of militants would visit the house of one of their

* Several companies do rely on psychometric tests. This is a good solution, provided the test has been designed with sophistication and understanding of the requirements. One method to evaluate a psychometric test before beginning to use it for new selections would be to administer it to employees whose traits are already well known and compare the outcomes for fidelity.

slain compatriots on the fourth day since the deaths. The company commander Capt Mahesh Bhure, a twenty-six-year-old bachelor from Pune, decided to lay an ambush to cover that possibility. His deputy was Lance Naik Nazir Ahmed Wani, a Territorial Army soldier who was a resident of Kulgam. Nazir had repeatedly displayed exemplary heroism and had been awarded the Sena Medal twice.

As the ambush party lay still, peering in the dark for any shape to emerge, Mahesh received a message from his commanding officer. There were near-confirmed reports of several militants in a house in Batagund. Would he prefer to move there instead?

Mahesh was excited. He knew the area well. The trick was to rush in without being detected, a tall order since the 'target' house stood at the village's periphery, with an orchard of trees utterly barren of leaves and a *kabristaan* around it. It was a clear night, and the moon began to wane two days ago. The area was awash with silvery light, bright enough to highlight any movement.

Capt Mahesh Bhure withdrew from the ambush site, collected the entire team of twenty soldiers in the dark and briefed them with the help of a map. Nazir was to lead the group of ten and approach the house from the north, and Mahesh would lead the rest and move in from the south.

But life – particularly in operations – rarely respects plans. A sudden shower of light caught the party crouching in the burial ground. A solitary bulb at a *ziarat* – a tombstone of a *pir* or saint – had suddenly lit up. It was a little past midnight when a lookout for the militants spotted the movement.

The cordon was settling into its positions, every pair of soldiers taking cover behind the smallest of bumps and peering hard into the darkness to ensure they knew where the neighbouring party was.

The area was too large for twenty soldiers to seal off the target house effectively. While on the move, Mahesh radioed back for reinforcements.

Instead of waiting for the inevitable firefight, the militants decided to sneak out, half-crawling close to the boundary wall of the house, making the tin rattle. Suddenly, the leading militant came within a few feet of Nazir. This face-to-face happened with such heartstopping suddenness that for nearly five seconds, neither side fired. And as if the inadvertent encounter had not already injected enough drama into the moment, a bulletproof, mine-resistant Casspir vehicle lumbered into view, carrying additional troops from another location. In the ensuing confusion, the militants sprayed the Casspir with bullets, and Nazir's men retaliated from close quarters. Two militants swivelled and rushed in Capt Bhure's direction. Mahesh fired and did not miss. The troops from the Cassspir opened up too, doing their best to avoid fratricide. The intense firefight lasted for a full minute.

Four militants died in the exchange. It wasn't known then, but two more had been injured and hurried back into the house. Of Capt Bhure's men, one soldier – Sepoy Sunil – had caught multiple splinters. His buddy Hav Rakesh got busy moving him to a safer place and providing first aid.

The company commander used the pause to take stock of the situation. Was everyone in his team unharmed? The troops from the Casspir began to move into the cordon, filling up voids. This sounds neater than in reality; darkness makes even the most minor coordination complex and perilous, mainly when everyone is jumpy, 'blinded' and armed with loaded AK-47s.

Not wanting to be left out of the battle, CO Col Naresh Gairola reached the scene. He brought with him policemen from the local station.

It turned out that Sunil's injury was more severe than had initially appeared. The blood loss had rendered his arm insensate. He was immediately moved out of the zone in the Casspir.*

As the night progressed, an uncomfortable silence fell over the area. The troops were ordered to lie still and wait for morning to

* A casualty evacuation helicopter flew in at dawn and moved Sunil to the military hospital. He recovered fully.

break before further search was mounted. But one of the surviving militants decided to take matters into his own hands. He climbed atop the house and fired bursts at random as if to ascertain whether the Army had left. When the deafening sound of the AK-47 firing from close proximity filled the night air, no one quite knew who had opened up. Was it one of the soldiers? Or could it have been a militant? No one from the Army's teams retaliated because the answers were unknowable at that juncture. This script is one that plays out in the battlefield with unerring regularity, and commanders are required to make sense of ambiguity and chaos. Fog is a permanent feature of wars, but more on that later.

Well before dawn, the house owner managed to get away and reached the policemen. 'There are two more,' he said. And they were unlikely to surrender.

Soon, the exchange of fire resumed. During this volley, a part of the target house began to burn. Could the militants have set it ablaze to cause confusion and escape? Capt Bhure ordered everyone to hold their fire while he made an effort to get close to the house with a small party. Nazir accompanied him.

Unable to take the heat, one of the militants rushed out, rapidly firing his automatic weapon as he approached. Nazir kept his cool and shot him dead. The house continued to burn and, save for one corner, soon turned into a hollow shell.

One of the parties, with Capt Bhure in the lead, sneaked up to a window. Unknown to them, the remaining militant had wet a mattress and lain down on it to avoid incineration. He was also poised, cradling his weapon, ready to fire at the first human who would venture near him.

Mahesh's party wondered if they should burst into what remained of the house. But the owner had informed them about the cooking gas cylinders that could explode any moment. And so, forcing a hole through the closed wooden window and sticking his weapon through it, Mahesh asked Nazir to hold on to his bulletproof jacket from behind. 'I am going to fire a burst inside,' he said, 'but if I am fired at in return, just yank me back to safety.' However, when he tried firing, the weapon stalled. It was a spine-chilling moment. After a brief struggle, Mahesh had no option but to withdraw the weapon. To complete what his company commander had started, Nazir stepped forward and decided to peer inside the hole. He was instantly shot and fell back. Mahesh changed the magazine and tried moving around to rescue Nazir – but he had already succumbed to the bullet injuries. The militant lobbed a grenade that fell on Nazir's mortal remains before blowing up. The team members in the vicinity were outraged over Nazir's death and stormed the house. The remaining militant was eliminated.

Of the six militants neutralized, one was a Pakistani. Another, one Abbas Bhatt, was wanted for the killing of Lt Ummar Fayaz, who had been abducted and murdered in May 2017.

'Teamwork' is not a platitude. Nor is it an idealistic expression worthy of motivational talks but a footnote in real life. It is a practical matter, an operational necessity for success. Soldiers get it because that is the culture they are steeped in. Everyone is better, safer and more secure for it.

In consequence, collectively, the Army wins.*

VI

Many citizens believe that the Indian soldier dies for the country with the image of a fluttering national flag flashing in his mind. One often hears the view that somehow soldiers are so deeply subsumed in the colour of patriotism that making the ultimate sacrifice becomes

* Lance Naik Nazir was posthumously awarded the Ashok Chakra, the nation's highest gallantry award other than in war. Capt Mahesh Bhure was decorated with a Shaurya Chakra while two others, Hav Rakesh and Sep Sunil, were awarded Sena Medals.

relatively easy. Or that there is something about the character of the people selected to don a uniform, reinforced by training, that turns them into heroes. Some of those sentiments may have a kernel of truth. But the secret of the Indian Army's robustness lies elsewhere. It is a secret that could immensely bolster any large organization's teamwork if imbibed.

The strength of the Indian Army is its 'unit'. Officers and men live, fight and, if required, die for their units – and in some cases, sub-units. The unit (or battalion, regiment, team – as it is variously called) is the highest cause for which officers and soldiers are willing to make any sacrifice. The fierce loyalty of all ranks is directed at the unit. And the sum of this paradigm is that the entire organization time after time performs effectively.

We will explore this further in 'Naam, Namak, Nishan'. But in the context of teamwork, a backdrop here would be instructive.

The primary unit of the Army is a battalion in the case of the infantry and a regiment for armoured corps, artillery, engineers and signals. The electrical & mechanical engineers (EME) and supply corps have battalions, while the ordnance simply calls their basic structure a unit.*

The idea of the unit's primacy has a British legacy. After many convulsions, the British had allowed Indian officers to command Indian companies, assisted by subedars, jemadars (now Junior Commissioned Officers) and several non-commissioned officers. The Indian officer who was later given the title of VCO – Viceroy's Commissioned Officer – was meant to be a critical link between the English officers and the indigenous sepoys. The link was vital, and while the British have long gone, it has retained its strength.

In his authoritative work on the Indian Army, American scholar Stephen Cohen spoke of how 'fierce clan or class pride was gradually transformed into identification with the unit, a transition which was

---

* In the description that follows, to obviate confusion, all these structures will be called ‚unit'.

made easier by the homogenous composition of many battalions or the pure class or caste composition of others.'[2] That also increasingly became the basis for the officer–jawan relationship.

But it isn't just class or caste loyalty that cemented the unit culture's fabric. The post-Independence Indian Army has consciously empowered units and accorded a status to its leader – the commanding officer – far above his rank in the hierarchy. In all matters of the unit, commanders respect the CO's word, up and down the chain. He has immense administrative and legal powers. For the unit, he is a larger-than-life father figure (despite his young years), the tales of whose tutelage will forever be told in the unit's oral and written history. And if the Army has installed the CO as the presiding deity, the company commanders and platoon commanders are demi-gods.*

This approach has created hundreds of units in the vein of closely knit families. The COs and the company commanders and everyone below them know not just the soldiers by name but their strengths, weaknesses, foibles, social backgrounds and personal problems. COs and other officers routinely go to great lengths to understand the men they command. In older regiments, it was customary to send newly commissioned officers to visit the catchment areas of recruitment and live with the unit's soldiers for a few days. Freshly minted young officers were also required to spend a few weeks in soldiers' barracks, sharing living space, bathrooms and dining halls.

The unit culture dictates that the officers participate in the social lives of the troops. This norm, too, is an inheritance from the Raj. Cohen mentions that the rank and file's religious festivals – in which the officers participated, irrespective of their religious moorings – '... were frequently given a strong military twist, and unit maulvis, pandits, or gurus blessed the weapons and the regiment', thus binding the leaders, and the led, to each other and the unit.

* If you drive through a cantonment, you might come across signboards that declare that certain roads are for a flag (senior commanders) and CO's vehicles only.

The apparent fallout is that a soldier does not see himself as a number on the payslip. The unit leadership acknowledges his identity. He is a living entity, recognized, celebrated, cared for and, when required, chastized, for who he is. He considers the unit his natural home and develops bonds that last his entire life.

That is precisely how a million-plus-strong Army retains high standards of motivation and teamwork. Unlike in large corporations, the leaders who give every individual personal attention and, by extension, make him feel wanted are his unit commanders. He neither has to look far for a reservoir of fellow feeling nor face a lack of identity.

That feeling is indistinguishable from the soldier's bond with his biological family during the service. Maj Gen Anil Sengar recounted to me the story of Subedar Major Dewan Singh, a practically unlettered soldier who rose to the seniormost rank in his battalion. The unit was deployed on the Siachen glacier. Siachen is one of the world's most unforgiving battlefields, where soldiers must combat the twin punishments of brutal weather conditions and the enemy's constant artillery fire from across the Line of Control.

One day, Pakistan's artillery shelling inflicted three fatal casualties on the battalion. Even as the unit was grappling with this tragedy, a telegram arrived. Back home, Subedar Major Dewan's daughter had died in an accident. Sengar, a young staff officer, had to break this news to the Subedar Major. Dewan was distraught and struggled to surmount his feelings. Since moving on foot meant a five-day walk through the glacier, Sengar offered to request a helicopter ride for him.

Dewan appeared to weigh the options. But his reflection had nothing to do with his move. He calmly replied that the three soldiers who had died were his family too, and he would wait until their mortal remains had been evacuated before he considered returning home.

In those days, the bodies of the fallen were cremated either at the Siachen base camp or, if the weather posed an obdurate challenge, at the post itself. This time, the latter was the only available option. It took days to drop sufficient firewood to conduct the last rites as, at rarified altitudes, wood takes ages to burn.

Subedar Major Dewan supervised the send-off without food or water, standing by the pyres as they slowly burnt for two days. Only then did he begin his trudge down the icy slopes to join his family to mourn the death of his child.

The culture of empowering units – or, in the corporate vocabulary, manufacturing plants, departments or verticals – is one of the least understood secrets of the Army's success. Its teamwork stems from the development and empowerment of the unit culture. The immense strength of the sub-unit and unit creates a sum far greater than simple maths would dictate.

A similar focus on creating a culture where verticals, departments and smaller teams within them have primacy could bring similar dividends to every civilian organization.

VII

One central tenet of a culture that encourages teamwork is trust: people should be able to trust each other and feel sure that their leaders and colleagues will never abandon them, no matter the cost. Leaders and colleagues that make us feel 'safe' – physically and psychologically – are considered trustworthy. They motivate the teams to raise their game and take risks for the benefit of the organization.

While in Jammu and Kashmir, anti-militant operations regularly embroiled a battalion of paratroopers. One of its teams (company) was in Tral, a bowl off the national highway surrounded by mountains. Tral is somewhat isolated from the surrounding areas of Awantipur and Pahalgam. That seclusion has always attracted militants to use it as a base.

On a bitterly cold February night, a Troop (about fifteen paratroopers) from this Team had climbed up a massif where, as per intelligence reports, militants were present. The party had split itself up and laid ambushes in different places.

At 4 a.m., one of the ambushes came to life. In the brief firefight, Havildar Rama Kant was shot by the militants. He lay grievously injured, bleeding from the abdomen, and it was evident that barring the miracle of early evacuation, he might soon be a dead man.

The location and timings of the gunshot injury created a dangerous situation. The wounded man was lying on the edge of a cliff. Physically carrying him was the only conceivable way to move him to a medical facility. That would take up to sixteen hours – clearly too long for him to survive the blood loss and internal injuries. And even that would be a Herculean enterprise.

Realistically, the man stood some chance only if he could be airlifted and flown to a hospital. The problem was that the terrain precluded that possibility. Army helicopters even attempt to land on 'stamp-sized' pieces of flat ground. Here, the cliff and the presence of trees would not allow that. Even while approaching the site, a helicopter's rotors were likely to slam into an obstruction.

Still, as dawn broke, a helicopter did make that near-impossible attempt. But the pilot soon came to the inevitable conclusion and flew back. The nearest helipad was eight to nine hours of trudge away – there was no way the havildar would make it.

Col Alin Saha, the CO, was in the loop of this unfolding tragedy. He had already reached the company base at Tral early in the morning and was figuring out what to do next. Three hours had already passed since the soldier had been wounded. The clock was ticking away.

Alin again spoke to the helicopter pilot and asked if they could try something different. After a few minutes of feverish discussion, they came to a 'solution' that was not only most unusual and dangerous but would flout every rule in the book. Since the helicopter could not land, they would attempt to carry the injured soldier slung with ropes under the belly of the helicopter. The prospect of a human being, lying on a makeshift stretcher, hanging from a helicopter – not the most stable of flying platforms in any case – swinging pendulously over mountains and ravines was hazardous for both man and machine.

And that was not even the end of the problems. Besides the fact that he would be violating every SOP and possibly imperil his job – and life – the pilot did not have a winch to carry the casualty. Colonel Alin promised that his party would make some arrangements. But at no cost would they leave an injured team member to die. After that brief confabulation, the pilot – reluctant for excellent reasons – was pulled into the moment's emotion and agreed to try. The CO said that he and another soldier would be on board the sortie to help.

Alin radioed the operation party to securely tie up Havildar Rama Kant in a harness. The plan was to use ropes and a carabiner to hook the injured to the helicopter and fly to the nearest piece of flat ground. Then the soldier would be unhooked and carried inside the craft for the rest of the journey.

As they approached the cliff, the complexity of the attempt became even more evident. A large pine tree was jutting out at an angle from the ridge. If the helicopter flew close enough for the evacuation, there was every chance the rotors would touch the tree. In such a scenario, an immediate crash was the only expected outcome. If the pilot could not fly to a point close enough to allow the soldiers to tie the rope to the fuselage, there would be no evacuation.

The pilot manoeuvred the helicopter as close to the cliff as he could. The Cheetah was now hovering between a pine tree and the cliff.* Even a gust of wind or slight wavering would be catastrophic.

* Manufactured by Hindustan Aeronautics Limited, the Cheetah is a five-seater helicopter. It is considered one of the best helicopters for operations in hot,

They had about thirty–forty tense seconds to lower the rope, secure the casualty, sling him and begin to fly away.

And that is what they did. The helicopter then flew slowly to the nearest ridge while the wounded soldier lay on the makeshift stretcher, slung at a dizzying height. The pilot spotted a tiny piece of flat ground. Again, the helicopter hovered, and the team members managed to remove the casualty from beneath. The pilot briefly landed the aircraft to accommodate the injured soldier.

The challenges were not yet over. Due to space constraints as well as weight restrictions when flying at higher altitudes, the helicopter could only carry the prone soldier. Colonel Saha told the pilot that it was not a problem. The CO and the other soldier would walk a few hours to the company base. 'But you are both unarmed, and this is a terrorist-infested area,' the pilot pointed out.*

He reluctantly agreed, but just before he taking off, the pilot asked the CO and the other soldier to squeeze in. 'Don't worry. I will do the best I can. I can't abandon you here.' At the nearest helipad, the CO and his buddy were dropped off. The load was too much for the helicopter to land gently; it came down with a nerve-wracking thud. But fortunately, there was no damage, and the aircraft flew safely to the military hospital in Srinagar.

Hav Rama Kant survived and eventually retired as a subedar.

The story has a great deal to say about the culture of risk-taking in the Army. But hidden in plain sight are also reasons for what fuels it. Why do officers and men consciously put themselves in harm's way as the helicopter's pilot, Colonel Alin Saha, and everyone else did? Moving as it is, need we underscore that neither this nor, indeed, any of the other stories in the book is a 'Param Vir Chakra' tale? They represent a broad swathe of the Army's culture and the propensity for teamwork fuelled by everyone watching each other's back.

---

tropical weather and missions at high altitudes.

* At that point, regulations did not permit carriage of weapons onboard sorties of this kind.

The knowledge that one is safe and will be cared for is perhaps the most significant catalyst for building winning teams – whether in the Army or in the corporate world.

VIII

Unit-based culture is a covenant that runs deep and strong among its rank and file and stays intact beyond retirement. The Army's traditions keep that stream flowing strongly forever. Units invite veterans to yearly 'raising day' functions and regimental reunions. No effort is spared to take care of veterans in distress. In return, The veterans routinely come together during raising day functions to contribute to the units financially, cover expenses and present momentoes. The desire to give back to the organization is a unique strand of the Army's culture.

Running marathons is a lonely undertaking. Unless the fire of self-motivation burns intensely, a million reasons – and an equal number of steps – can compel a runner to give up. So what can drive an individual who volunteers to run not one but fifty marathons in his fiftieth year without seeking wins, rewards or self-promotion?

On 23 April 2016, retired Lt Col Sundaresan lumbered along a gruelling marathon route from Deepor Beel to Chandubi Lake, near Guwahati. The memory of his father was fresh in his mind. As did the need to summon the willpower to push each sinew in his body. Sundaresan's father had passed away a mere three days ago. But this Indian Army veteran was determined to fulfil his promise to himself – running fifty arduous marathons in one year for the families of the soldiers that had fallen while in harness.

Sundaresan isn't a retired senior officer of the Army. Indeed, he exited the service prematurely when it became evident that he may already have reached the end of the road professionally. When he left, he was forty-five years old.

By all accounts, Sundaresan had been a tiny link in a long chain. One individual in a million-plus-strong Army. Someone whose sacrifices and privations were no less than those of others but, seen purely from the prism of ranks and rewards, who had reached a dead end in the prime of his life. So what sustains the motivation of the Sundaresans of the Army long after they have walked into the sunset? What fuels their commitment to bend the arc of possibilities as a homage to the organization?

Sundaresan came from a purely civilian background; no one in his middle-class family had ever considered donning olive greens. He is the youngest of six siblings, brought up by a father who worked at Indian Airlines and a homemaker mother. Nothing in his academic background – a bachelor's in Chemistry – pointed to a career in the military. But a fortuitous stint in the National Cadet Corps nudged him towards the Army. At the age of twenty-three, he was commissioned into the infantry.

Two decades of service took him all over the country with notable tours of duty at Poonch, Siachen, Srinagar, Doda and Nathu La. By 2012, it had become clear to him that in the sharp pyramidical structure of the Army, he was unlikely to attain further promotions. At that point, he was a lieutenant colonel. So he sought premature retirement and joined the private sector.

As it happens almost without exception with every veteran, the Army never leaves your being. Its robust culture seeps into its members' DNA. It is an unbreakable bond. A truly remarkable fact is that, by and large, this is equally so with those who have risen to higher ranks and those who could not achieve their aspirations. Of course, hierarchy and ranks are crucial to the military men as bonuses, monetary raises and promotions are to the corporate world. But the magic of the Army's culture is that it celebrates identities and enriches memories, possibly the stuff of utmost importance to all of us as we progress in life.

Sundaresan was not a regular runner. He liked to run but always at his own pace. Yet, after he left the Army, thoughts of jawans who had lost their lives in operations and the shadow their absence must cast on the families never left him. He told me that the Army does a great deal for the martyrs' families, but that shouldn't stop us, as their leaders, from stepping up and putting our shoulders to the wheel. So he thought about what he could do.

Running was his strong suit, albeit as an enthusiast pursuing a hobby. He was never in it for competition, much less for rewards. This pursuit had taken him to places as far away as Pietermaritzburg and Durban in South Africa, where he had been among 20,000 runners ambling across five mountain ranges for eighty-nine kilometres in twelve hours. Gruelling, but essentially fun.

How could he weave this into a project that would bring succour to the kin of the fallen soldiers?

He was turning fifty in 2017. Why not run fifty marathons in that one year to raise and donate funds for this cause? It was a one-person show, from planning to logistics to execution. The enterprise would cost a fair amount, so he approached over a hundred companies for sponsorship. None were interested; in fact, no one even cared to respond.

Driven by his passion, in December 2016, he launched a fifty-marathon effort called 'Run With a Soldier' by running the Vasai–Virar marathon in Mumbai. Marathon after marathon followed, taking him to distant locales – including Ahemdabad, Summit Sutpara, Delhi, Kolkata, Jaipur, along the Auroville trail, Raipur, Bangalore, Patiala, Manipur, Guwahati, Dehradun, Raipur, Simla, Hyderabad, Prabalgarh, Vijayawada, Kargil, Matheran, Chennai, Kanchipuram, Durshet, Nainital, Ludhiana, Pune, Songarh, Chandigarh, Indore and Goa.

When he was running the fifth marathon of the series, a certain CEO came forward and offered him flight tickets. Some organizers waived the entry fee, others provided free accommodation. Gradually, the money began to trickle in.

On 20 April 2017, Sundaresan lost his eighty-nine-year-old father. He had returned home to Mumbai after completing his nineteenth marathon in Amritsar when the tragedy struck. The next run was slated for the 23rd. A day after his father's demise, Sundaresan boarded a flight to Guwahati and ran his twentieth, as scheduled.

As donations began to arrive in bits and pieces, friends recommended that he use 10 per cent to fund his expenses – travel, lodging, entry fees and so on. Sundaresan refused. 'My conscience would never have permitted me,' he told me. The money was meant for the families. And even though the project was denting his resources, the collections were exclusive and sacred.

After a year-long quest, Sundaresan raised ₹27 lakh. Sundaresan had researched the details of fatal casualties and reached out to twenty-seven families whose kin had made the supreme sacrifice – each family received an equal amount of money.

The story of these fifty marathons is unknown mainly because Sundaresan had no intention of garnering personal attention. What prompts an organization's unsung heroes to display such commitment and fellow feeling?

That brings us to the question of identity and a sense of belonging in large corporations. How do you create a culture where the last nameless worker or soldier is so intrinsically attached to the organization's identity? Take a step further. How does an organization make its countless members feel so wanted and cared for that their identities are subsumed into the organization's? The Army's culture that celebrates the unit provides a powerful clue.

Can companies in the business world replicate unit-based culture? Yes and no. There is an inherent lack of permanence in civilian organizations, particularly in the private sector. That makes the creation of such a culture somewhat challenging. But despite the transitory nature of jobs, departments, verticals and units will immeasurably benefit from such a culture. Every individual works for one's identity and dignity. That is not to discount the lure of financial rewards, but arguably, the corporate has self-seduced itself into believing that money is the sole motivator. If human beings worldwide had only the pull of money on their minds, what would explain the behaviour of many iconic workers in every company who appear to display outstanding dedication without the attendant monetary progress? How would we decipher the selflessness of the Army's soldiers? Could it be that 'people work for money alone' is a lazy answer? An intellectual rationalization for the abdication of effort by leaders?

People strive for many reasons. Money is the most visible marker, but it alone is insufficient for fostering even 'job satisfaction', leave alone creating high motivation levels. There are other things at play here. A focus on departments and verticals as powerful entities is one such idea. Pick the right people to lead these sub-units and empower them to take care of their teams and produce results. Ensure that leading by example becomes an article of faith. And train them not just to become good managers but leaders who are tough yet empathetic.

IX

The Adivasi JCO from Jharkhand had been handpicked to lead one of the two ambush parties. A strapping young captain, eager to make his mark, was the commander of the other team.

The area was Ganderbal and the year 1997. Militancy was raging.

The two parties were briefed. There were several reports that freshly minted Pakistani militants had infiltrated Indian territory and taken refuge in the thick forest of the Safalpur mountain range. As was often the case, there was little actionable intelligence; only strands of information that needed analysis to weave discernible patterns.

Villagers had reported that the cattle grazers spotted a few foreigners. A couple of ex-militants or Ikhwans – rehabilitated after surrendering to the police – brought some news. They had heard on the grapevine that at night, these militants sporadically came into villages on the foothills to gather provisions and more. The ambush party planned to occupy two houses on two different streets in the densely populated village of Damura* and lie doggo. If nothing transpired, the ambush would be repeated after a few days in other locations. Anti-terrorism operations are a game of patience. T. E. Lawrence's aphorism that 'making war upon insurgents is messy and slow, like eating soup with a knife'[3] is accurate. Ask soldiers who, after a few dozen ambushes, stagger back at dawn, unwashed, sleepy and without anything to show for night-long endeavours.

The CO, Colonel (later Brigadier) Pradeep Rathee, an incorrigible optimist, routinely told his officers that Damura was a success waiting to happen. But weeks passed, and Damura remained trenchantly unproductive. It was frustrating because wisps of intelligence about the continuing militant forays were regularly floating in.

And then, the ambush happened. Almost.

A little past 1 a.m., the party led by the JCO perked up. The street, bereft of any light, was coal dark. But in the distance, a dog barked. That was probably a reaction to the movement of an outsider.

Ambush parties follow a cast-iron discipline. Soldiers are not allowed to open fire until the commander – in this case, the Adivasi subedar – fires the first burst. The rationale is that no one should fire prematurely, alerting the militants and triggering their escape. The restraint also obviates collateral damage if the movement happens to be by civilians. In the Valley, after nightfall, the latter is a rarity. But exceptions can always be made, for example, to move an ailing person for medical attention.

* Name changed.

Outside the window was an eerie silence; not even the sound of approaching footfalls could be heard. The team waited, their tension ebbing and flowing by turns.

Suddenly, a party of four shadowy figures appeared. Dressed in *phirans* and with flowing beards, they had AK-47s on the ready. They looked alert, almost as if they had anticipated trouble and were prepared to retaliate in a flash. Moving nimbly, almost on a half-trot, the four scanned the area as they approached. The subedar had already raised a hand to signal his team not to open fire until he did. The militants kept moving forward and would soon be within touching distance of the subedar. He lay in wait behind the cover of the wall and the half-open window.

The militants reached the house and continued to move in single file. One by one, they swiftly passed by the window. The ambush party waited, perplexed by the lack of signal to open fire. They glanced at the subedar, who had his AK-47 poised in the direction of the receding footsteps. But to their utter astonishment, the signal never came.

The militants got away.

After the failed ambush, the next morning's debriefing was very tense. Colonel Rathee was puzzled at the JCO's non-response. The young captain was livid. The men were silent with their heads hanging down, as if searching for something around their feet.

The CO repeatedly asked the party why it had squandered the opportunity. The men shook their heads from side to side. Someone mumbled that the all-important signal to permit assault never came. The subedar also stood in silence, clearly shamefaced.

'I got scared,' he finally said, uttering a word that most soldiers feel but rarely admit during the length of their service.

'Scared?'

'Yes, sir. I froze with fear. I don't know what came upon me, but I feared for our safety at the very last moment. They were too close. I can't explain this any better. I am sorry.'

The subedar broke down and kept asking for another chance for redemption.

Later in the day, the CO met with his senior company commanders and discussed this unusual occurrence. The words most heard during the conference were 'shame', 'terrible let-down', even 'court martial'. There is no other recourse to dealing with cowardice but court martial – a process that can send army personnel to jail with remarkable despatch. The findings cannot be overturned even by the highest civilian court in the land, except on purely technical grounds of form and procedure.

There was near-unanimity among the officers. The JCO would most certainly face legal fire. And if the precedent was any indication, he could be dismissed and possibly jailed.

What does the Army's unwritten culture dictate in such situations? Like all matters that need to be deciphered based on 'culture' – or 'precedent', if you prefer a pedantic expression – the answers are never readily apparent. In leadership matters, intuition and gut are the norms, not a headlong plunge into the innards of the rulebook. If the latter were to adjudicate all issues, a computer could replace the CO. Or any decision-maker. In life's real situations, particularly in war, you must stare at the dichotomy of gut versus rules in its eye and wrestle it to the ground.

Colonel Rathee took a call that the subedar had shown the sort of contrition – and authenticity – that demanded a treatment different from pursuing the narrow path of legality. If given another opportunity, the JCO might compensate for his failure. The CO also instinctively felt that the man's self-esteem needed shoring up for the next chance to succeed. He inducted the subedar as Commander of the CO's Quick Reaction Team, a group of the best in the battalion. The QRT commander is the most top-notch JCO in the battalion. This smelt like a promotion! It was hardly a popular decision with the rank and file. But that was the CO's stance, and it sent a message to all, especially the JCO himself.

The 'gut option' paid off, and the story ended well after all. The subedar covered himself with enough glory in so many operations that recommending him for a gallantry award became the easiest decision to make.

X

The story of Major Nitin Leetul Gogoi – a controversial tale that has excited many passions – is also instructive in strengthening team motivation and initiative.

In April 2017, by-elections were underway in the Budgam constituency in conflict-ridden Kashmir. Gogoi's company was deployed in the town's proximity. It was among the several contingents of the Army, paramilitary and police that were on the ready to provide an umbrella of security to the process.

At 3 p.m., while Maj Gogoi was in his company location, he received a frantic telephonic call from the Indo-Tibetan Border Police (ITBP) officer in charge of protecting the polling booth at Gundi Pora village. The officer reported that 400–500 agitating civilians had surrounded the booth and were attempting to cause a disruption by pelting stones at the civilian staff and the ITBP soldiers.

Gogoi led his QRT into the vortex of the gathering trouble and managed to disperse the mob without using force. With four of his men, he reached out to the polling staff to ascertain their well-being. But he received another distress call from the neighbouring polling station of Ootligam. About 1,200 civilians had surrounded the booth and were hurling petrol bombs to burn it down.

Maj Gogoi's team made its way to the next hotspot, removing artificial barricades put up by the crowd. When they arrived on the scene, a volley of stones greeted them. Stones were also raining down from rooftops. A mixed group of men, women and children appeared determined to cause damage. Megaphone announcements made no impact on the mob. The QRT was unable to disembark from the vehicles. The situation was incredibly tense and appeared to be slipping into further chaos. The choices at the QRT's disposal were few and unclear.

Gogoi spotted a stone-pelter who had advanced ahead of the crowd and was at roughly thirty metres from the QRT. The major and a few soldiers rushed towards him, braving the rain of stones that came down on them. It appeared that the civilian, Farooq Ahmed Dar, a resident of a village some twenty kilometres away, was there to foment trouble. He tried to decamp, but the party nabbed him and brought him to the leading vehicle.

The next few minutes were a blur of several events.

Amid the continued stone-pelting, a petrol bomb landed among the soldiers but, mercifully, did not explode. The team managed to rescue four members of the polling staff, seven ITBP soldiers and a member of the J&K Police. In the meantime, someone began to make announcements from a nearby mosque, exhorting more locals to join the stone-pelting effort. An Army mine-protected vehicle broke down and added to the drama. All the while, Gogoi kept making requests through his megaphone to allow everyone safe passage. His entreaties fell on deaf ears.

At this point, Major Gogoi took the controversial decision that lit up the Indian electronic media and political firmament for the next many days. He decided to tie Farooq Ahmed Dar onto the bonnet of the leading vehicle, a stratagem that he later said 'just came to my mind' to ensure that the forces could exit without resorting to firing and bloodshed. The latter would have created an unfortunate situation because the Army manual on the subject forbids soldiers to fire in the air. Shoot to kill is the only option listed, the rationale being that if the Army's intervention has been necessitated, then the police tactics of firing in the air would already have failed to deter a mob. In any case, Army soldiers must not deviate from their core learning; you shoot to kill, not for effect. Of course, the use of such force has to be minimal and rare.

Farooq Dar, an embroidery artisan, later denied that he had any allegiance with the crowd, claiming that he was on his way to cast his vote. A storm erupted in both print and electronic media the next day. Social media took up the cause with its usual – and mostly feckless – passion. Politicians weighed in on using a civilian 'as a human shield'. And eventually, the J&K State Human Rights Commission's doorbell was rung by petitioners.

No one seemed to admit that this tactic had prevented violence and casualties. The pressure on the Army to act against the 'unseemly', 'un-soldier-like' and 'disgraceful' conduct of the officer must have been immense. While there was some support for Gogoi's actions, broad swathes of the media and opposition politicians were unanimous in their denunciation. A few retired Army officers, including the respected Lt Gen H. S. Panag, expressed unambiguous disapproval. 'Image of a "stone pelter" tied in front of a jeep as a "human shield", will forever haunt the Indian Army and the nation,' he tweeted.[4]

The point of this story is not to justify Maj Gogoi's actions. It is not even to weigh the incident on any scale, particularly moral or ethical. The 'human-shield' tactic is not an Army practice; in the four decades of my uniformed service, including twelve years fighting insurgency, I have never come across another instance that could even remotely fall into this category. Everyone – including those who have never faced a mob – is entitled to a view. No opinion is being judged as inferior to another.

My point, in fact, is quite different.

Even as the Court of Inquiry ordered by the Army was completing its work, the Army chief late General Bipin Rawat visited Srinagar and awarded the Chief's Commendation to Major Gogoi. The decision surprised some and angered many more. What was the Chief of the Army Staff doing? He followed the Army's culture of rewarding initiative instead of smothering it. It is not the Army's tradition to throw a soldier, trained to make decisions and initiative, under the bus because the option he took looked bad from a distance.

Here is an approach from the Army's culture that is pregnant with wisdom. All errors are not equal. And, therefore, different errors need different responses. Errors of judgement must not be responded to in the same manner as one would to errors of intent, commission and even omission and laziness.

Punishing people for judgement errors is the shortest cut to smothering all initiative. When an initiative invites criticism or punitive action, a culture of 'personal safety first' and 'taking no call is better than trying something new' will inevitably develop. And it will show up in the outcome of wars – and the performance of companies.

This might sound easier said than done. It is hard to discern motivation that can beget an error, and harder still to exercise restraint in dealing with such an error, particularly when the world is baying for blood, or the numbers on the sheet may be adversely affected. That is where true leadership comes into play. The hallmark of sound leadership is the ability to take responsibility for a subordinate's actions when errors of judgement occur. The converse only denotes timidity – hardly an attribute of leadership.

How do you balance the multiple pulls of upholding the rule of law and the need to ensure that the response does not dampen initiative? All while aligning to values? The culture helps you do it. Provided it is a culture that has been envisioned, designed and cultivated with care and not allowed to grow unattended like wild mushrooms.

XI

The lessons from this chapter bear repeating.

Motivated teams do not evolve in a vacuum. Unless the organization's leadership propels a culture wherein every individual counts and each team member has clarity on their larger role and contribution, team spirit will not even begin to germinate.

Leaders who believe they are not obligated to set excellent personal examples and that their words are enough should not expect to build successful teams. Organizations that do not focus on character issues and attitudes while creating teams will forever struggle. Pushing an unwilling horse up the slope is not the best way to gather momentum.

Only leaders and organizations that consistently reward cooperation, coordination and teamwork will succeed in creating an enabling culture. Such enterprises must also expeditiously rap on the knuckles of those who believe personal success is more important than teamwork. I have met CEOs who yearn for better team spirit but are fuelling unhealthy intra-departmental competition by favouring one over the other. Or letting gossip go unpunished. And, ironically, the same CEOs lament office politics, a bit like an arsonist complaining about the heat after lighting a fire.

Everyone in the company must feel safe and protected – not only on the days when the gentle sun is out and the birds are singing, but also when a crisis erupts. The feeling of psychological safety translates as being treated with fairness, knowing that merit and hard work will protect interests and that their leader is accessible. Leaders who believe in being mysterious and seldom demonstrate their human side are obstacles to building great teams. As are those who are so self-serving and timid that they would punish every error of judgement, no matter how well-intentioned the effort behind it was. They do not understand this simple framework: forgive mistakes of judgement, resolutely act on errors of omission and laziness, severely punish errors of intention.

Leaders who pray for a team of proactive tigers but end up crushing initiative and team spirit inevitably end up rearing rabbits.

4

THE FOG THAT HANGS FOREVER

'War is the realm of uncertainty; three-quarters of the factors on which action is based are wrapped in a fog of greater or lesser uncertainty.'

– KARL VON CLAUSEWITZ

I

ONE OF THE PRIMARY roles of leadership is to create sense out of chaos. Life does not come in neat patterns that proffer themselves for easy deciphering. Anyone who has invested time and effort in a complex project, a business, or managed a family knows this seminal reality – uncertainty and ambiguity are the norms. That cute geometrical label called 'linear' is a rarity; 'wildly unpredictable' is a more accurate description of our existence.

And it is exponentially so for those engaged in the business of warfighting. The fog of war is unfailingly thick. Every soldier knows that upon crossing the start line (an imaginary line that troops cross to begin an assault on the enemy), the transpiring dynamic reduces all plans to mere guidelines. Once the bullets begin to fly, the shells whistle overhead and land to devastate. And smokescreens add to the blackness of the night. The soldier's battle thus is not merely against the enemy – it is against incertitude and chaos.

The Indian Army is wedded to order and neatness in peacetime. How does it then cope with the messiness of the battlefield's unfolding unknown? Indeed, critics of the Army's way of life – and there does exist such a tribe among thinking people – often deride the organization for its obsession with appearances and spit and polish. Isn't it counterintuitive to spend decades focusing on order when war will test the soldier for chaos? The psychologist Norman F. Dixon called it a manifestation of 'impressive levels of irrationality'.[1]

The point is not to join issues with these critics or extol the Army's investment in orderliness. Indeed, the two exist in impressive measure – the life of clearly established patterns during peace and a seamless shift into handling the swirling mess of uncertainty during operations. The idea here is to point to the phenomenon that an organization's culture can combine and encompass disparate elements – in the case of the Army – 'good order' and 'preparation for combatting randomness'. A business's equivalent would be dedication to processes and meticulous analysis, co-existing with the propensity to take bold risks and managing rapidly changing market conditions.

How well do these competing elements thrive in the Army's culture? And more importantly, how does the culture manage this seemingly mutually exclusive contradiction?

II

Captain Sai Shankar's unit was deployed in Mutur, in the Trincomalee district in eastern Sri Lanka. The year was 1989, and the conflagration of LTTE-led insurgency was at its most intense.

Commissioned barely two years ago onto a battalion of Sikh soldiers, Sai was the first from his family to join the Army. He was the intelligence officer posted at the battalion HQ. His mandate was to interrogate LTTE suspects, and while he liked the job, he yearned to go out into the field and operate with a company. Infantry officers rarely consider desk jobs to be listed in the 'glorious' column. Given a slight whiff of an opportunity, most young officers would rather be out taking risks than stay rooted to a chair in an operational area.

'I longed to go out with the troops on independent operations like cordon and search, to patrol, and ambush. I kept pestering my CO to relieve me from the HQ and send me to any rifle company,' Sai said to me, as expected. His prayers were answered when a company commander in an area called LB3 needed to be relieved temporarily. Sai was elated when he got his marching orders. 'I was overjoyed, even though these were only for a month.' He immediately packed up to move.

LB3 was a remote area with a heavy LTTE presence. The incumbent company commander briefed him and stayed back to operate for a few days to break Sai in. He explained that the company was required to dominate the area of about ten square kilometres, patrolling it day and night, laying ambushes, moving to cordoned-off areas and searching for terrorists on actionable intelligence. Thick jungles and small waterlogged cultivated fields were excellent places for terrorists to hide and spring ambushes on the army patrols as these challenging for patrols to negotiate.

Once in the saddle, Sai began to accompany his troops on patrols. On a hot and humid August afternoon, with temperatures pushing 35°C, he was with one such party on the outskirts of a village. The column was crossing an irrigation canal. A single log straddled the two banks, and the party was required to tread over it carefully, in ones and twos.

The scouts were on the log when the staccato sounds of rifle firing shattered the calm. Bullets hit the leading scout, smashing and bloodying his shin. Before the troops could react, a volley of fire enveloped their location.

This was the first time ever young Sai had faced live enemy fire. He experienced an initial shock not unlike any other soldier who similarly finds himself amidst life-threatening enemy assault. There is always momentary paralysis. But it recedes in a few seconds when training and the pull of culture kicks in.

Beyond assessing the broad direction of the firing, it is almost impossible to discern the source with pinpoint certainty. All one hears is the debilitating sound. No bullets are visible, of course, and the closest one can come to making any sense of the target is if the bullets kick up dust around you. In this case, even that clue was unavailable.

The soldiers picked up whatever cover they could find, some lying behind mere nine-inch-high bumps in the ground, and began retaliating. Sai realized that his party's counter-fire was scattered and perhaps wasteful. 'Most of them appeared to be firing into thin air,' he recollected later. No one had located the enemy, though it appeared that the fire was emanating from the village, behind a ring of palm trees and thick foliage. The best they could hope from the undirected shooting was that some of it might deter the enemy.

It took Sai a few minutes to get a firm hold on the situation. He shouted over the din to order his men to stop firing. Moments later, the location of the terrorists became more explicit. The LTTE cadres might have been firing from a vacant house on the village's periphery. The patrol peppered the house with aimed fire, but it did not affect the enemy who had taken sanctuary behind the thick walls. Sai had to take the subsequent decision to end the impasse. He decided to use a rocket launcher to blow a hole in one of the walls. That did the trick. The firing stopped, at least for the moment. But the unpredictability of when and from where the next hail of bullets might come loomed large.

The immediate problem was evacuating the wounded soldier who was still bleeding. First aid had been but a temporary measure. Sai radioed back to the headquarters and requested a helicopter for evacuation. The nearest clearing for a helipad was two kilometres away, and the route went through areas where the enemy could potentially be lying in an ambush.

The captain made a quick assessment. There was no time to lose. The risk of running into more fire was unavoidable. But faced with ambiguity, situations often brook a yes-or-no answer. This was one such moment. The patrol must move quickly to the helipad, Sai decided.

To ensure the highest possible vigil while on the move and sensing that this was time for a display of even more significant leadership to shore up morale, Sai replaced the injured scout and began to lead the patrol. This was, he reckoned, not the time to take counsel of one's worst fears. It was his job to eke sense out of chaos to the extent possible. That is what leaders do. He was the first to cross over the log on the canal.

'Strangely, I felt no fear after I began to lead. Whatever trepidation had entered my mind seemed to have evaporated. As if my mind and body intrinsically knew it was my responsibility to ensure a good ending for the injured soldier and the rest of the team.'

The casualty was successfully evacuated.

This is obviously a story of leadership. But it is also a tale of another cardinal mandate leaders have – dealing with uncertainty and ambiguity.

To be sure, this case study is not the most indicative example of the fog of war. Maybe the story is not even unique. But it gives a flavour of what soldiers face perpetually at a tactical level. Every operation, especially in the blackness of night and unrelenting weather conditions, is fraught with the unforeseeable and the unpredictable. The original plans serve as a datum, guidance to ensure that the aim remains firmly in the crosshairs and direction is not lost. But the burden of unravelling patterns and making minute-to-minute decisions falls squarely on the shoulders of the leaders.

The paradigm is valid for the business world and many other walks of life where leaders must cut through the foliage and darkness to arrive at 'good' decisions. Of course, the functioning reality in the business world is starkly different from what soldiers confront during operations. Senior leaders are also required to trudge through a great deal of fog at strategic levels, but it is not to say that the rest of the employees can be impervious to learning how to grapple with it. Many of these 'tactical-level' employees will eventually grow to shoulder higher designations and responsibilities. The framework for the approach to leading through ambiguity is priceless. The Army's stories throw up several compelling and relevant lessons.

What, then, are the secret ingredients of the culture that led Sai – and thousands of others before and after him – to grab an extremely volatile situation by the scruff and shake it until a more precise picture emerged? We will come to that formulation in a bit. But first, here's another story of enormous uncertainty.

III

The Indian Army's bloody war with the LTTE in Sri Lanka began on a deceptively quiet note. Then, like an untameable flame racing across a film of oil, it brutally hit one of the first units to land on the island – a battalion of the Sikh Light Infantry, the 13 SIKH LI.

This unit was a relatively new outfit. Raised in 1979, within four years it had served on the Siachen glacier. Later it moved to Gwalior. In 1987, the year that changed the battalion's collective memory forever, its CO was Lt Col Sethi, an officer of outstanding professionalism. Even though he had been 'imported' from another regiment and had never commanded troops of the Sikh Light Infantry in his career, Lt Col Sethi had eased into the role with remarkable felicity. Previously, while the battalion was at Kargil, an unfortunate fight between two intoxicated soldiers had led to fratricide; that must have been a significant setback for the new

CO because the Army regards such incidents as 'command failure'. Lt Col Sethi must have experienced a culture shock when he arrived to command this unfamiliar set of troops. This incident which led to court martials with their accompanying hullabaloo, would have affected any professional. But, as his staff officer Rajeev Shirwalkar recounts, Lt Col Sethi was undeterred. 'He took to us like fish to water, hitting his stride without loss of time. He was a hard taskmaster, and did he make us slog! His focus was entirely on transforming the professional culture of the battalion. He plunged into setting procedures and SOPs. The battalion started winning competitions in the new location. We were a happy team. As a youngster, I realized how critical the top man is for impacting the unit's culture.'

But this growing sense of stability was about to be shattered in a manner the battalion could never have predicted.

The year was 1987. While 13 SIKH LI was settled into the peacetime routine at Gwalior, 3,000 kilometres away in another country, the events were set into motion to test the battalion as never before.

Since 1983, in neighbouring Sri Lanka, the LTTE, led by the charismatic Vellupillai Prabhakaran, had unleashed an intermittent but brutal insurgency. The internecine battles were claiming lives; the country was in grave turmoil. In July 1987, the LTTE upped the ante and introduced the concept of suicide attacks.

Many observers believe that the Indian government, through its intelligence agency, the Research and Analysis Wing (R&AW), had actively armed and supported the LTTE and several other militant groups. In an overt display of India's support, on 5 June 1987, the Indian Air Force airdropped twenty-five tons of food and medicine by parachute into LTTE-held areas in Jaffna, while it was under siege by the Sri Lankan army. If any evidence of Indian affinity with the LTTE was needed, this airdrop was it – and no one in India could have read the situation in any other manner.

Subsequently, another event further cemented the view that the LTTE was amenable to India's influence. After intense negotiations, the Indo-Sri Lanka Peace Accord was signed on 29 July 1987 by Indian prime minister Rajiv Gandhi and Sri Lankan president J. R. Jayewardene. The Sri Lankan government agreed to make several concessions to key Tamil demands. India agreed to assist in establishing peace in the affected regions of the north and east through the Indian Peace Keeping Force. Harmony, finally, appeared to be on the scene.

But the LTTE had agreed to this deal with barely concealed reluctance. In his pronouncements, Prabhakaran hinted at the group's displeasure. But since the LTTE – India's ally – had agreed to surrender their weapons to the IPKF, everyone had concluded that the war was over.

That was the prevailing sentiment when 13 SIKH LI received its marching orders to move to Sri Lanka for overseeing the maintenance of peace. In May 1987, the unit was put on notice to go to the island. After the accord was signed, on 30 July the battalion boarded the IL-36 and AN-32 aircraft. Its peacekeeping task appeared straightforward enough. Little, if any, resistance was expected from the LTTE. Among the uniforms that the personnel carried, were formal – or ceremonial – outfits.

The aircraft flew from Gwalior to Bangalore, where it stopped to refuel. But as suddenly as it had embarked on this journey, fresh orders to halt arrived. The unit moved into an Army area and spent two months, awaiting the dissipation of this 'strategic haze' and further instructions. During this period of precariousness, Lt Col Sethi put the officers and soldiers through the peacetime routine of building physical fitness, weapon training and honing fieldcraft skills.

On 1 October, the battalion was informed that it was no longer required to deploy to Sri Lanka. The troops boarded a 'military special' train with all attendant equipment and baggage and landed back in Gwalior, happy to resume their 'family lives'.

Suddenly, on 10 October, the last order was revoked. The unit boarded Air Force aircrafts that same night and flew to Trincomalee in eastern Sri Lanka. When the planes landed for refuelling at the Tambram airfield in the early hours of the following day, the battalion received a change in its mandate – it was to now fly to Jaffna.

The Jaffna airfield is at Pallali, on the outskirts of the city. On 11 October, two companies and officers from the battalion headquarters of 13 SIKH LI landed at Pallali, unaware of the violence that was about to be unleashed against them in a few hours. Two other companies had been rerouted to Agra as the IL-76 aircraft had developed a technical snag.

The brigade HQ had landed a couple of hours ahead; its officers were waiting for Lt Col Sethi to arrive and for further orders. As the troops unloaded the aircraft, there was some fuzzy information in the air about a planned operation.

A battalion of Gurkhas – the 4/5 GR – had also landed at the airport, and was awaiting orders.

Lt Col Sethi returned at 5 p.m. The HQ had handed him a 1923 edition map – the only map available at that point – to plan the operations. The CO of 10 Para Special Forces – SF are more colloquially known as commandos – was also present. Lt Col Sethi briefed the officers using that outdated map, which provided clearly inadequate information and even less actionable intelligence.

There was some unverified information that Prabhakaran had called for a meeting of the LTTE leadership on the University of Jaffna campus. The Army planned to drop a team of Special Forces on the university grounds – ostensibly an LTTE stronghold – and secure a landing zone for the forces following in the wake. The area identified was a football field from where, on many previous occasions, Indian Air Force helicopters had picked up LTTE commanders for talks.

As per the plan, the SF troops would fly to the 'landing zone' and secure it. The 13 SIKH LI's Charlie company, led by Maj Sri Chand would follow, in helicopters, and drop at the exact location.

The Special Forces were then to hand over the landing zone to the Sikhs, whose task was to disarm the squeamish LTTE leadership about the peace accord.

'To tell you the truth, we did not have an obvious picture of what was happening on the island,' Shirwalkar, then the battalion adjutant, told me. 'As part of the briefing, we were told breakfast would be delivered to the university the next morning. It added to what everyone believed – that this would be a cakewalk.'

But as the CO wound up his briefing, fate intervened. Maj Birendra of the Delta Company volunteered to replace Maj Sri Chand in the operation. Reason being? The former had previously attended training in heliborne operations. The CO accepted his suggestion. A few hours later, Maj Birendra had fallen to the LTTE's bullets.

The operation began at midnight. Six helicopters were to ferry the troops of Special Forces – the commandos – to secure the landing zone where the follow-up company of the 13 SIKH LI was slated to land.

The two Mi-8 helicopters carrying SF troops flew for a few minutes and soon began to hover over the landing zone. Even though the half-moon was up, conditions were close to near-darkness. The troops, poised to slither ten metres from the helicopters, were oblivious to the fact that the LTTE had intercepted radio communications about the operation and deployed several .50 calibre machine guns on the first and second floors of the university to greet the incoming troops.

But the stringent discipline of the first two helicopter pilots – Sapre and Vinayraj – in not switching on any lights resulted in safe landing and disembarkation. The LTTE shooters were deployed at a relative height and would have shot at the hovering helicopters with ease. Sensing this, the pilots abandoned the initial plan to hover and instead landed briefly. Of course, the din had drawn the LTTE's attention to the precise location of the troops. The moment the two helicopters took off, a volley of fire carpeted the area. The helicopters flew away unscathed, but the snipers' fire, using telescopic rifles and machines, pinned the troops to the ground. As the mayhem unfolded, it became clear that this wave of soldiers would have to abort the efforts to 'mark' the landing zone for subsequent sorties.

The next wave of helicopters – flown again by the original pilots as they were now 'familiar' with the murderous challenge – carrying the SF troops came in. All that the pilots could see were flashes of fire and grenade blasts punctuating the pitch-dark night.

Undeterred, the army formations embarked on the next attempt to insert 13 SIKH LI and SF troops into the battle. Even more deadly fire, including the RPG rocket launcher, met this attempt to land. The helicopters managed to drop the troops but sustained heavy damage. Riven with bullet holes, they barely made it back to the base.

One of the first casualties of the intense LTTE fire was the radio operator of the Sikhs. That debilitated the passage of instructions. If the SIKH LI platoon had to communicate anything to its base, the Special Forces contingent was the only channel.

The SF troops were ordered to continue the mission of capturing the LTTE leadership, while the SIKH LI platoon – one-third of the initially planned company – would protect the landing zone.

This situation had arisen in the middle of the night, where troops – only a fraction of the planned strength – were fighting an unseen enemy, proving deadlier than every estimate, in an area whose configuration they had never seen. In this swirling mass of uncertainty, and a bloodied chaotic scenario, the commanders were required to extract a cogent picture.

Is this an unusual situation on the battlefield or even during fights against militants in strife-ridden areas? While every situation is different, there is rarely an engagement where leaders are not required to slash through the thick foliage of ambiguity and rapidly come to grips with the scenario.

And it isn't just leaders who must possess the propensity to do that; each soldier has to play that role because in the fog of battle, and the accompanying din, noise and darkness, often even communication is scarce or patchy. Naturally, to put it mildly, the passage of accurate instructions is challenging.

To be clear, corporate entities, too, have to operate in an uncertain environment, even though they are not usually faced with crises that unfold minute to minute. That is where a culture that acknowledges and embraces preparation for uncertainty steps in to propel an organization's plans forward.

Back to the University of Jaffna.

Now with a platoon, Maj Birendra was still waiting for the rest of the company. He decided the area needed to be defended for the subsequent troops to land safely. At one point, the commander of the Special Forces team suggested that the major should abandon the landing zone and move into the nearby buildings. But Birendra refused. He was expecting the remainder of his company to land. In his understanding, leaving the landing zone then would imperil the incoming soldiers.

Meanwhile, the SF team – a truncated version of the originally planned size – began moving towards the spots where the LTTE militants were expected to be holed up. This party, too, was waylaid and took up positions in neighbouring buildings.

Over the course of the night, Maj Birendra Singh and his next-in-command succumbed to enemy bullets. By morning, only three of the thirty soldiers were alive; they charged the LTTE positions with naked bayonets. Two of them were killed, and Sepoy Gora Singh was taken prisoner, ostensibly to send a grim message.* Six SF soldiers, too, had perished in the battle. No Sikh Light Infantry soldier remained in action by noon the next day.†

---

* Gora Singh was never forgotten by the Army – not during the days following the battle and, as we will see in chapter 6, not even twenty-four years later.

† The commandos continued on their mission, moving out to destroy a communication tower and eliminate LTTE cadres in the built-up area of Kokkuvil. They incurred several casualties.

In the middle of the night, mindful that a dire situation was unfolding at the university, the Gurkha battalion and the remainder of the available 13 SIKH LI troops began to march along the Palaly–Kokkuvil route to reach the beleaguered platoon some sixteen kilometres away. But barely a kilometre outside the airport, the leading troops came under heavy fire from LTTE militants. The Gurkhas lost their company commander, and the company temporarily halted its progress to devise an alternative plan. Quickly, the Gurkhas planned a detour through the fields around a place called Chunnakam to reach Kokkuvil.

Jaffna was a picture of normalcy when the marching columns entered the outskirts; people were moving about freely and calmly, and children were headed for school. 'All this made us very wary,' Shirwalker told me.

That wariness was well founded. The leading troops barely broke a sweat when firing erupted from a grape vineyard, followed by ceaseless sniping. The advancing soldiers replied in ample measure; there was palpable anxiety to eliminate the opposition expeditiously and link up with the platoon at the university. But these skirmishes were slowing down the advance.

That ambush was not the end of the enemy resistance. The LTTE had sited several such positions, heavily armed with machine guns, that were to inflict casualties at each step. The crossing between Chunnakam and Urumpirai was one such potential death trap. In the heavy volume of fire that descended, the SIKH LI lost five to six soldiers, and several others sustained gunshot wounds. The time was ten in the morning, and the efforts to establish a link-up had clearly stalled.

There is a dictum in the Army to 'never reinforce a failure'. The commanders decided to pivot to another approach to resume their advance to the university. The 4/5 GR and 65 Armoured Regiment, a tank unit that was operating with the brigade, attempted to extricate the troops at the crossing. By 4 p.m., this manoeuvre succeeded.

Some of the casualties were loaded onto tanks for evacuation. The column made its way along the railway line to Jaffna and reached a place known as the Scissors Crossing by nightfall. Bereft of radio linkage, no one knew the fate that had already befallen the platoon at the university.

The next day, a SIKH LI company that had arrived after being stranded at Agra, along with one tank of 65 Armoured Regiment commanded by Major Anil Kaul, made further progress. The 4/5 GR was mandated to move along a different axis, leading from Urelu to Urumpirai and finally to Kokkuvil, a distance that under normal circumstances, would need under two hours to traverse. But these were no ordinary circumstances. The estimated hours turned into days. This march was in the open with minimal cover, and troops came under LTTE fire repeatedly. The 4/5 GR suffered several casualties of officers and soldiers; the CO Lt Col Inderbal Bawa, was shot just below the heart. The soldiers moved him behind the cover of a well, where the unit doctor struggled to save him in vain. The advance had become painstakingly slow.

In the midst of swirling confusion and disorientation, Maj Anil Kaul suspected that the LTTE would have mined the routes to the university with IEDs. He decided to drive his tanks over a railway line that passed in close proximity to the campus. That move proved brave and prescient. It helped the eventual link-up with the Special Forces. But an RPG rocket hit the turret of Anil Kaul's tank, and the splinters took away his eye and severed his ring finger. His troops put him on morphine and pressed ahead with the operation.

Eventually, the action of tanks and a brave push forward by Lt Col Dalvir Singh of the Special Forces led to the eventual link-up with the troops at the university.

Between them, the 13 SIKH LI and 4/5 GR incurred over a hundred casualties.

After three days in the university area, where they learnt the gory tale of the decimation of the platoon, the 13 SIKH LI was moved around in Sri Lanka, first to Palali, then to Vavuniya, Mannar and eventually to Muttur near Trincomalee. Each of these areas is different, and every time a unit is inducted, it must rapidly familiarize itself with the terrain and the local dynamics.

Rajeev Shirwalkar reminisced, 'During this bloody experience, I realized that we *faujis* revel in chaos. We know how to sort it out. We stayed motivated, and there was no loss of morale. The first ambush at Chunakkam came as a shock – but we took it in our stride from there. We instinctively knew that we would succeed.'

Which ingredient of the culture empowers the Army to meet head-on the challenge of uncertainty? Is it training – not just academic instruction, but exercises and wargames based on conditions that mirror the anticipated reality as closely as possible? Suppose this activity is at the heart of the matter. Can the business world refashion its approach and focus on making the simulation of unpredictability and role-playing intrinsic to its training curriculum?

Training has a significant hand in shaping culture to facilitate combating uncertainty. But it is not the only element – I would argue that it is not even on the top of the list of cultural attributes for this purpose.

It is also important to develop mindsets that can approach situations of ambiguity with courage. Doubt can devour the timid. And leaders who, by their inconsiderate and selfish conduct, end up creating teams full of the faint-hearted are priming their organizations for paralysis when uncertainty strikes. Leadership, therefore, plays a role in creating a culture where their teams do not crumble at the first signs of a fog descending upon them.

IV

No matter how detailed, any plan – based on all the factors we can know before firing the first shot – can only serve as broad guidance. As soon as the attacking troops cross the start line, and the first volley flies through the air – sometimes even before it is heard – several possibilities begin to erupt, on some occasions by the minute. Not all contingencies can be visualized in advance. Indeed, to plan for too many contingencies can be self-defeating; it is impossible to refer to each contingency when the factors are hardly apple to apple. In the swirling fog of ambiguity, leaders are often called upon to make split-second decisions.

On the forbidding snow-laden upper reaches of the Chittibande forests, north of Bandipur town in Kashmir, on a freezing night, commanders were forced into a harrowingly uncertain situation that was deteriorating by the hour. A Jammu and Kashmir Rifles battalion team had planned to move up the mountain slopes to act on a tip-off. The local civilian source had proffered a juicy piece of intelligence that militants had established a hideout near the top. It was underground and well built. In the severe winter, it was unlikely that the militants would leave the warmth of their den and venture into the valley. It was an opportune time to strike, if only the team could accurately locate the hideout.

Such an operation could last for days. So, as has been the practice, a few paid civilian porters accompanied the team to carry backpacks of purely logistical supplies, freeing the troops to haul the maximum load of weapons and ammunition. Being a civilian porter for the Army is an attractive profession along the Line of Control and the mountainous parts of the Valley. The hardy nomadic tribes flock to join this temporary vocation whenever required. The arrangement has always been mutually beneficial.

All night, the team cautiously footslogged up the slopes, careful not to give the game away, much less blindly stumble upon the target. As the first hint of dawn filtered through the forest, the source indicated the likely location of the hideout.

In the brigade headquarters, the commander Brig (later Maj Gen) S. V. Bhide received the first information about the developing operation. The battalion's CO called on the radio set and informed him that a gunfight had broken out. There was a possibility that a few militants had escaped to the west. That was not as per the scripted plan. But they were unlikely to get far because the team had a cordon of stops for precisely that eventuality. In the meanwhile, efforts were on to neutralize the remaining hideout.

Two hours later, the CO was back on the call. After the first skirmish, the hideout had fallen silent. But as the team had crouched and crawled to it, the foxhole had come alive with volleys of automatic fire, killing two of our soldiers at the hideout's entrance. More militants had tried to scamper away, but our constant firing had driven them back. Perhaps there were casualties among the militants too. The team was regrouping, and reinforcements were on their way.

In the next few hours, there was complete silence on the radio waves. Brig Bhide started climbing towards the operation's site with a small team. He was not inclined to interfere or control the operations – that was the CO's privilege. He wanted to be visibly at hand to provide reassurance to the troops.

The CO informed Bhide that there had been intermittent firing from the haven. The lay of the ground was such that it was not prudent to approach the hideout in daylight to retrieve the bodies of the fallen soldiers. It was also evident that some militants were still inside. The modified plan was to try again after darkness had fallen. Nothing was likely to happen over the next several hours, so Bhide walked back to the headquarters.

But through the night, the situation only became murkier. The troops fired several rounds of rocket launcher ammunition, but the hideout remained intact. The rocket launchers need a clear path to the target and the rear to allow the fiery blowback. The presence of dense foliage constricted the options. It appeared to Bhide that the operating team was running out of ideas. He asked the CO to try and physically approach the hideout from above. That would be substantially more perilous compared to firing from a distance, but sustaining casualties is considered a part of the cost of reaching the objective. The troops had now been out for forty-eight hours. Further delay was hardly the solution to the standoff.

Throughout the previous day, the troops had manoeuvred closer to the hideout and retrieved one of the two bodies of their compatriots. The commander assessed that the team needed support after two days of continuous operations. He ordered a party of Special Forces to move up. It was to carry enough explosives to blow up the foxhole. They, too, had a few porters to help ferry stores other than the ammunition.

The terrorists had built an elaborate hideout. It had been set behind a rock face with a small loophole meant to be used as an observation point and to fire at anyone approaching it. On the inside was a cave fortified with rocks and tree trunks forming a ceiling. The structure did not end there. The cave led to an underground shelter that could easily house ten men.

Eventually, the team destroyed the hideout completely. A preliminary search indicated that no one could have survived the assault, and the ensuing silence seemed to confirm it. But not everything in war – or the business of life – is as crystal clear as it first appears.

Catastrophe struck when it was least expected. The troops and porters began clearing the rubble to find the body of the second dead soldier. Suddenly, firing erupted from inside the hideout, killing two of the civilian porters. When this report went up the channel, orders were communicated to ensure that no other civilian was allowed to be in harm's way. But in the murkiness of battle, three more porters had perished by the time the caution could be relayed to the troops near the hideout.

It was no doubt a tragedy for the families of the porters. But it had grim consequences for the battalion as well. Such large-scale casualties of porters were unheard of, and everyone knew that the media would go to town painting it as a case of using humans as a shield. No unit ever wants the opprobrium of that tag. And no one in the chain would forgive it. After two days of energy-sapping effort and injury, that was the last thing any battalion needed.

The Army headquarters ordered an inquiry. In the meanwhile, the highest headquarters in the Valley – the corps HQ – contemplated future SOP. The operational staff advised corps commander Lt Gen Nirbhay Sharma that a signal be sent to all, placing an immediate embargo on the use of porters by the units anywhere in Kashmir. Given the humongous task of supplying logistics in the forbidding mountainous terrain, this change would have severely impacted the deployed units. The soldiers would now have to lug loads instead of maintaining a round-the-clock vigil on the Line of Control. Others suggested that the language of the new instructions be slightly tempered to indicate that porters should not be employed where a militant or enemy action was anticipated.

The corps commander's response contains a powerful hint of what makes leaders in the Army operate in uncertainty and ambiguity with courage and decisiveness.

He ordered no such communication be made for at least a few months. Officers already understood that we cannot afford civilian casualties. 'Reinforcing the point at this stage would have caused two damages: drive leaders at all levels to take extreme caution and signal that I was upset with the unit under whose watch the casualties had occurred. And the latter would be profoundly erroneous because I was not upset. If we are not prepared to absorb such setbacks – no matter how horrendous – we cannot impel our people to fight. Unless it is a mistake of intention, I am prepared to bury it with a mild rap on the knuckles. As for the storm in the media, let me face that – not the troops.'

A culture that makes you feel safe, so long as your errors are born out of judgement and not intention or gross dereliction of the mandate, allows its adherents to be fearless in times of uncertainty. It tells them that indecisiveness or timidity will cause them trouble, not the boldness of their calls. In this lies the most powerful lesson for creating bold leadership at every rung of the hierarchy. Leaders in most professions do not understand the difference between judgement, omission and intention errors. The culture of covering my posterior creates a Pavlovian impulse to treat all mistakes alike – and dissociate from subordinates' foul-ups. It is also born out of another infirmity that plagues the corporate world – most people treat all relationships as transactional. In the Army, most leader-led equations are relational. They last lifetimes. Isn't it evident that it is hard to feel protective of your team members when you don't mean anything to each other except for putting one another to work?

Errors of intention – matters of probity, letting down the team or company, indulging in illegal or unethical practices – should invite expeditious punishment. Errors of omission and laziness – the most prevalent breed – should be treated as subjects for improvement until the employee shows trenchant disinclination to improve. The treatment for errors of judgement holds the key to creating reservoirs of initiative within the organization. Always overlook errors made purely out of judgment, except for guidance for the future. Discouraging people who act, crushes the spirit of entrepreneurship and proactive action. It is the death knell for courage and, by extension, the ability to step up during doubt and danger.

When uncertainty looms, you need a team of tigers not a colony of rabbits caught in imaginary headlights.

V

On a coal-black night in May 1999 in north Kashmir, the ambush party of the 2nd battalion of the Rajputana Rifles was patiently waiting for its quarry near the village of Kandi. It was 4 a.m. already, and the chances of success were dimming. Only a handful of ambushes are ever sprung because operations of this kind are based chiefly on informed analysis rather than actionable intelligence. It is like hitting several balls on a billiards table to pocket one.

The radio set of the party commander Maj Mohit Saxena crackled. It was most unusual for the commanding officer to be online. Lt Col M. B. Ravindernath asked the officer to quickly roll up the ambush party and return to his company base.

On reaching his company, Mohit found that his JCO was supervising the packing of the stores. There was a palpable air of urgency, though no one seemed to know why they had received orders to mount a convoy of vehicles and reach the battalion HQ.

The picture was only a shade less foggy at the headquarters. The higher HQ had summoned the CO. All that the second-in-command could tell them in a hushed tone was that the word Kargil was being whispered. No one knew what happened in that sector, some 250 kilometres away. Unknown to the battalion, it would be injected into a bloody battle.

At this point, the Indian intelligence had confirmed that a few intruders had occupied the heights vacated by the Indian Army in Kargil. The situation was far from clear. The estimates of the intelligence agencies were varied; initially, reports placed the proportion of jihadi militants at 70 per cent and the regular Army at 30 per cent. Within days, the intelligence apparatus had to swap those figures.

Back at the Rajputana Rifles HQ (or 2 RAJ RIF), the CO called from the brigade HQ, telling everyone to 'stand down'. The battalion was no longer required in Kargil. But to avoid rumours, he addressed all the troops to explain the change in orders. Amidst all this, an intelligence source turned up with the news that there were militants in a nearby village. The CO ordered an immediate cordon and search. In a few short hours, the unit had mentally switched from counterinsurgency to regular warfighting – two completely different operations – and was now back to fighting militants.

But the following day came another reversal. The troops were to reel back, load and prepare for Kargil. This time, to keep the move's secrecy intact, the Army had requisitioned civilian trucks.

The scenario of a change of orders is neither unique nor uncommon. The fog of war is not partial only to tactical situations; arguably, it envelops the strategic levels even more because any error in decisions at the highest rungs could easily be catastrophic for all. Intelligence rarely provides a picture so perfect that leaders can take clear-eyed calls. It is no different in the business world, though it can be argued that, regarding human cost and national prestige, the uncertainties for the armed forces can have a far more profound impact. The lack of actionable data adds to the shifting sands of decision-making and creates the perpetual dust storm.

By noon, the battalion was ordered to begin moving towards Srinagar to a final destination that was yet undisclosed. Further clarity would follow, the troops were told. Just short of Srinagar, the convoy halted outside Nishat and Shalimar gardens and, before anybody could start to feel touristy, wheeled towards Sonamarg.

On 26 May, the unit reached Sonamarg Transit Camp in the wee hours. The camp was agog with whispers of several casualties. It was the first realization for 2 RAJ RIF of the seriousness of the Kargil situation. Another rumour claimed that the Pakistanis were so well ensconced at the Kargil heights that they were living there with women!

The CO decided to insulate his troops from speculation and ordered the battalion to set up a tented camp away from the transit camp. He also set acclimatization into the process – usually a fourteen-day regimen that the Army legislates before induction into heights exceeding 4,500 metres. But the unfolding script of war seldom affords such luxury to its participants; two days into acclimatization, the unit was again ordered to move forward, this time to Dras.

The unit's 'battle inoculation' came sooner than expected. As the convoy halted near the Div HQ at Meenamarg, just east of the Zozi La pass on NH1, it came under Pakistani artillery shelling. So far from the known objectives, the fiery welcome took the inducting unit by surprise. Troops scampered off the vehicles and dashed to the ground to crawl behind the cover for safety. Mercifully, the fall of rounds appeared to be inching towards the Div HQ but could inflict no damage as the headquarter was sited well protected by the folds of the mountain. After this baptism, the convoy resumed its progress and halted near Dras. 'Set up a camp,' the CO ordered.

Switching profiles from fighting militants to assaulting regular troops follows entirely different paradigms. It is like suddenly switching overnight from retail to wholesale or B2C to B2B. The unit began to rapidly reconfigure its internal organization, overhaul the distribution of weapons, ammunition and equipment, and conduct refresher training on 'undiscriminating' weapons like the MMG, AGL and Mortars that are not employed against militants to obviate civilian collateral damage. By 30 May, the battalion received instructions to commence reconnaissance of Tololing, its objective for capture.

At this juncture, it was unknown to 2 RAJ RIF that another unit had already attacked Tololing twice. A Grenadiers battalion, without the benefit of complete acclimatization, had been launched on the night of 22 and 23 May. The information about the enemy was scanty, but it was believed that six to eight Pakistanis were at each post. But when the battalion, approaching from three directions, reached near the top, a barrage of artillery fire, MMGs and HMGs pinned down the troops, now strung out in the open and shielded only by boulders. The soldiers refused to leave the area they had secured, even though they were 'thirsty, hungry and soaking wet due to snow'.[2] One of its NCOs had repeatedly come out in the open to fire several dozen rounds from his rocket launcher. After five days of stalemate, during which superhuman effort helped evacuate the wounded, the battalion had launched a second attack. Maj R. S. Adhikari, one of the company commanders, led the assault and made it within twenty-five metres of the enemy positions before he was cut down by bullets raining from above. The Grenadiers battalion had kept on defying the murderous firing from the bunkers and charged repeatedly. At last, the attack stalled, though a valuable foothold on the ridge was now available to launch fresh assaults. For several days to follow, the officers and the soldiers of the Grenadiers battalion remained in their new locations, utterly bereft of cover, except for the boulders and no food other than a meal delivered in the hours of darkness. Two pup tents had been erected, and a few soldiers, in rotation, took shelter from the bone-chilling cold. But when a party of 2 RAJ RIF first climbed up to them, the morale of their company commander, his skin broken from exposure to inclement weather, was still surprisingly sky-high. Maj Saxena remembers that he even pointed out the probable location of enemy bunkers.

The body of Maj Adhikari was lying a few metres from the Pakistani emplacements; the enemy had regularly brought down accurate lethal fire to ensure that no one could retrieve the mortal remains. That was the stage set for 2 RAJ RIF when it received its orders on 30 May to attack Tololing and bring down its well-entrenched enemy.

The CO decided that two companies moving on two separate axes would lead the attack. Major Mohit Saxena's D Company was tasked to attack Point 4590 along the southwestern approach. Major Vivek Gupta's C company would mount an attack on Tololing Top from the southeastern direction. Indeed, the terrain forbade an approach from any other side. Both units had a company each in reserve. Keeping the ethnic composition of the companies in mind, the CO christened the two approaches as the Jat axis and the Rajput axis. Maj Gen Sandeep Bajaj, who served in the battalion in Kargil recalled, 'Soldiers fight for the izzat of their battalions, companies, villages and regions they hail from. They fight and die for that identity. As the then second-in-command, I sensed what the CO was doing. He was lighting the fuel of motivation because he understood what plays on our men's psyche.'

But before the battalion set these plans in stone, officers were ordered to do extensive reconnaissance on respective approaches. And then they were swapped to look at the objectives from the other's direction. One stratagem to lessen unpredictability is to ensure that leaders have a 360° view, as objectives can appear completely different from the 'other' perspective.

Also, a part of the operation plans was the Ghatak (or Commando) platoon, led by a firebrand Naga officer – commissioned in ASC, but temporarily on the rolls of 2 RAJ RIF – whose name, Captain N. Kenguruse, could hardly roll off the tongues of the Jats and the Rajputs. He was called Nembu Sahab and the name stuck forever.

Incidentally, when the battalion was readying for the attack of its life, it had eleven officers – other than the CO and the second-in-command, none had completed more than seven years of service. Four had finished less than six months of commissioned service. Maj Mohit Saxena, who was to lead the opening assault, had been an officer for four years; he was twenty-six years old and a bachelor.

During the reconnaissance, the patrols closed in as much as they could without revealing their hand. They studied the ground, took pictures and returned to create sand models to present as realistic a feel as possible to the rest of the attacking parties. The ability to graphically visualize the scene of action is a powerful antidote to ambiguity. A few went up in a Cheetah helicopter for an aerial view; an Mi-17 armed IAF helicopter had only recently been shot down by a Stinger, and the Cheetah had to fly at a safe distance. And while these intrepid teams were visually probing the likely enemy positions, the rest of the battalion was training hard to oil the wheels of battle drills and procedures at the base HQ.

By 6 June, the CO and the officers had drawn up the plans. The attack was slated for 11 June, a Friday.

The first task was to haul ammunition up the steep slopes to set up a base for fire support. It was a colossal task – estimates put the requirement of porters at 1500. Even if all the troops were to make a back-breaking effort, it would be hard. And the village of Dras had long been evacuated; no able-bodied porters were available.

Many in the unit rose to meet this challenge. All soldiers were sent up at least once with the ammunition and supplies so that each person could see the peaks they had to assault. Two companies would haul stores each night while the other two practised drills and procedures. The quartermaster, Capt Bhanwer Singh Rathore, noticed that the fleeing civilian population had abandoned its horses. He commandeered all the animals, saddled them up with makeshift blankets and employed them to haul ammunition. He ensured that 100 per cent of the equipment and rations were in place before the attack.* The Grenadiers unit chipped in too. Whatever ammunition was remaining was offered without as much as a receipt.

Two days before the attack, the GOC Maj Gen Mohinder Puri spoke to an assembly of troops. He talked about the battalion's history, mentioning that 2 RAJ RIF had never lost a battle.† He stirred everyone by reminding them of that lineage. 'Your parents are awaiting your return,' he said. 'When you do well here, your name will resonate not just in your village but the entire area. What you achieve will reflect your parenting – at home and in the unit.'

During tea after the address, a jawan pointed out something to the general: 2 RAJ RIF was to attack on Friday – a day considered

* The unit still relates the story of Naik Uttam Singh, a carpenter who pitched in with gusto. Apparently, he had extremely poor eyesight and was practically blind at night. He made six trips with loads, tying himself to the leading soldier and allowing himself to be guided by the one following him.

† Maj Gen Sandeep Bajaj told me that the battalion had an unbroken 175-year record of succeeding in every attack which was playing on the officers' minds. The Army thrives on its traditions, and the battalion was determined not to break that chain.

'auspicious' by the Pakistanis. The GOC merely smiled. But later that evening came the orders – to honour the point made by that soldier, the attack was postponed by a day.*

On 12 June, Maj Mohit Saxena's company crept up the slopes and took cover behind the boulders. There was, of course, no treeline and nothing else that would shield them from observation or the enemy's fire from further atop the hill on Point 4590. To ensure maximum possible ammunition for the attack, the troops brought only drinking water and no food. All soldiers carry a personal weapon – mostly a rifle or a carbine. Hav Maj Yashbir Singh, who had primarily served in the battalion's band platoon as a musician, decided that his proficiency with his personal weapon 'being what it was', he would discard it and instead carry an additional load of twenty grenades for the company.†

The unit remained there all day, scattered, absolutely still and silent, peering at the massif that loomed above. The Pakistanis did not indicate whether they knew of the impending attack.

At 5 p.m., over a hundred guns of the Indian artillery began to pound the objective. Simultaneously, the troops began the ascent, moving practically in single file because of the constricted space. They could see the artillery barrage fall on Tololing as well. Soon, the Bofors guns opened up in a direct firing role. As they laboriously trudged up, Maj Saxena's troops would hear the boom behind, then sense the rounds whistle overhead, and smash into the hilltop with another bang. When a shell splintered the boulders, stones were thrown up, sparkling in the setting sun. Mohit remembers that the spectacle was reassuring and a treat to watch. No one would survive this fire assault, he could tell.

---

* To be clear, the point being made by the soldier was specific to the Pakistanis and not a general comment on the Islamic practice of treating it as a sacred day, as ruled by the Holy Quran in a chapter called 'Al Jumu'ah'. For more on the secular strain of the Indian Army's culture and how it sees Fridays, see chapter 7.

† He managed to throw twelve or so during the battle and died in the effort.

But the Pakistanis had sensed the artillery fire would have to lift, just before the assaulting Indian troops entered the objective. They temporarily vacated the post, and moved on to the reverse slopes to remove themselves from beneath the murderous barrage. From afar, Capt Nembu's Ghatak platoon had seen that manoeuvre and reported it to the assaulting company. The enemy fired an illuminating round as they came close to the top. The glare set the entire slope awash with a bright yellow glow, stripping the troops of their only cover. The first shock of being lit up always freezes even the most trained soldiers. Before they could react, the enemy was bringing down a volley of fire. Looking up, the company could see more than fifteen silhouettes along the crest, yelling the war cry of 'Allah hu Akbar' and raining bullets on the attackers. It was a few seconds of sheer mayhem, the longest ten to twelve seconds of Maj Mohit Saxena's life.

A second illuminating round followed. By now, the troops had learnt their lesson. They immediately dashed to the ground and crawled to whatever fold would accommodate a part of their body. But as per the teaching, the attackers held their fire and continued to crawl upwards. A few had suffered bullet wounds, and in the darkness and doubt, it was impossible to tell the extent of the injuries; mercifully, there were no fatalities.

One of the machine gunners, Hav Sultan Singh Narwalia, volunteered to climb closer to the enemy and provide covering fire. He suggested that while he engaged the Pakistani post, the rest of the platoon should approach it from another direction. Accompanied by his LMG detachment buddy, Sultan reached within forty-five metres of the enemy, plonked down his LMG and opened fire. An illuminating third round went up, this one right above the LMG, rendering Sultan Singh's location starkly exposed. He took a bullet in the chest and died. The buddy moved up, used Sultan's mortal remains as cover, took over the LMG and resumed shooting.

The situation was increasingly turning dire. The space was too constricted to dodge enemy fire. One of the platoons tried to change directions and move to a flank. Two of its havaldars, Om Pal and Vinod, attempted to climb a near-vertical slope. They even sling-armed their weapons and were thus completely vulnerable during the climb. The company commander Mohit joined the effort, but it soon became clear that they would not make any headway. The slant of the slope made the approach impassable.

Never reinforcing a failure is one of the many tactical dictums that, due to sheer repetition, have entered the fabric of the Army's culture. Mohit decided that at least a part of the company should pivot towards an adjacent area called Barbad Bunker. An MMG would support their attempt.

The outcome of the initial assault did not augur well for the new approach. Again, the narrow ridge permitted only three soldiers to move astride. The first three assaulting soldiers died in a hail of bullets.

The battle was already mired in a stalemate. The two platoons of the company attacking Point 4590 and Barbad Bunker were held up. The third was lurking in the shadows as a reserve. And what was happening on the other side where Maj Vivek Gupta's C company had been mandated to capture Tololing?

By design, the company had commenced its attack an hour later than the Delta Company. The Charlie company was simultaneously attacking Tololing Top and an adjoining post known as Area Flat. The staggering of the timings proved fortuitous. Since all had been quiet along this direction, when the battle elsewhere began to rage, the enemy had vacated Area Flat to reinforce Barbad Bunker and Point 4590. The first platoon of the C company, led by Subedar Dharamveer, entered the post uncontested. He immediately set up two LMGs to engage Barbad Bunker and Tololing Top.

Dharamveer's location was barely thirty to forty metres from Barbad Bunker. Amid firing, a verbal shouting spat started between the Pakistanis and Dharamveer's men, peppered with the subcontinent's most popular incendiary abuses.

By inserting the platoon into the vacated Area Flat, the C company had effectively driven a wedge between the enemy's defences. By midnight, the second platoon of this company was still under fire from Tololing Top. But the platoon was refusing to get bogged down. From its location, the outline of an enemy bunker was visible. The platoon commander, a subedar, decided that the time had come to storm the post. Two scouts crawled up and reached a spot fifteen metres from the it, with the subedar close behind. No fire was drawn. The three rose and charged at the bunker, their weapons firing as they rushed. The Pakistanis must have been watching the group's movement. When the trio was only ten metres away, the enemy opened up with a machine gun – all three Indians perished on the spot.

To maintain whatever little momentum had been gained, the company commander Maj Vivek Gupta decided that this setback must not be allowed to stall the attack. From his location, he could make out the faint outline of three more bunkers. Again, the approach was constricted, and only two to three attackers could move up simultaneously. Maj Gupta asked a havaldar and a jawan to accompany him and charged one of the bunkers from the rear. For a few seconds, a heartstopping melee ensued inside, where soldiers of the two sides exchanged fire in the pitch dark. Two Pakistani soldiers were killed and the unit had its first foothold on the Tololing complex.

With the first bunker captured, Maj Vivek Gupta and his team of two soldiers assaulted the neighbouring one. A bloody exchange took place amid thick smoke. Maj Gupta was hit, and collapsed on the spot. The havaldar sustained gunshot injuries but lived to tell the tale. The heroic attempt to capture the spot had come to nought.

Progress on the other axis, where Maj Mohit Saxena's D company had now been attacking for hours, was painstakingly slow. The CO,

Lt Col M B Ravindernath, and the second-in-command, Maj (now Maj Gen) Sandeep Bajaj, had been staging up from two different directions behind the assaulting companies. In the total darkness, the unfolding narrative of the battle had to be pieced together from snatches of radio conversation above crackling static, the booms and staccato firing, and flashes in the distance.

Sensing that D company's efforts needed a boost, Maj Bajaj – who was in charge of the fire support to the troops tackling Point 4590 – launched a second company, Alpha, in its wake. Bajaj later revealed that his rationale was twofold: he estimated that the attack needed reinforcements to ensure success before daylight again exposed the troops. More importantly, this stratagem was part of a mind game. Bajaj visualized that the Pakistanis watching through their night-vision devices would suddenly see the doubling of the attackers creeping up the slopes, which could dent the defender's morale. As they inched up, defying near-certain death, the troops were to fire constantly so that the enemy was forced to take cover. Thus, the torrent of bullets coming from above would pause.

Mohit Saxena recalls that 'the most difficult part of the battle was the last twenty-five metres. You do not know who is on your left or right. And you realize that bullets do not discriminate – they fly in all directions! Sometimes you see a tracer hurtling through the dark, and sometimes you see just a flash. Amidst all this, you hear someone yell that his weapon had developed a stoppage and would not fire; the tone loaded with jitters.'

When the attacking troops were a few metres away, the Pakistani soldiers began to thin out from Point 4590 and retreated towards Tololing Top. Then they regrouped and launched a ferocious counter-attack on the very bunker that Maj Vivek Gupta had captured at the cost of lives, including his own. The enemy managed to regain its hold on that bunker and, after a night-long fight, 2 RAJ RIF had been divested of its only foothold.

The night of mayhem continued. At 3 a.m., the contours of the battle became somewhat less hazy. The battle for Point 4590 was far from over. No part of the post had yet been captured even though the attacking troops had reached the doorstep. 'We were inching forward – in centimetres and millimetres,' Mohit told me. 'The unit had captured neither Tololing Top nor Barbad Bunker on the other axis. We did not even know whether Barbad Bunker had any enemy troops left to defend it. Area Flat was the only post where the battalion had notched its presence.'

By now, the CO had reached Area Flat. In the swirling fog of the battle, he was constantly stitching together a patchwork of information. At Area Flat, he decided to summon an MMG and a few LMGs from the firebase and engage Tololing Top. But by 4 a.m., he decided to cease all firing and let a deathly silence prevail on the entire battlefield. The idea was to confound the Pakistanis and send jitters among them. After this 'strategic pause', all the companies – or what was left after the casualties – would simultaneously recommence the attack.

Maj P. Acharya's Alpha company now led the final assault on Point 4590 – Maj Gupta having laid down his life an hour ago. Mohit Saxena's Delta company was targeting Barbad Bunker. And the mandate of leading the attack on Tololing Top had fallen on the young commander of the Bravo company, Lieutenant Rautela, who had all of three months of commissioned service under his belt.*

* Twenty-three years after the battle, Mohit Saxena, now a serving Brigadier and a decorated soldier (he was awarded the Vir Chakra), broke down while recounting the story. 'What is most horrifying to you as a leader are the sights of your men suffering – blood bursting forth like a fountain, grown-up men crying out in such severe pain, soldiers with shrapnel on their faces, gunshot wounds on all limbs, removing a man's bullet-proof jacket to tear up his shirt to make a bandage to stench the bleeding, your people dying around you ... It shakes your being. These men follow us blindly on the decisions that we make. They are the family you have. And amid the battle, you feel helpless that you can't do more to help them. Those feelings have never left me – and I am sure others who lead troops in battle carry the same burden of responsibility. I lost four boys. After the war, I went to visit their families, of course. It was heartbreaking. All you can do is recount the story of their

By 5:30 a.m., when dawn broke over the bloodied slopes, 2 RAJ RIF had captured Point 4590 and Barbad Bunker, but the battle for Tololing Top was still ongoing; the objective continued to attract counter-attacks by the enemy. By 6 a.m., Tololing Top, too, was in the bag. But it was hardly the end of the unit's travails.

A unit of bone-weary soldiers, who had just had a tryst with the longest night of their lives, were packed in an area with barely any room for a platoon. Within a few minutes, the enemy artillery began to pound the area. There was no cover, no place to take shelter. Men ran helter-skelter and crawled into whatever fold of ground offered even inches of protection. Before withdrawing, the enemy had scattered mines; one soldier's foot blew off, a part of his leg attached to his body by a bloodied tendon.

The CO ordered two companies to disperse from the area. Several casualties needed immediate evacuation, but helicopters could not land due to artillery shelling. Ultimately, the jawans made stretchers out of rifles and carried their buddies down. Some rode piggyback on the more fortunate. This effort was extremely arduous at altitudes where oxygen is rare. One jawan died while extricating Maj Adhikari, the Grenadiers officer who had been killed in the previous operation. Pakistanis had booby-trapped his body with explosives.

The victory on Tololing was won at a formidable cost: one officer, two JCOs and twenty-seven Other Ranks killed and over sixty seriously injured. Several awards were conferred – four Maha Vir Chakras (including Maj Vivek Gupta and Hav Nagendra), seven Vir Chakras (Maj Mohit Saxena was one), nine Sena Medals and two Mentioned-in-Despatches. The unit was awarded the Theatre Honour of Kargil and the Battle Honours of Tololing and Dras.

So, this is the canvas of the 'fog of war'. At different stages of

---

courage – it is hard to face the family, especially the wife and the mother.'

Watching him wipe his tears, I was reminded of the powerful the culture of the Army – and that in great organizations, relationships are not transactional but authentic and bereft of mere momentary extraneous advantages.

the run-up to the battle, there is less-than-complete clarity about the enemy, timings and objectives. And once the battle is joined, these shifting targets can only be identified and hit after making tremendous sacrifices. Yet, leaders are expected not to drop the ball. They must be competent when it comes to reading patterns, making sense of the randomness thrown at them and never lose their nerve.

It is no different in the business world, except that the fluidity of the situation may be less dynamic, and the sacrifices entailed of an entirely different type and magnitude.

What injects the ability to deal with such uncertainty into an organization's culture?

VI

As I mentioned at the beginning of this chapter, there is an aspect of the Army's culture that should detract from its ability to deal with the swirling uncertainties that envelop any battlefield.

Dr Norman F. Dixon, a British psychologist, devoted a chapter to it in his celebrated work, *On the Psychology of Military Incompetence*. The chapter is titled 'Bullshit'.

'Why one of the more striking features of militarism should be associated with bovine excreta remains a matter for debate,' he begins. Whatever the answer to that query, wrapped inside the Army's obsession with extreme orderliness is another more telling dichotomy.

To be fair, Dixon is not off the mark that 'manifestations of "bull" range from such minor apparent absurdities as the polishing of the badges of rank until they emit a blinding glare' or painting of tree trunks for a forthcoming inspection – or simply for the appearance of neatness. The compulsive concern with cleanliness, he says, alone may qualify for 'impressive levels of irrationality'. He admits that the 'bull' is not without its payoffs. The orderliness and discipline achieve 'a level of uniformity that makes for solidarity and group cohesiveness'.

But what does it do for the preparation to fight in conditions that are anything but orderly? If chaos is the real test, should not year after year of preoccupation with orderliness militate against creating the right mindset for war? Indeed, doesn't it make it harder to combat the utter lack of order that must ensue after the first bullet has gone off?

Even when it comes to the written word, the Army is obsessed with using just the correct abbreviations, leaving the prescribed space between lines, paragraphs and pages, implicitly obeying the diktats of the templates, and never straying into jargon. The entire cornucopia goes by the delightful expression of Minor SD (or Staff Duties), and there is nothing minor about the centrality of its importance in Army life. In the Defence Services Staff College, where I have taught, it is considered the ultimate art form. Even the slightest deviation is promptly pointed out.*

General V. P. Malik, an ex-Chief of Army Staff (COAS) widely respected for his intellectual probity, explained why an Army that inhabits a world obsessed with order and neatness is so proficient at combatting ambiguity. He is in fact confident that the two seemingly mutually exclusive pulls are not competing elements. In practice, the 'fixation' with systems, order and clear patterns in thought and display feed the collective competence to deal with the fog of war.

Here is how it works: orderliness is at the core of the 'discipline' that the Army is famed for; the word 'uniform' connotes precisely

---

* I once used what I thought was the correct abbreviation for 'meeting' in a demi-official letter to a senior. 'Though I have not had the pleasure of mtg you,' I began, 'I am writing for some guidance.' Alas, I did not know that in those days 'mtg' was not an abbreviation for 'meeting', as it now is. It used to stand only for 'mounting'. The officer replied, 'While I will be more than happy to guide you, I don't think that our relationship will ever reach the levels of intimacy that you seem to imply.'

that. Living an orderly existence trains minds to sift what is critical from what is merely necessary and dispensable. It subliminally teaches one to think sequentially and settle life's myriad activities into patterns.

'We do things in a manner that makes sense – following correct sequences as it saves energy and time, the two attributes that are critical on the battlefield. So, when thrown into situations of chaos and uncertainty, our minds rapidly bring the information into sequence and order and respond in that "trained" manner.'

The Army also places battle drills and procedures at the centre of all its tactical training. Right from the day a recruit joins the service, the tenets of good basic practices during operations are drummed into him, ad infinitum. These drills and procedures are considered inviolable, no matter how high or low the levels of training for war. 'One leg on the ground', 'create and re-create reserves', 'dash-down-crawl-cover-observe-fire' and many other tenets – big and small – are part of the collective DNA of Army men. Other frameworks form the core of operational practices, such as the primacy of having and recreating reserves at each battle stage and making viable contingency plans. These act as a robust bulwark against haphazard responses in situations that demand the greatest mental discipline. In practice, though, these are nothing but discipline in conduct; decades of repetition have woven them into the fabric of culture. They are like good habits. If you have them, your mind is free to deal with other complexities when a crisis brews. You deal with uncertainties relatively better because even in the middle of ambiguity, the mind is still thinking as per an orderly format acquired over the years.

Of course, training feeds this strength. Arguably, the Army does this more than any other organization in the country. The aspects that stand out the most are the 'collective training' – more colloquially known as 'exercises' – where units and large formations move out of cantonments for months and train in conditions that approximate their projected area of operation. These are as close to realism as possible. The inevitable absence of live firing and casualties certainly dilutes the authenticity to that extent. Still, the fact that these exercises are considered 'make-or-break' for progressing in one's career adds to the seriousness exponentially.

And then, there is the aspect of leadership from the front and by example that soothes nerves and obviates panic, thus creating a certain calm for people to think straight. Veterans of the 13 SIKH LI – the unit whose University of Jaffna story we learnt earlier – recount that the leadership of the CO, Lt Col Randhir Singh Sethi, was a crucial factor in the eventual accomplishment of the mission. His officers recall that he was always in the front, moving in the centre of the route and sometimes not even taking cover in order to remain visible to his troops. It inspired the rank and file.

After the bloodbath of the University of Jaffna operation, the battalion moved to Muttur. The COAS visited the unit. Having listened to the CO's briefing, he asked what made him accept the mission when he wasn't provided with the most basic intelligence or wherewithal. Col Sethi replied, 'It is for the commanders to give us tasks after due thought; it is not for the followers to pick and choose. If I hadn't accepted the task, it would have gone to someone else with all the possibility of glory. Where would that have left me in the eyes of my troops?'

Three decades later, Col Sethi told me, 'Not doing the task was not an option I would have considered. The naam and izzat of my battalion – and the one where I had earlier been commissioned – would have been dented. I would have let 13 SIKH LI down – I would rather commit suicide than let that happen.'

A few days after the fateful university operation, 13 SIKH LI had a short period of rest and reorganization. Once the unit had recovered its breath, Col Sethi sent a signal to the Army commander: 'Request assign fresh assignment; 13 SIKH LI will not let you down.'

The murkiness of battle is inevitable. Rapidly unfolding situations, the unpredictability of your competitor's response, the infirmity in planning for contingencies, the sheer need to maintain secrecy and the perennial problem of acquiring specific intelligence all contribute to the uncertainty, even on a clear day.

And then there is always the weather!

VII

In life, precariousness is the norm. The higher a leader rises, the wider the canvas and the more complex the dynamics. Each moving part appears to have a mind of its own. Each dune in this desert is perpetually shifting.

What can we learn from the Army's culture to be battle-ready?

Such a culture comes about at the back of cast iron procedures, processes and norms. Orderliness and an inviolable fidelity to good basic practices is a great place to begin. Much vagueness can be blunted when leaders and teams have no ambiguity about the basics. In cultures where routine actions are ad hoc and inconsistent, the culture of haphazard response prevails. Indeed, consistency must be a keyword. Otherwise, when confronted with uncertain situations, team members will be stranded in the zone of confusion.

Continuous visualization of the challenges that lie ahead and training for them is valuable to building such a culture. By and large, the current approach to training in the corporate world is not suitable for this purpose. A system of wargaming and brainstorming scenarios will sensitize leaders at different levels to think ahead and anticipate surprises.

Among the many frameworks that the Army follows, there are two that can help surmount uncertainty in the business world most effectively. One is detailed contingency planning. Every plan – made on specific timelines, objectives, resources and anticipated sacrifices

– has a couple of contingency plans that answer the questions. If it does not go as per the plan, what next? The alternative strategies are not mere formality. Each contingency must pass every test of validity that the mother plan has. And every eventuality must be known, and nominated team members must rehearse the response as far as realistically possible.

And how can we succeed if the company's culture gives short shrift to learning about the competition? In most companies, competitive intelligence is either handled by a nondescript cell with little access to strategy or no one from within feeds it meaningful data. Management treats it as another overhead, an appendix in the backdrop, occasionally making presentations to market their wisdom. In the Indian environment, part of this infirmity is due to our obsession with stray gossip and strands of information as serious inputs. Can you imagine success without knowing the enemy? 2 RAJ RIF had the shortest of notices to attack – and one of its prime focuses was 360° reconnaissance.

There is another attitude that militates against creating a culture to defeat ambiguity. It is called 'duplication of work'. In too many companies, leaders routinely give overlapping roles and responsibilities to the team members. Nothing is more debilitating for efficiency, long-term growth and morale. Such lack of role clarity paralyses even the best during moments of crisis. But where leaders are crystal clear about their responsibilities, even those with little experience – the examples of 2 RAJ RIF again come to mind – will do their job with aplomb. This is how, gradually, a robust culture takes shape.

But a culture of responsibility does not develop in a void. It comes about in an environment where leaders conduct themselves with authenticity and care for their team members. Regrettably, transactional behaviour is the norm outside the Army in much of the world, and that can never lead to extraordinary leadership. Responsibility grows in tandem with the freedom to take the initiative. Does the behaviour of a company's leader promote making independent decisions and even mistakes of judgement, or is the leader intolerant of anything but straitjacketed adherence to the path he has laid down? Does the company's culture rear tigers or rabbits?

Finally, there is that bulwark called tradition. The business world is at a disadvantage here. Unlike in the Army, the workforce is not permanent. But think again – even within the Army, soldiers and officers constantly move from one unit to another. Eventually, it is the tradition of the unit that outlasts everyone.

And keeps its culture going.

5

TAKE TWO RISKS AND SEE ME TOMORROW

'The time to take counsel of your fears is before you make an important battle decision. That's the time to listen to every fear you can imagine! When you have collected all the facts and fears and made your decision, turn off all your fears and go ahead!'

– GENERAL GEORGE S. PATTON, JR.

I

THE NIGHT SEA WAS far choppier than the wildest estimates of the paratroopers riding the four fragile twelve-foot boats. The relentless waves battered and tossed the tiny flotilla with supreme indifference; its tumult impeding the covert move of the raiders towards Delft Island. Dancing under a half-moonlit sky, the violent sea threatened to collide and overturn the boats. The handful of men sailing in them were all hardened soldiers – among the best in the Army. But queasiness rose to their throats, as the air around grew rife with apprehension.

The year was 1989. The Indian Peace Keeping Force had been fighting bloody battles against the Tamil separatists for nearly two years. As counter-insurgency operations almost always do, this war had acquired the appearance of a bruising stalemate. The militants and the Army continuously learned tough lessons and upped their game. Major (later Lieutenant General) T. S. Gill's company had been operating on a string of islands north of the Jaffna peninsula, where the remainder of the Parachute Regiment's 5th Battalion had been deployed.

By all accounts, Delft made for an excellent base for the LTTE. The oval-shaped island, spread over fifty-square-kilometres, sits just thirty-five kilometres off the Jaffna peninsula in the Palk Strait. It is at one-third of the distance to Rameswaram, India. The island wasn't always called Delft. It was known as Neduntheevu, or Nedunthivu, before the Portuguese occupied it, and later the Dutch gave it the name Delft. That is how it has always figured on the charts of seafarers. Its isolation from the mainland made it an excellent hideout and training ground for the militants, and its proximity to India offered the possibility of rapid transit.

While conceiving the plan for the raid, Major Gill (popularly known as 'Tanker') had considered the relatively safer option of helicopter-borne assault on the LTTE militants situated on the island. But loss of surprise and the consequent disappearance of the cadre were not acceptable prospects. A previous heliborne operation had in fact failed, as approaching helicopters had given sufficient forewarning to the LTTE to decamp. The other option of mounting more powerful boats off a jetty was also fraught with similar obstacles; civilians looking out for the militants invariably tipped them off. These challenges only added to the problem of the militants being dispersed across several houses; homing on to them was a needle-in-the-haystack situation.

The Army's script needed a change based on the lessons from the previous missions. Major Gill opted for a far riskier option.

Low-power fibre-glass boats – hardly the best vessels for navigating rough seas – were chosen for the operation. The higher probability of achieving the mission trumped personal safety considerations.

Tanker Gill's plan reflected that change – and a propensity to opt for a bigger gamble. The paratroopers had discarded the relative safety of movement by helicopters or powerful sea vessels. As even full fuel tanks on these rudimentary boats were insufficient to complete the journey, additional fuel was loaded. The boats were not built for sophisticated navigation either, so the paratroopers carried along primitive compasses. Even a slight miscalculation could potentially strand the tiny vessels in the middle of nowhere.

Well ahead of the operation, the troops quietly identified fishermen who owned boats that could be requisitioned for the move. Instead of a regular jetty, the selected point of the launch was the nondescript southern coast of Punkudutivu island, some twenty kilometres from Delft. The task force was eventually expected to land at a point on the island that the fishermen rarely used.

On the day of the operation, a platoon of paratroopers moved to Punkudutivu in the guise of conducting other activities. They waited until the dead of night and then moved in to commandeer the boats. Those same boats were now flailing about in the high seas.

The raiding party had left another platoon at Punkudutivu. It was to be in 'reserve' – a critical component of any Army plan. The platoon's continued presence on Punkudutivu, would be the smokescreen that hid the initial move to Delft. This party would take the government ferries the following day and join the first party, led by Gill.

Back in the rough waters, when the party started, the waters of Palk Strait had given every indication of being calm. But within a few minutes, waves had begun to rise. Now ten-foot high, the waves were buffeting and lashing the boats, lifting and lowering them by turns, like a giant out-of-control carousel in an amusement park.

But there was nothing amusing about the next event. Midway to Delft, the task force was in for a horrendous surprise. Literally out of nowhere, emerged the menacing outline of a Sri Lankan navy gunboat. 'It looked like a monster,' Gen Gill recounted to me later.

The sailors aboard the gunship did not have the slightest indication that riding those primitive fishermen's boats at night were Indian Army soldiers. Since the government had outlawed all nocturnal fishing activity, the platoon assumed that LTTE militants were moving around on the high seas. To render matters even more perilous for the Indians, the LTTE was often known to dress up in Indian Army-like fatigues. The confluence of all these factors made it evident that a fusillade of gunfire from the naval ship was imminent. In such situations, the navy was known to shoot first and investigate later.

Amid the din on the swirling seas, no sound could reach the approaching gunboat. Within minutes, the boats were in the crosshairs of harsh searchlights. The paratroopers could hear the cocking of machine guns.

Tanker Gill did the first thing that came to his mind. Propped up by his deputy, Subedar Narain, the major rose to his full six-foot-one stature and began to wave his arms. He was, of course, immediately putting himself in harm's way. But his fervent, if desperate, hope was that the visage of a tall, bearded Sikh might sow doubts long enough for the sailors to postpone mowing down the boats' passengers.

The stratagem worked.

A naval officer recognized Gill from a previous meeting and shouted through his megaphone, 'Consider this to be your most fortunate day! I was about to give orders to fire at your lot.'

At 2 a.m., the boats carrying the now eminently seasick paratroopers reached the shallow waters of the coral-covered eastern beach. Having made it thus far, the team wanted to ensure the element of surprise. They turned all the boats back to Punkudutivu. The two dozen soldiers of the raiding party were now on an unknown island, and had effectively cut themselves off from the mainland.

When they hit solid ground, Gill first asked the soldiers to do a few crunches to dispel nausea. Then they swiftly moved inland. Delft has a scattering of hamlets, and each house there is unique. The troops first approached the house of Sangrapillai. A school headmaster and known, committed LTTE sympathizer, he hedged at first but soon broke down and agreed to lead the team to the LTTE militants. But Sangrapillai's resistance wasn't over yet. He misled the men to several decoy houses before the team commander used his persuasive powers to make the headmaster see the futility of his subterfuge.

The night was passing fast. They had much to accomplish in the remaining few hours of darkness. Gill split the team into three smaller groups for a simultaneous raid on three different targets.

During the next few hours, several target houses were cordoned off and searched for the LTTE. Sharpshooters covered each target window, and some doors were broken down.

When the leader of the pack, Ravi, was accosted by Maj Gill, he swallowed a cyanide capsule and died before he could be nabbed. His deputy Ariamalai also reached for the deadly capsule, but an alert paratrooper wrestled it out of his grasp. Ariamalai proved to be a mine of information.

By daybreak, all seven militants on the island had been captured. The paratroopers suffered no losses.

The enormous risk had paid off.

Every Army operation is a story of risk. Some of these have a degree of risk so great that it would be considered extraordinary even by those with extensive operational experience. You might argue that there is nothing unusual about it. After all, isn't that the very nature of the beast? Something that soldiers sign up for?

You would at once be right and off the mark. It is not the inherent quality of risk in the Army that makes the phenomenon 'glorious'. Instead, what stands out is the Army's culture that encourages its adherents to embrace risks more readily than is the case in other organizations. It prompts the commander of an uncertain flotilla to discard the safer options in order to increase the chances of success. It militates against 'playing it safe' and prompts soldiers to consciously take risks to win. But what forges such a culture?

Risks for a business can come in many shapes and sizes and inflict such injuries as loss of reputation, revenue, clientele, brand damage and employee attrition. It could also embroil a company in litigation. No one is supposed to pine for risk. For it is the fearful enemy that must be avoided. The corporate often looks at it with caution, disdain and, in some cases, even fear.

The Army's culture views risk differently. Unnecessary risk is to be avoided with the same vehemence and resolve as in the world of business. But the Army also realizes that you can hardly win a battle unless you proactively seek risk, even though its connotation for the Army is far more severe – loss of limb, life, reputation and even the country's prestige. But risk is also a friend that needs to be understood and co-opted, not merely 'managed'. At the same time, it is impossible to embark on this potentially perilous path if an organization's culture does not support it. Appetite for risk and the supportiveness of a company's culture have to be in lockstep, marching to the tune of a common drummer.

Is it possible to create a culture that has a high propensity for taking thoughtful risks? One that shuns unnecessary timidity since only boldness of thought and action will bring profit and victory?

Developing such a culture requires visionary thinking at the very apex of an organization. Designing it can be a painstaking process – and culture needs a drawing board too. It is a sum of many parts, and we will turn to those parts in a bit.

A culture of risk-taking manifests in many avatars, and the almost Pavlovian – in the best sense of the expression – readiness of the rank and file to voluntarily, almost instinctively, assume higher roles and responsibilities, is one of them.

It also shows up in the gorges on the Line of Control, where a 'commander' with no prior operations experience decides that he must assume the mantle in the absence of a superior.

II

Beyond the picturesque town of Gulmarg are forbidding mountains, steep cliffs and deep ravines that separate India from a territory currently held by Pakistan – Pakistan Occupied Kashmir. Both armies on either side man the peaks and a few troughs. But it is not possible to have a physical presence on large tracts; neither the availability of troops in such gargantuan numbers nor the logistics would support such a wild endeavour. But none is required because, in modern warfare, soldiers do not have to deploy atop formidable walls to dominate the forts protected by moats. The areas are kept under observation by manned patrols, surveillance equipment, including infrared and thermal imagers and, lately, drones and sensors.

The Maginot Line and every other linear defence conceived by military strategists worldwide have taught us one common lesson – all defences, no matter how intimidating and sophisticated, can be breached. Nothing defeats human ingenuity and determination, particularly when coloured with extreme ideologies. The border fencing put up by the Army all along the Line of Control has radically reduced the infiltration of Pakistani militants. But it can never eliminate the trickling in of intruders altogether, particularly when the Pakistan Army thoroughly patronizes the terrorists.

But our story is from a period when border fencing was yet to be conceived. The expressions 'Line of Control' and 'porous' had much greater currency in single sentences. This was the summer of 1990, just a while after some militants had murdered Air Force personnel at Rawalpora. The Pakistan-fuelled militancy was in its incipient stage, but the conflagration had already seared all the actors.

Before I continue, a quick aside. Every Army unit has an officers' mess (as well as a JCOs' mess and an NCOs' club). The officers' mess is an institute beholden with pride and sentiment. Its smooth functioning is the result of a corporate effort by all the officers. To supervize its operations, a mess havildar – a non-commissioned officer considered decorous, efficient and dynamic – is appointed by selection. The flip side is that unless his career progression is planned carefully, he could reach 'Peter Principle level of incompetence' – an excellent mess manager, not proficient at much else as a junior leader.

Havildar Kanshi Ram graduated to become a subedar. Still, in the eyes of many of his compatriots, he had only won his spurs easily by remaining in the proximity of the officers for years. He did not have any experience of 'real soldiering', an expression that is among the most disparaging epithets conferred on a soldier who has somehow escaped the trials and tribulations of field operations. You cannot rewind and replay the past, and Subedar Kanshi Ram, who was now in charge of a forward post of a company (deliciously named Litchi) facing the enemy, had to live with it.

The posts were strung on massive mountain features, their heights ranging from 12,000 to 14,000 feet. Patrols regularly moved between the posts to keep a watchful eye on the gaps. On this day, one such four-man patrol, led by a naik, was on the move. They first climbed down to a fast-flowing stream, then trudged up the forbidding slope. Their progress was relayed to the company HQ over a radio set.

Over the crackle, the HQ heard a message that made everyone sit up. The patrol had come upon a telltale sign of fresh infiltration – footmarks that had freshly beaten a path, toffee wrappers and, after they pursued it further, even remains of human excreta. There was no doubt that militants had recently crossed over.

With the company commander away, the mantle of decision-making fell on Kanshi Ram. He was to plan the next move, allocate a team that would go into pursuit from the top and brief its commander before leaving.

Kanshi Ram picked himself to lead that effort. He didn't have to, but soldiers are driven by a word in the Army's lexicon that carries a meaning exponentially greater than its direct translation – izzat, or honour. Quite literally, lives are lost at the altar of the unit's izzat. This is not honour at the narrow personal level, but the kind that is maintained by not betraying an ideal. Notwithstanding his lack of experience, Kanshi Ram felt that, in the absence of the company commander, he had to ensure the company wasn't let down.

He led a small party down the slopes and into a gorge, the direction roughly pointed to him by the patrol. They approached slowly and carefully, mindful that infiltrators could appear without notice.

Which they did. A large group of militants, scattered along the slope, had paused to rest, when Kanshi Ram's party reached the patch. Sensing no way to avoid a confrontation, he drew his weapon and challenged the men.

Subedar Kanshi Ram died that day from a long burst of AK-47 hitting him in the chest. In the follow-up operation, all the militants were killed too. Kanshi Ram's son later joined his father's regiment and is currently a serving soldier.

What prompts soldiers to put their hands into the beehive of danger, voluntarily?

Several pieces complete this cultural picture. But before taking a look at those, here are three stories from one battalion to give us more insight into the phenomenon of embracing risk.

III

In 1998, two young officers joined the 1st Battalion of the Parachute Regiment in Manipur. They were course-mates who had stepped into the service from slightly different training backgrounds. One of them was Subbu, or R. Subramanium, a first-generation Army entry from Mumbai who had graduated from the Indian Military Academy after the first three years at the NDA in Khadakvasla, near Pune. The other, Uday Singh, was a 'direct entry' who had joined the IMA straight after graduation.

Why did they opt for one of the most formidable outfits – the Special Forces – where everyone is a volunteer and known for its gruelling probation period that not all survive? 'We want to take part in operations against the enemy,' both had replied. That is a sentiment consistently shared by most newly commissioned officers.

A ceasefire accord, signed in 1997 by the rebel group NSCN (IM)* with the Government of India, was in force. But the insurgents of the Kuki National Army were still active.

After Subbu returned from the Young Officers' Course, he was attached to one of the paratrooper Teams to gain exposure to live operations. He was required to observe and learn, not participate. Within days of his return, the Team raided an insurgent camp. An intense firefight followed, and the paratroopers eliminated the militants. Two soldiers were also injured. On returning to the base, Subbu vocally expressed his disappointment to all the officers – as an observer, the Team had held him back, he could not fire even one round. Being denied the opportunity to participate in the thrillingly risky operation had rankled him.

The following year, Subbu was nominated to attend the prestigious Freefall course. Meanwhile, the battalion was redeployed for a Kargil mission – Operation Vijay. When Subbu learnt this, he created a ruckus at the training institution and argued his way back to the unit. That unusual move did not fulfil his dreams, though. Subbu's Troop (or platoon – a sub-unit of more than thirty soldiers) was

---

* The National Socialist Council of Nagalim – Isak-Muivah (IM) is a faction of the National Socialist Council of Nagaland (NSCN), the Naga nationalist and separatist group.

mainly deployed for surveillance tasks in the Mashkoh sector. Once again, he felt deprived of the opportunity to fight the enemy. After the Kargil conflict, Subbu returned for the freefall training.

Young officers are frequently required to attend training courses. It has a direct bearing on the growth of their career. Subbu found his name listed for the next course just as another one of the battalion's Teams, which he did not belong to, received orders to move to Kashmir. Subbu again threw a fit. He wanted the unit to approach higher authorities so that his name could be struck off from the course – incidentally not an easy enterprise – so that he could fight militants instead. Like many young officers, he was eager to experience the thrill of peril. The CO relented.

The Team had moved to Kupwara and was soon operating in the dense jungles of Haphruda. The inaccessibility inside the wilderness made Haphruda a preferred militant haven and stronghold.

Since Subbu had returned after a short leave, prevailing norms dictated that he could not immediately be part of an active operation. But the same night, when the Team decided to insert itself into the forest following an actionable piece of intelligence, Subbu insisted that he be allowed to participate in the skirmish.

In the dead of night, a firefight broke out between the terrorists and the Team. There were indications that three to four militants had been killed by dawn. Were there more lurking amidst the foliage? The confirmation could, of course, only come once there was enough visibility.

Subbu was included in the search party that began to move cautiously across the undulating terrain. The men started to go down the slope, vigilant, lest any unpleasant surprises occur. Two soldiers, who were at the head of the column, had reached a patch where a large fallen tree trunk was obscuring the view ahead. From his position above, Subbu saw something that the leading duo could not – surreptitious movement behind that massive log. If he had shouted to caution the two scouts, it might have alerted the militants and elicited an immediate reaction. Instead, Subbu chose to put himself in harm's way. He rushed down the slopes, sliding through the undergrowth, and physically stopped the two pointsmen from going ahead.

The frenetic activity did tip the militants but, at least for now, the initiative was with the paratroopers. Subbu fired and killed the terrorist in his line of vision. But camouflaged among the vegetation was a second one, hidden from the line of sight, who fired and injured Subbu. The wounded young officer crawled to a better position and shot the militant, even though he was already bleeding from the gunshot. Then he engaged and killed another.

Subbu – Captain R. Subramanium – was all of twenty-four years when he died of blood loss. He was posthumously awarded the Kirti Chakra. The other officer participating in the operation, his batchmate Maj Uday, carried Subbu's mortal remains home to his family.*

An ex-CO of the battalion, Brig Alin Saha, told me that scrawled on a wall in Subbu's room was a line he had authored to motivate himself: 'You have never lived until you have almost died. And for those who choose to fight, life has a special flavour that the protected will never know.'

Still in Jammu and Kashmir, the same battalion – the 1st Parachute Regiment – was mandated to combat militants infiltrating from Pakistan Occupied Kashmir in the picturesque Lolab Valley. Passing through the thickly forested higher reaches of Lolab, their plan entailed staying in the jungles for a few days and then staging forward into the Valley. The inaccessibility of the area made it a safe haven.

A civilian informer told the commander of a 1st Para Team that a group of militants was staying on the ridge in tarpaulin structures. The informer appeared confident, and the tip-off was seemingly fresh. The Team decided to follow through.

---

* Three years later, Maj Uday Singh too laid down his life in an anti-militant operation in Jammu and Kashmir's Rajouri.

Up they went at night, moving ever so warily, conscious of traps and accidentally stumbling into militants. The soldiers had searched several likely hideouts by dawn but did not come across even one telltale sign, much less a militant or munition. Still, the Team persisted in scouring the area. But when the afternoon sun rose above the treetops, they eventually concluded that the lead had been a dud. It was time to call off the operation and return to base. But no operation is ever considered complete until the last man has returned to the barracks, the weapons cleaned and deposited in the armoury and the boots taken off weary feet.

The Team began to inch down the slopes, traversing tactically along a winding trail and alert for any unusual signs. One of the scouts halted as the trail descended within a kilometre of a village. He then silently gestured to the rest of the party to stop. It was the early hours of the evening and there was a strange smell wafting down the slope. He reported this to Maj (now Brig) Alin Saha, who was in the leading group. It wasn't clear what the scent was, but it was an indicator of human presence. The source of the smell was hidden amidst the foliage up the slope to the left.

Alin conjectured that there were explosives nearby. On one side of the trail was a sharp fall. The slope rose steeply through thick vegetation toward the object of their attention. He decided that a small party would scale ten metres to get closer to whatever was emanating the odour. If the smell seemed more intense, the Team would then do a planned search, perhaps by skirting the location and approaching from above.

A havildar, a naik and three paratroopers began to move up. The remaining party dispersed, poised to strike. The search party had barely moved a few metres when a sudden shower of gunfire violently punctuated the eerie silence. In no time, murderous bullets carpeted the entire area. It was like attending a firepower demonstration, Alin recalled later. Shots from AK-47s, rocket-propelled grenade launchers and machine guns was incessantly raining down. It was a scene out of an apocalyptic movie!

While the rest of the Team was figuring out the next move, there was a brief pause in the din. On the radio set, Maj Alin caught the voice of the naik; Hav Subhash was down, hit by a bullet in the neck.

Before Alin could react, another firestorm broke out. It was utter pandemonium. The militants had pinned down the leading troops, and the rest of the party was towards the bottom of the slope – they could not shoot without risking fratricide. But the status quo was hardly the prescription for this developing trouble. Alin ordered a round to be fired from a rocket launcher. The thunderous boom had the desired effect. The enemy's firing began to recede somewhat, and the paratroopers saw their leading soldiers moving down to rejoin the main party.

Thankfully, the unit doctor had accompanied the Team for his initial orientation – or onboarding – and was at hand. He tended to Hav Subhash, arresting the flow of blood and resuscitating the NCO. Some members of the party carried the injured to the village. On the slopes, the firefight continued to rage.

At the end of the operation, during the formal debrief, the story of those tumultuous first few minutes became clear. Hav Subhash had suffered a gunshot wound in the first few seconds of the battle. The volume of fire was unprecedented. Every second of the stay in the area meant an extremely high probability of death. But amid the murderous barrage, Naik Chander Vijay decided that the remaining four soldiers would not retreat without pulling out the bleeding NCO.

The ensuing minutes are a tale of a human being stretching the boundaries of risk-taking. The four soldiers, led by the naik, chose to remain in location, unmindful of the direction from where the next volley of bullets might arrive. Every millisecond's pause in the firing was used to crawl closer to their buddy. And, miraculously, they managed to pull him out to relative safety.

Not everyone is awarded medals for what they do in an operation. The system is mainly fair – but conservative. And soldiers in the

Indian Army understand that. Naik Chander Vijay did not receive any medal for his action. 'But the respect for him within the unit became immense. He was forever a hero for everyone.' The fact that Brig Saha could passionately recount this story to me two decades after the incident is an indicator of why the Army's culture remains robust; awards or no awards, the individuals continue to be idolized and celebrated. Folklore grows around them and bestows a subliminal raison d'être for taking risks.

And yet, in many organizations, acts of selflessness are treated transactionally and allowed to evaporate from collective memory.*

IV

One of the commonest laments within organizations is this: people do not step up to take charge. Even in routine situations that are bereft of noticeable risk, employees often dodge the bullet of additional responsibility. Waiting for orders is the norm. And if the task is pregnant with risky possibilities, the chances of proactiveness rapidly recede.

This should have been the unfolding scenario on a bright November 1999 morning near Sopore along the Kupwara–Srinagar highway. Maj Shirish Pandey and his small party were moving to Awantipura to rejoin the battalion's base. Everything appeared quiet, but Shireesh had an inexplicable gut feeling about impending violence. Such a premonition is not unprecedented for soldiers in the Valley – firefights often break out without notice.

As the vehicles approached Sopore, another stationary convoy blocked its progress. An ongoing encounter's proximity had halted

* The Team managed to evacuate Hav Subhash from the village in a mine-proof Casspir vehicle. He survived and rose to the rank of a subedar and eventually retired as an honorary captain. Naik Chander Vijay progressed too and retired as a subedar.

the convoy. Shireesh could hear the rat-a-tat of AK-47s in the distance. Information was filtering back in penny packets: militant fire had grievously wounded a BSF officer.

Shirish was a mere bystander for all intent and purposes. He had nothing to do with the BSF troops involved in the operation or the convoy's security. But, instinctively, he moved forward with his deputy Capt Ashish Agarwal and a few of his men to take better stock of the situation. And help.

'*Sahab ko goli lag gayi* – the officer has been shot' were the first words he heard from the BSF head constable, who appeared to be now in command. The firing came from a nearby house with a sloping roof ringed by a tall boundary wall, just fifty metres off the road. By all accounts, a mix of Pakistani and local terrorists had taken on the BSF party.

'Do you need our help?' Shirish asked the BSF trooper. He replied in the affirmative. The major needed that confirmation to ensure his soldiers would not end up complicating an ongoing operation.

As Shirish and two of his soldiers cautiously moved forward, taking cover as they went along, the militants spotted them and fired an automatic burst. The head constable relayed that there were possibly four or more militants holed up inside the two-storeyed house. In all probability, they were ensconced in the small outhouse in the courtyard, but some could well be in the main building.

Shirish's party lobbed a grenade and immediately elicited another volley in response. Once it became clear that at least a few terrorists were in the outhouse, Shirish decided to storm it. It was a move fraught with danger but one that could bring the episode to its quickest possible end. The soldiers rushed in and surprised the militants. After a brief firefight, four militants lay dead.

But that did not bring the curtain down on that fiery afternoon. Afterwards, a few militants began to shoot intermittently from the top floor. As was learnt later, there were two of them, and they had taken refuge inside the house. It became clear to Shirish that his party needed to quickly neutralize the militants' upper hand by firing from a place of dominance. The militants could observe and fire, a patently disadvantageous situation for the soldiers. The two rebels could have caused maximum damage.

The major asked the head constable to keep his soldiers deployed in the cordon and directed his deputy Capt Ashish to move to the rear of the building. The plan was to open fire from another direction to divert and eventually suppress the barrage originating from the house. He also radioed back for a rocket launcher with high-explosive ammunition.

An hour and a half elapsed, but the stalemate continued. Maj Pandey decided to get as close to the house as possible. This risky manoeuvre aimed to ascertain if any civilians were trapped or held hostage and to seek a surrender. The assessment of civilian presence is always a crucial part of any such operation to avoid collateral damage.

Shirish shouted his advice to the militants to surrender peacefully. But they refused and continued to show belligerence by firing back. The time had come to make the next move.

A rocket launcher fired a high-explosive round at the first-floor window, demolishing a part of the wall with an ear-splitting boom. Before the din and dust could settle, the soldiers tossed Molotov cocktails through the gaping hole. That follow-up was designed to force the militants to climb down and lose the advantage of their elevation in the process.

As the day progressed, soldiers from other Army units and policemen from neighbouring outposts poured in. By afternoon, the BSF company commander arrived on the scene with additional troops. He and Shirish went into a huddle for a situational briefing. Earlier in the day, they had already discussed storming the house and carrying out 'room interventions' – clearing each space inside the building. They had, however, jettisoned the idea because it involved traversing through an open courtyard and inevitably incurring casualties. But unaware of this reservation, late in the evening, the remaining terrorists blinked. First, they set the kitchen on fire. The thunderous blast of the gas cylinder added to the drama and confusion. The militants also hoped to divert the troops' attention in the cordon. And then they rushed out from two directions to shoot their way to escape.

In no time, the troops felled them. Maj Shirish Pandey and his men handed over the follow-up to the other Army unit now present there, and to the police and the BSF before leaving for their destination.

What creates a culture wherein team members, who are expected to do nothing to solve a bad situation, step up to help? Cultures develop based on what we treat as important. Not merely in our pronouncements – they are worth little – but by our actions. The Army treats many attributes as critical. The powerful impulse to lead by example, of course, was instilled right from the training days at the NDA, the IMA and the Officers Training Academy. Leaving a compatriot vulnerable to harm is unthinkable. Each proactive action during operations attracts appreciation. Not every act can win a medal, but tales of heroism always enter the unit's folklore.

Which set of behaviour is likely to win glory in a company in the business world? Are people genuinely rewarded and celebrated for going out on a limb? Or is the organizations focused on winning the battle of numbers, without any attention towards creating of incentives for initiative, risk-taking and stepping into the breach? No leadership can fake this exercise or confuse it with exhortations from the pulpit. What you want to build culturally must be reflected in SOPs, processes, norms, traditions and symbolism. Above all, the culture of risk-taking and initiative can only be built on the back of rewards and punishments. Do not overlook the fact that, eventually, people work for their self-interest.

And it is not always about money.

V

The superhuman efforts of the 2 RAJ RIF (as detailed in chapter 4), bloodied and bruised during the capture of Tololing, should have brought that story to an end for the battalion, like a piece of classical music ending with a flourish. But the template of wars can change abruptly. The end of one battle may just be a hiatus, barely long enough for a deep breath before the next risk-ridden enterprise summons the soldiers. This is what happened to 2 RAJ RIF on 13 June 1999, the day it had surmounted all odds to secure Tololing.

Almost always, the attackers come in more significant numbers than the defenders. On top of the Tololing ridge, the density of troops was such that any artillery shell could have caused multiple casualties. The enemy sensed this and immediately began to pound the area.

The CO asked two companies to move down the slopes and out of harm's way. The trudge was hardly free of risk. The enemy had scattered mines in the area, and several troops were injured. Army helicopters attempted to reach the location to evacuate the wounded, but the Pakistani artillery's constant counter-bombardment made it impossible. While some of the wounded were carried down on stretchers, others were lifted by compatriots on their backs, and a few were brought to safety on makeshift gurneys made by stringing rifles and sheets together. A few hobbled their way to the base.

On 14 June, a Grenadiers battalion relieved the 2 RAJ RIF companies. By next evening, all the attacking troops were down at the base. Time to rest and nurse your injuries, they were told. Look after the wounded, make arrangements to transport all mortal remains and complete the documentation for the deceased.

A maelstrom of antithetical feelings overcame everyone. The soldiers were understandably weary to the bone, but their morale was sky-high. After all, Tololing was not just a victory for the battalion, it was the nation's first success in the war. At the same time, the officers could sense unease rippling just below the calm. The spectre of dead bodies being returned to their homes, visions of how they would be received and the families' devastation were playing on every mind.

The unit had lost an officer, two JCOs and five Other Rank. Many more had been severely wounded. A party from the battalion, led at least by a JCO, accompanied each of the mortal remains. The dead received rousing receptions; villages and towns celebrated the accompanying parties as heroes.

Mohit Saxena* recalled the moment: 'While the nation was celebrating, we in the battalion could not. The loss of men haunts you for a long time.'

Soldiers are taught not to draw any motivation from feelings of vengeance. Instead, the discipline of soldiering prides itself on its professionalism. But one could sense that these soldiers wanted to deliver retribution to those who had felled their comrades. Of course, the unit had done its bit and was waiting to be de-inducted from the sector. The possibility of being employed for another attack did not as much as flit across anybody's mind. The date was 19 June – four days since the battalion had reached the base.

That day, the CO was summoned to the higher HQ and ordered to prepare his men to attack another enemy-held complex called 3 Pimple. No date was given, but the task had to be accomplished without delay.

The officers were surprised that the battalion, physically battered after the first attack, was to launch the next one in such quick succession. But no one questioned the decision. Instead, the battalion immediately sent off reconnaissance parties.

Here is the macro topographical picture of the area of operations. The initial intrusions had taken place on three parallel ridges. The one closest to the national highway – the Tololing ridge –

* The same Major Mohit Saxena who in chapter 4 had figured in the story of the attack on Tololing. He is now a Brigadier.

had already been captured. The next was the 3 Pimple area, and echeloned further to the depth was the ridge that housed the Tiger Hill complex. The rationale for occupying these ridges was simple: it provided an observation deep into the Indian territory and allowed the Pakistanis to bring down artillery fire onto the national highway. Any daytime movement of vehicles invited fiery attention. While movement at night was possible only without headlights, using just the dimmer convoy lights.

In the area where 2 RAJ RIF was operating, between the Pakistani deployment and the nearest Indian Army battalion, the 16 Grenadiers Regiment, rose a formidable mountain called Kajal 1. The final objective could only be achieved by scaling Kajal 1, moving down into Tololing Nala, and attacking the Pakistanis uphill.

Of the main objectives, only two enemy posts known as 3 Pimples and Knoll were visible from the highway. But another feature, Lone Hill, could not be viewed unless the reconnaissance parties went beyond the 16 Grenadiers' positions and towards Kajal 1.

It was decided to get a closer look at the objective from two different directions. Maj Mohit Saxena's D Company was tasked to approach it from the west, while A Company, led by Maj Padmapani Acharya and Capt Vijayant Thapar, were to take the easterly direction. Captain N. Kenguruse (everyone in the battalion had simplified his name to 'Nembu') was to infiltrate with his Ghatak platoon* to assess possible routes for enemy reinforcements.

The 2 RAJ RIF reconnaissance parties climbed up towards Kajal 1. Short of that hill, they met up with a company of Grenadiers that had been holding the area. One of the parties that had come up to liaise with the Grenadiers was led by a young officer, Lt Routella, who had completed all of three months of commissioned service at that point. Was there any enemy present on Kajal 1? The answer was unclear. There was a brief discussion regarding the possibilities.

---

* Infantry subunits comprising the toughest officers and soldiers, and trained to execute 'commando type' actions.

'Let us go there and find out,' an exuberant Routella suggested. His party of ten, led by the young lieutenant, then began to move down a slope that reached a nullah before ascending upwards towards Kajal 1. But the moment they were exposed to the enemy deployed on 3 Pimples, a hail of bullets was showered upon them. Instead of retreating, Routella and his men took counsel of courage and ran down, until they were no longer visible to the Pakistanis. Then they began to climb up towards Kajal 1 and, much to their pleasant surprise, were able to reach it without any further engagement with the enemy. Kajal 1 was unoccupied. It gave the troops an excellent vantage point and a firm base for future attacks.

Days of reconnaissance, often extremely risky, and planning followed. Eventually, the plan was cast. Maj Acharya's A Company would lead the assault on 3 Pimple/Knoll, and Maj Mohit Saxena's D Company would follow. Since C Company had lost its commander a few days ago and incurred several casualties, the CO placed it in reserve to follow the assaulting troops and remain poised to join the action when needed.

There were multiple objectives to assault, but geography dictated that Knoll must be the first in the sequence. Captain Kenguruse, who had taken a closer look at the target area, suggested simultaneously tackling Lone Hill. This manoeuvre would need a company infiltrating behind enemy lines and coming up from the rear.*

On 26 June, the GOC Maj Gen Mohinder Puri spoke to the troops. 'You are my *Brahmastra*,' he told them. 'You have already given the Indian Army its first success. You have a rich history and you've never lost a battle,' he reminded the gathering.

The next four days saw hectic activity in hauling ammunition and other equipment up the slopes. A series of efforts over forbidding terrain aligned the preparation meticulously with the plans. The

---

* The 2 RAJ RIF attack was part of a larger brigade attack. Since the purpose of this narrative is not to recount military history, those details have not been included here.

quartermaster Maj Rathore again pressed the locally marshalled ponies into service. The unit deployed weapons that were to provide support to the attacking troops. One of the many risks in store was the direction of supporting fire from the medium machine guns and automatic grenade launchers; the lay of the ground dictated that the movement of the supporting fire and attack would be the same. Bullets would fly over the attacking troops once they moved ahead of Kajal 1. The attacking troops would be advancing right under the canopy of machine gunfire. Even the slightest error in aim could cause fratricide and prove catastrophic.

On the night of 26 June, the troops enjoyed their last hot meal – the unit had set up langars at the lower end of the slopes – and everyone filled up on water from the stream. The build-up could not have gone unnoticed from the enemy's far higher perch; the troops knew that they were probably getting ready to counter-attack. But it was an inevitable risk. There was no getting around it.

On the 27th, the stage was set for the attack. The companies were positioned at Kajal 1. The doctor, Capt Somnath Basu, had set up a regimental aid post (RAP) to receive casualties that would surely follow.* In the evening, all officers – including the CO who had moved up – sat together, bantering and laughing. The unspoken reason was apparent – they were creating a light-hearted atmosphere that would act as a bulwark against the tension of the ensuing task. The officers also decided to write letters and carry them in the pockets of their combat outfit. If an officer died in the attack, his comrades would deliver this last letter to his home.†

* 'Anybody and everybody who reached this RAP survived, irrespective of the severity of wounds,' Brig Mohit Saxena told me.

† One of the youngest officers, Capt Vijayant Thapar (Robin), wrote this in a Forces Letter envelope addressed simply to 'My Family':
Dearest Papa, Mama, Birdie and Granny,

By the time you get this letter I'll be observing you all from the sky, enjoying the hospitality of Apsaras.

Though the officers engaged in cheerful, high-spirited conversation – often punctuated with laughter – deep inside, uncertainties swirled. Mohit Saxena was fully aware of the gaps in the information at hand. He had hardly any idea of the number of enemy soldiers on the post and would be attacking from a rear direction that no one was

---

I have no regrets; in fact even if I become a human again I'll join the army again and fight for my nation.

If you can, please come and see where the Indian army fought for your tomorrow.

As far as the unit is concerned, the new chaps should be told about this sacrifice. I hope my photo will be kept in the 'A' coy mandir with Karni Mata.

Whatever organ can be taken, should be done.

Contribute some money to the orphanage and keep on giving Rs 50/- to Ruksana per month and meet Yogi Baba.

Best of luck to Birdie, never forget this sacrifice of these men. Papa, you should feel proud. Mama, so should you, meet Preeti [name changed] (I loved her). Mamaji, forgive me for everything wrong I did.

Ok then its time for me to join my clan of the Dirty Dozen. My aslt party has 12 chaps.

Best of luck to you all.

Live life king size.

Yours

Robin

[Note: Ruksana was a six-year-old Kashmiri girl whose father had been killed by terrorists. Capt Thapar had met her when he was posted in Kupwara. When Capt Thapar heard about Ruksana's plight, he made daily visits to her school. Accompanied by his helper, Sepoy Jagmal Singh, he would bring sweets and chocolates and talk to the child. The two slowly bonded, and he even took Ruksana to see a doctor. Colonel Thapar, who is now in his seventies, has continued to honour the wishes of their late son, stayed in touch with Ruksana, and sends her money annually.

In fact, Col Thapar had met Ruksana and her mother in 2015 and was happy to see that she was going to school regularly.]

Another officer, Maj Padmapani Acharya, wrote in his letter: 'Dear Papa … don't worry about casualties – it's a professional hazard beyond our control. At least it is for a good cause.

Tell mamma that combat is an honour of a lifetime, and I could not think of anything less. What better way to serve the nation? Tell a story a day from the Mahabharata to Charu so that your grandchild imbibes good values.'

familiar with. It was deduced from the available facts that there was a track which could help them navigate their way up to the objective. It was a risk to assume the attackers did not have the luxury of circumventing. But this risk could be somewhat mitigated – by taking a different risk! Mohit took along three well-trained soldiers and crept up as close to Knoll as possible to make greater sense of the situation. Two shots were fired from the post as the party probed the slopes leading up to Knoll. Even in the darkness of night, the enemy possibly spotted the soldiers' movement and blasted a few rounds. Or was it routine speculative firing?

The attack commenced on the evening of 28 June. A barrage of artillery carpeted the estimated Pakistani locations. The enemy promptly responded in kind. As the leading A company began its move, it was confronted with a truth that every attacker has faced since warfare began. The plans you make are just that, a framework for guidance. From the moment the first bullet is fired, all plans risk obsolescence. The science of planning is imperfect because so many dynamic factors are at play on the battlefield that it is impossible to adhere to the original script. That is the risk – and uncertainty – that military commanders must surmount with discipline, cool heads and courage.

A Company found that the terrain permitted only a single-file advance. The timeline was rapidly dissolving into a delay. The CO decided that matters needed to be hastened by modifying the ploy and simultaneously launching Mohit's D Company. Since the initial descent was steep, the company decided that soldiers would use their raincoats as a platform to slide down right to the nullah.

As the troops reached the Tololing Nullah, the enemy artillery began to greet them with fairly accurate bombardment. One of the rounds fell close to the artillery fire observation officer and wounded him. He later lost his arm. At the very start of the battle, the chief fire controller had been rendered inoperative.

Both companies were nearly an hour behind schedule. One of them began climbing to Knoll and reached its vicinity just before midnight. It was a moonlit night; the slopes were a patchwork of shadows and gleaming rocks. The Pakistanis could see the play of shadows but had chosen to hold their fire. When the first platoon, led by Capt Thapar, began to close in, a fusillade of bullets greeted it. Thapar's platoon, caught in the open, took tactical cover behind rocks and retaliated.

While this action was underway, Mohit's D Company had been negotiating the nullah to begin climbing towards Lone Hill. A scout noticed a field telephone cable running across the nullah and up the slope towards the Pakistani post. The attackers slashed the cable.

As the party closed in on Lone Hill, it was confronted with a phenomenon that hits most climbers – false ridge lines. As you move up, fresh outlines begin to loom, and it is often hard to discern whether or not the final destination has been reached. It is common to cross several such 'mirages' before finally ascending to the peak. The night only magnifies the risk inherent in such incertitude. One can attack the wrong objective or prematurely come under enemy fire. In this case, three distinct 'bumps' were visible, but there was no clarity as to whether these were a part of the final objective.

Capt Nembu, physically leading the forwardmost platoon, offered to tactically approach the first of these bumps. Several gut-wrenching moments later, Nembu's party had reached this feature, unopposed and undetected. The enemy was farther away.

The script was repeated when the next platoon, with Maj Mohit Saxena at the helm, crept up to the second bump. Nembu's party had deployed itself to cover the move of the second platoon with fire, but that, in the end, was not needed. It turned out that the remaining 'bump' was Lone Hill, the ultimate prize. The company readied its automatic weapons and prepared to throw itself into the final battle. The time was 1 a.m. on 29 June.

Earlier, at 11 p.m. on 28 June, the leading platoon of Acharya's D Company had been unable to progress towards its objective; accurate firing from Knoll had pinned it down. The company commander decided to move the next platoon to open that door. But the moment he moved from another direction, lethal fire enveloped the soldiers. A dangerous situation had developed – Maj Acharya's men were a mere fifty metres from the first fire-spewing bunker. The company's second-in-command, Capt Thapar, was 150 metres away from his first objective. The climb to the post was steep and could only be negotiated one person at a time. That is what had made the final approach hazardous.

Maj Acharya ordered that a grenade be lobbed at the enemy post. The almighty bang was effective, stopping the firing. But the moment the platoon commenced its ponderous move up the fiery slope, the Pakistanis resumed their attack. Maj Acharya's party responded with a few more grenades, hoping to rush up the last few metres before the din subsided. But the firing from above was relentless. One of the soldiers managed to move another ten metres and took cover behind a boulder. The party was tantalizingly – and perilously – close to the post's first bunker.

Perhaps taking a cue from the grenade assault that had hit them, the Pakistani troops in the bunker began to lob grenades down the slope. One of the grenades burst right in front of Maj Acharya, killing him on the spot.*

The radio operator who had seen Maj Acharya perish switched the radio set to a secure frequency and informed the CO. In another location, the same communication was heard by Capt Thapar too. The youngster decided that he must immediately assume command and lead the charge to the bunker that had halted their progress. He headed right to the front, firing from a light machine gun while on the move. But his progress was cut short by another hail of bullets.

---

* Maj Acharya's wife was expecting their child when he died. Aparajita was born two months after her father's death and has written a moving book in his memory. Mrs Acharya still attends the battalion's Raising Day functions.

Capt Thapar received a gunshot wound in the head and instantly lost his life.* In a span of half an hour, the entire officer leadership of the company was gone.

One of the subedars – Sunayak Singh – decided to step up and take charge. He knew that the soldiers' morale was bound to have been dented. It was time to ensure that the sortie did not get stalled. The CO spoke to Sub Sunayak on the radio set and told him he was also moving up to be with the beleaguered company. He asked the JCO whether artillery fire should be brought to pound the bunker. 'No,' said the JCO. 'We are so close that before any shelling, our troops must vacate the position and move down first.' Even a temporary withdrawal to a safer place was not advisable from the morale standpoint, or the subsequent effort needed to recommence the attack. Risking assault without artillery support was the better option.

After taking stock of the situation, the CO reached Sunayak's platoon and moved to Thapar's too. The troops that the enemy fusillade had pinned down saw their CO among them. It is not hard to fathom what effect it would have had on their morale. To be visible among your team when the chips are down is one of the primary rules of leading by example. It motivates the rank and file because it fosters a sense of security.

The CO decided that the time was ripe to bring down the direct cannonade of the formidable Bofors. The plan now was to move both the platoons out of the danger zone, fire a few rounds before the enemy regained its wits and charge the bunkers within moments of the shells landing on the target.

The entire hill shook at 3 a.m. when the Bofors rounds pummelled the hilltop. Before the dust and reverberations settled, the platoons began their charge into the enemy bunkers.

One of the units reached within five metres of the objective when the Pakistani bunker began to spew lethal fire. The assaulting troops

* In 2016, Colonel (retired) Vijendra Thapar climbed 16,000 feet to fulfil his son's wish expressed in his last letter.

took cover behind the nearest boulders, awaiting the opportune moment to rush in. The other unit too was similarly placed – within a few metres of the Pakistani bunker. That was the situation at 3:30 a.m. – still pregnant with humongous risk and uncertainty.

In the other attack – on Lone Hill by Mohit Saxena's D Company – a greater peril was about to unveil itself. Having occupied two bumps without firing a shot, the company was poised to capture the third and last. That peak lay 200 metres away, with a near-vertical eighty-metre slope in the final approach. The moon was behind the looming Lone Hill, and shadows were darkening the entire area where Mohit's men waited. There was no sign of the enemy's presence on the slopes of Lone Hill. This presented a grave risk.

Capt Nembu led the platoon with a couple of Ghataks and began to ascend. The Pakistanis instantly opened gunfire, targeted at the firebase on the first bump. Nembu's party was defiladed from observation and thus, for the moment, not in the line of fire. The medium machine gun from Bump 1 retaliated, generally firing towards the top of Lone Hill because it was impossible to pinpoint the precise location of the enemy's automatic weapons from the occasional flash.

One of the soldiers manning the MMG at Bump 1, Rifleman Jai Hind Prakash, was hit in the face by a bullet. He lost his left eye, nostril and upper lip. Instantly, his complete face was covered in blood. Little could be done to help him except wrap his severely mauled face with a shell dressing to stench the blood flow. The injured rifleman's demeanour struck Mohit – even in severe pain and trauma, he was able to remain calm. The extent of his injuries was such that it appeared he would not survive. Later, when the party decided to leave the location and attack the enemy, the injured rifleman held Mohit's hand and made a quiet promise, 'Come back. I will stay alive.'*

---

* Rifleman Jai Hind Prakash remained true to his word. He survived and was later evacuated. He spent eight years under treatment at the Army's Research

Nembu began his arduous climb. As a Naga, he was naturally adept at scaling mountains. But the incline was treacherously steep and the progress slow. Mohit also left the firebase and, with a few soldiers, began to go up after him. Soon, the Pakistani firing became increasingly intense. The climbers realized it would be impossible to make any progress without using their hands and feet. Weapons had to be slung over the shoulder, which rendered them useless during the ascent. They had to periodically stop to shoot a few rounds and then begin scaling the mountain again. The lack of oxygen in the rarified atmosphere made each step a torturous enterprise.

As the parties made their way up, the enemy fire rose to a crescendo. It was apparent that they were closing in on the objective, and the defenders were aware of their presence.

When Nembu's party reached within a hundred metres of the target, they came onto a patch of snow hidden from the sun due to its location. But the moment the soldiers negotiated that area, their silhouettes stood out against the whiteness and the enemy began to carpet the place with bullets. Nembu's party had to retreat a bit to escape the barrage.

Nembu requisitioned a rocket launcher, which was brought to him from the rear and passed up one man at a time. It was difficult to aim and fire upwards and, finally, when the trigger was pressed, there was a massive boom and a fiery backblast – but the round sailed over Lone Hill without damage to the enemy.

It was clear to the captain that there was no more time to lose. In a couple of hours, dawn would break over the horizon, exposing

---

and Referral Hospital in Delhi, undergoing three dozen surgeries for grafts. Muscles were transplanted from his thighs, arms and hips. When Maj Mohit visited him in the hospital, he had only one tongue-in-cheek complaint. 'With a face like mine,' he said, 'no one will ever marry me!' But he couldn't have been more wrong. He married, served out his entire seventeen years in the Army, was re-employed with the DRDO and now has a son and daughter-in-law.

everyone in stark relief. They returned to the snow patch and discovered it was a slippery ice sheet. The skid and slither was making progress backbreakingly slow.

He decided to discard his shoes to move faster.

The NCO beside him saw his leader do it and removed his shoes as well. Both of them now began to mount the height faster. Fifty metres from the top, they saw the outline of a bunker – a makeshift structure of heavy boulders, commonly known as *sangar*, with a corrugated sheet for a roof. Flashes of fire spewed forth from a loophole. The duo was in no position to respond – they were using all fours to climb, their weapons uselessly hanging from the shoulders. The rest of the platoon, only a little bit behind, was also closing in. Capt Nembu reached within five metres of the enemy bunker. It must have been clear to the Pakistanis that the end was near.

That is when the battle turned ugly for the Raj Rif company.

The Pakistanis decided to start pushing the boulders of the bunker downslope. Each massive rock, now hurtling down at the soldiers desperately climbing up, became a lethal missile. Nembu was among the first to be hammered by a boulder, and he fell 200 metres back to the starting point. One by one, other men began to fall, thoroughly unable to save their lives in the apocalyptic moment – the giant rocks rolling down on them were accompanied by hellfire out of nowhere.

The suddenness of this catastrophe perplexed those who were still climbing. Mohit soon realized what was happening; the number of men falling off the slope was far too many to be a one-off phenomenon. But by the time he could make sense of the mayhem, the entire platoon of nearly twenty – except for one soldier ahead of the group – had been pummelled and pushed down. Severely wounded soldiers, smashing against rocks on their way to the bottom, lay scattered at the base of the bump. The only soldier still unscathed was Sepoy Jaipal Singh, and he did the unthinkable. Standing up on a ledge, he began to shoot upslope in the direction of the enemy with his light machine gun. Within a few minutes, he too was hit and rolled down to the valley.*

It was a horrific scene. Soldiers were screaming in pain, some were quietly suffering, yet others remembered their near and dear ones. While the sounds of anguish wafted up to the company commander, he had no idea how many of his men had died. There was nothing he could do to help them; it was arguably the most challenging moment of his life. And he was the only one in that dark and forbidding terrain who had to summon all he had to alleviate the situation. Somewhere from the deepest recesses of his memory came the reminder that 2 RAJ RIF had never lost a battle in 175 years. He had heard this fact recounted on so many occasions in the battalion. The thought was encouragement enough for him to fight on and do the right thing. But what was that right thing anyway? Should he climb down and look up at the injured? Find a few survivors in the dark and renew the attack? Or reach out to his third platoon, which was now on the radio with the news that they were under fire from an entirely unexpected direction? Then there was the risk of delay and getting caught in the open in daylight.

Mohit decided to join the platoon under enemy fire. He ordered area fresh round of salvo that lit up the area. Unfortunately, despite all precautions, the illumination burst over the enemy and Mohit's soldiers. An intense firefight ensued but suddenly ended after two–three minutes. Maj Mohit later learnt that some enemy soldiers had slithered down from Lone Hill and were running away. They were the ones who had engaged the platoon from an unexpected direction.†

---

* Sep Jaipal Singh was later awarded the Vir Chakra.

† After the battle, three Pakistani soldiers' bodies, including that of the company commander, were recovered. The company commander was carrying a large rucksack with chocolates, civilian dresses and other items – all made in England.

The time now was 4 a.m. Maj Mohit Saxena managed to reach the CO by radio set via the A Company – incidentally, this is when he learnt that both the officers of A Company had been killed – and informed him of the situation. He also learnt that the company, now led by the JCO, was still attacking its objective.

Maj Mohit decided that the remaining company must recommence the attack despite what had transpired through the night. The first attempt had been made along one spur coming down from Lone Hill. There was another that led to the top from a different direction. Never reinforce a failure – the Army's culture teaches you. The major decided to lead his men along the second spur.

He had to descend to the valley to take that fresh direction. En route, he saw Nembu's mortal remains – his eyes closed, his face composed. Near him was the other dead barefoot leader, Hav Sengar, calm as if in sleep but still clenching a grenade. The major saw a soldier bleeding and crying in pain not too far away. 'He seemed a bit relieved as I approached him, as if the mere appearance of his leader was somehow going to improve his parlous situation,' Mohit recalled. A fourth soldier seemed to have broken his spine, yet another was moaning in pain – his hands and legs fractured. Major Mohit Saxena summoned the second platoon and ordered that everyone be given morphine injections to reduce their suffering and bandaged up.

The uppermost thought in the company commander's mind was this: time was running out, and there was still nothing to show for the night-long efforts. He remembers that his paramount thought was that a failure would be a blot on the battalion's izzat. It was not an option. He requested some reinforcements and decided to prosecute a fresh attack along the second spine leading up to Lone Hill.

By 4:30 a.m., a platoon led by Capt Routella reached the bone-weary soldiers of D Company – the CO had released the reserves to assist Mohit's company. The climb started afresh. The party moved from one boulder to the other, walking along a telephone cable, and gradually came within fifty metres of Lone Hill.

The Pakistani troops in the post sensed that another assault was imminent. They unleashed all their weapons, but this time the quantum and intensity of fire seemed much lower. Was the enemy fearful of exhausting its ammunition? Or were they exercising better fire discipline to release the full force of lethality when the attacking party was much closer and easier to pick? Or was the attacker so close that aiming and firing downslope from inside the safety of a bunker had become difficult?

The company kept moving and finally the three leading soldiers charged into the first bunker, their weapons blazing. Once inside, they shot the Pakistani soldier who had been firing at them intermittently.

Dawn was breaking above the desolate battlefield. At last, Raj Rif had gained a tenuous foothold on its objective.

In the other battle, rendered bereft of officers, the Alpha company had been pressing on to reach the top of Knoll and 3 Pimples. Around 3 a.m., a barrage from the Bofors had carpeted the enemy post. The ear-splitting booms, the dance of the splinters and direct hits had inflicted significant damage – including dismantling one of the bunkers – but, more crucially, created enough deterrence to keep the defender's fire suppressed. By 5 a.m., the A company too had captured its first bunkers, one each on Knoll and 3 Pimples. An exorbitant price paid through the long night had earned a nascent victory. Even in the last moments of the assault, point-blank firing from the bunkers had killed two Indian soldiers. The foothold was flimsy at best, and the risk of enemy counterattacks loomed on the unimaginably sapped troops.

By this point, nine men of the assaulting companies had died, three of them officers. Countless soldiers with grave injuries were on different slopes, awaiting evacuation or succour. As daylight began to spread down the mountains and into the valley, the Bravo

Company, led by Capt Routella, arrived and began to expeditiously ferry the injured to medical facilities.

Back at Lone Hill, Mohit Saxena's company began to move towards the next bunker. The enemy immediately opened fire from a shelter higher up the slope. The charging troops decided to crawl up to minimize the risk of getting hit. The loophole was now visible, and the retaliatory fire was more accurate. The Pakistanis, sensing the desperate situation as the first three soldiers closed in, lobbed a grenade at the advancing troops. One of the soldiers died instantly. The other two hoisted themselves onto their feet and charged at the bunker. When the melee subsided, two enemy soldiers had perished.

After capturing the second bunker, the company moved towards the third in the rear. It overlooked a slope in a different direction, and a streak of blood was flowing towards it. Sporadic fire initially emanated from that the inside, followed by silence. As the attackers entered, they realized that the bunker had been a makeshift cookhouse. Using ropes, the occupants had slithered down to safety. They had left a clumsy kitchen – with rations and oil scattered all over, artillery-damaged utensils rendered useless and water that seemed contaminated. Also left behind a cleverly hidden IED that went off when the troops entered. Fortunately, no one was injured.

The enemy's resistance was diminishing by the minute. The soldiers of Alpha company went from bunker to bunker, tactically entering and eliminating the defenders. By 11 a.m. on 29 June, they had captured the entire objective – all the enemy troops were either dead or had escaped.*

* The capture of a Fibre Reinforced Plastic hut, where the Pakistani company commander had stayed, brought out the stark contrast between the cultures of the two armies. While the Pakistani soldiers had lived in challenging – even pathetic – conditions, the company commander's abode was a picture of relative luxury, with a music system, several uniforms and a supply of chocolates. On the other hand, the troops lived in filthy conditions, wearing clothes of indifferent quality that were originally white but had turned jet-black, sleeping bags in tatters and not even proper blankets to sleep on.

On the other objective, the CO had ordered that the Alpha Company, now assisted by the Capt Tomar-led Charlie Company, maintain the momentum and continue attacking the remaining bunkers. Under cover of ferocious automatic fire, the troops began to charge the bunkers. Capt Tomar and three soldiers rushed towards one of the first shelters; a soldier died in the attempt and another was wounded. But Tomar and the remaining soldiers charged inside it and killed the two Pakistani soldiers stalling the attack. One after another, the bunkers fell to the attackers. By 4 p.m., Raj Rif had captured 3 Pimples and Knoll.

The battalion lost four officers, two JCOs and seventeen Other Rank. A hundred and ninety were wounded. The battalion was honoured with multiple awards, as were several officers and soldiers.*†

Two decades later, Brig Mohit Saxena said to me, 'But none of the awards are worth it when you lose soldiers. If only we could get them back.'

VI

This brings us to the heart of the matter: what creates a culture that willingly embraces risk and wins? Why do people steeped in such a culture step up to take charge instead of awaiting orders or shrinking from acting? An equally important question is what

* Much heroism was displayed by the wounded and those evacuating them. One party carrying a critically wounded soldier – he had been hit in the face – lost its way into the Tololing Nullah. It eventually took seventeen hours to reach a surgeon operating under a tent. Eight soldiers carried the wounded and administered morphine injections to alleviate his suffering. The man ultimately survived.

† Among others, Major Acharya, Capt Vivek Gupta, Capt N. Kenguruse and Hav Jitender were posthumously awarded the Maha Vir Chakra. Maj Mohit Saxena was decorated with a Vir Chakra.

creates a culture wherein teams persist in achieving objectives amidst risk and adversities, no matter the sacrifice involved?

First, a caveat. It may not be prudent to compare and contrast risks in the business world with the ones faced by soldiers in battle. Nor is this chapter a prescription to copy the Army's culture. The aim here is to merely point out what lies beneath a robust culture – frameworks, practices, ideas – that can give us clues for creating our own culture.

The first secret is to create an ecosystem that has the propensity for taking and stomaching risks. This requires behavioural adjustments: does the leadership encourage and reward risk-taking and support the team when things go south? Or is the leadership's collective spirit so brittle and timid that every slip-up invites criticism and worse? If the latter is true, you can bid goodbye to a culture of courage and initiative.

Next comes the independence to act. In the Army, the unit – and likewise, in a large company, the department or vertical – is considered supreme. COs are appointed after meticulous selection and then elevated, in a manner of speaking, to the status of demi-gods. The Army entrusts the CO to train his battalion, look after the logistics and ensure high morale. Echoing the sentiment of almost every soldier, Alin Saha told me, 'Our kith and kin are secondary, and the unit becomes the primary family.'

Incidentally, the CO of each battalion is called Tiger by its officers and men – and the rest of the Army. Each battalion develops an ethos (2 RAJ RIF knew they had never lost a battle), producing a self-pride that drives it to take superhuman risks. Given the impermanence of personnel in the business world, that model cannot be replicated. But what can be done is to accord primacy to each department, allow the leader sufficient space to operate, and kindle a sense of pride among the team members. This may sound like a fundamental idea, but in far too many organizations, department or plant heads are mere water bearers. The management violates the channel of hierarchies with impunity. Where micro-managing is king, the head of the vertical is bound to lose motivation. That is hardly the prescription to rear a tiger.

This is the oft-heard counter-refrain: how can we give freedom to every leader when they do not have the competence? That lament is wrong on many planes. Did we pick the leader with care? Did we train them sufficiently to lead their department – which is why we hired them in the first place? Most importantly, are we acting out of our timidity, the inability to 'let go' (a debilitating strain, particularly in many family-owned businesses) and lack of trust? And if a leader is considered weak, the approach must be to handhold until they gain the wherewithal to act independently. In other words, in every contingency, the goal is to foster freedom to act and take initiative, not a vice-like control.

Creating a culture of initiative- and risk-taking is an act of sustained courage. It cannot develop in a faithless vacuum.

We must also look at a whole bucket of leadership issues. Is the leadership visible to the rank and file, especially during a crisis? Does the CEO choose to stay back in his office past midnight – without interfering – simply because the business development or sales team is working on a crucial bid? Do leaders reach out to employees – preferably in person and certainly by video call or email – when the company is going through a rough patch? Can employees even put a face to the leaders at the apex? Some would contest the viability of such an effort. 'But we are too busy with work to pay attention to all this,' they say. I would venture that this, above all, is their actual 'work'. It is what will build a winning culture. And countless business leaders – Ratan Tata, Narayan Murthy and Sam Walton of Walmart, to name a few – have shown us that it can be done with the outcome of immense profit.

Does the organization overlook fallouts of risks taken with good intent? Does it have a policy of rewarding those who step up in moments of difficulty? Are such individuals celebrated in public –

preferably in the presence of their families? People work for money. But the laziest thought in the corporate world is that they work for money alone. No one would be willing to die in the Army if that formulation was the whole truth. There are no end-of-the-year appraisals in the Army – nor any bonuses.

We must recognize that the motivation to work also comes from the fulfilment of many agendas that are invisible to the naked eye: attention, a sense of identity, love, appreciation, an innate desire to achieve, to secure growth and recognition. The list is indicative but not comprehensive. To develop a culture of courage, we must focus on developing top leaders that acknowledge the above.

Even creating a culture of storytelling can help. Given the transitory nature of employees, companies must develop a repository of tales of times when outstanding action was taken. Corporate communication departments must compile such stories and circulate and recount them during celebrations and appropriate company events. Even stray lessons and comments can ignite motivation.

Finally, a culture of courage and risk-taking is built on thoughtful assessments – not blind plunges for glory. And one of the central stratagem to develop it is based on brainstorming future scenarios and responses. Organizations that devote time and effort to discussing various options and putting contingencies in place are far more likely to win than those merely sitting on a roller coaster of daily action. Because while roller coasters are an exciting boost to adrenaline, the rider sees only a blur, never a focused view.

6

IT ISN'T JUST ABOUT THE BROTHERHOOD

> 'I am both sad and happy. I am happy that my son sacrificed his life for the country, but I grieve his loss as a mother. He is my only son.'
>
> – MANJULA, mother of Col Santosh Babu, who laid down his life during the Galwan clashes

I

In June 2017, Nagaland's Mon district was abuzz with rumours about a militant group belonging to the Paresh Baruah faction of the ULFA and the SS Khaplang faction of the NSCN-K. The coming together of the two groups was widely considered a potent mix – ULFA had held out for decades, while the Khaplang faction were masters of the terrain. If there was any truth to the murmurs, it was entirely likely that violence would soon erupt.

During the years of insurgency, the Army had raised a new set of territorial units – the Home and Hearth battalions. These entities drew their rank and file from the military men in local areas. Initially, the charter of these new units was to funnel local intelligence to the regular Army, but with the passage of time, the intelligence had dried up. Locals had become wary that if they continued to support the Home and Hearth battalions, the spectre of retaliation by militants would loom large on their lives. The new units had begun to dominate the area instead of providing actionable intelligence.

Maj David Manlun had served his time with the battalion and was due to move for the next tour of duty. Instead of returning to his battalion, the 1st Naga Regiment, he had opted for another operational tenure with the Special Services Group. He was on the cusp of marrying his childhood sweetheart, possibly in his hometown in Churachandpur, a Manipur district from where his father, the Army veteran Subedar (Honorary Captain) M. Khamzalam, and the rest of the family hailed.

In the late evening of 6 June, a few strands of information arrived – the outlaws were lurking close to the Myanmar border in the Lappa area. Another report suggested their move along the villages of Oting and Tizit was imminent.

David's team of soldiers from the Home and Hearth battalion teamed up with the crack troops of a Special Forces battalion. But as darkness fell on the thick forests that enveloped the winding road, it appeared that the information might have been less than accurate. Suggestions were made to David to call off the operation. He refused.

A little past midnight, the penny dropped. Armed with rifles and long-range grenades, the militants emerged from the darkness, riding in autorickshaws as a ruse. The two adversaries noticed each other almost simultaneously. The militants were the first to fire – as is invariably the case, since, unlike them, soldiers are identifiable by uniform. The Army men, on the other hand, must first be sure, lest they be hurting civilians. Once the intense exchange of fire began, David led the charge. During the operation, he was hit in the chest but managed to inflict damage in return – four militants perished in the ensuing firefight. David died on the spot, and a dozen others were wounded. The operation was expensive, but the Army does not count costs. David's team had eliminated the entire militant group.

This story of courage and sacrifice is inspiring in itself. But there is more here that points to a relatively lesser-known aspect of the Army – how soldiers' families get closely woven into its culture and become an immense support system. The degree to which the families of serving soldiers and veterans identify with the Indian Army is a uniquely remarkable phenomenon. It is not limited to families that have served for more than one generation in uniform – rather it extends to every family, and is an immense contributor to the morale and motivation of those who serve. By extension, it is a source of significant support to the Army's success.

In the previous chapter, we saw how the propensity to take risks is intrinsic to the Army's culture. We also noticed the bouquet of elements that gives its soldiers the leverage to take risks. One such element is the support Army families give to the institution and how it returns the gesture.

The guitar-playing polyglot (David spoke English, Hindi, his mother tongue Zou, Mizo, Kuki and Paitewas) was gone. The seniormost officer in the northeast, the commander of Eastern Army, Lt Gen Praveen Bakshi, visited his parents in Shillong. He went quietly, bereft of fanfare and the trappings of protocol. He was there to simply share in their grief. After he trooped up to their modest home's first floor, David's proud but stoic parents met Praveen. No tears were shed. They told him stories of David's childhood and his pride in being commissioned as an officer into the 1st Naga Regiment. They showed David's pictures. And then, when the lieutenant general got up to leave, the mother presented him with a shawl, as she would on any other day to a guest. They asked for nothing and expressed no rancour. Only at the very end, David's mother held Praveen's hand and gently asked if her son's name would become famous among soldiers. There was nothing but dignity in her manner, not a hint of plea or suggestion, a mere expression of motherly instinct. Her husband looked at her with disapproval.

There is a structured process for awarding gallantry medals in the Army. No one person, no matter how high, can ensure that they get conferred with medals. But in this case, mindful that he was not to make the promise lightly, the general said that her son's valour would be announced to the whole nation and that they would witness it.

The courage shown by Army families plays a part in fuelling the organization's culture of bravery and risk-taking. There are other factors as well, but the role of the families is among the most powerful on that list. Why wouldn't an Army embrace risk when it knows that the entire service and their families support the endeavour? Or will, at the very least, feel proud of their sacrifice?.

On his return, General Bakshi spoke to the commanding officer of the Special Forces battalion that had also incurred a dozen wounded in the operation. He wanted to know all the details. Towards the end, the CO requested that a citation only for Major David be forwarded so that he stood the best possible chance of being decorated.

In 2018, David's parents received the Kirti Chakra, the nation's second-highest gallantry award, from President Ram Nath Kovind. David's bust was unveiled in the Shillong museum the same year.

The story of the quiet courage shown by David's parents has been – and is being – repeated in countless homes. I experienced it first-hand when I visited the family of Major Mohit Whig, who had died in the IED blast in 1997. Mohit was the only son of a retired brigadier, a Maha Vir Chakra recipient, and a mother who hailed from the Nepalese royal line. The parents lived in a multi-storeyed building in Delhi's Som Vihar at the time. Before I visited them, Mohit's father had undergone a bypass surgery.

It therefore took me by surprise when I climbed out of the Army vehicle to see old Brigadier Whig standing outside on the ground floor to receive me. I was flustered. I asked him, 'Why did you come down from the fourth floor, sir?'

'Neeraj, you are Mohit's commanding officer. And commanding officers are to be treated with respect.'

Notice the Brigadier Whig's reference to his late son in the present tense. And adherence to an unwritten cultural norm – of treating a CO as not just any other officer but a custodian of the Army's values in its most important segment, a unit.

We went up by the lift, and I sat face-to-face with the grieving parents. There was not a shred of rancour, no whiff of anger, not a single request for anything. Mohit's mother had only one question for me: Did he suffer before he died?

Brigadier Whig wanted me to see Mohit's room and sit in his chair. 'I can't tell you how proud I felt when Sam Manekshaw called me in person and said I should be proud of my contribution to the country.' Then, pointing to the street below, he continued: 'The place was full of cars. So many retired Army officers came for his funeral.'

My next stop was to meet Mohit's wife Tina and his in-laws. The same story of stoicism repeated itself at their house in Chandigarh. Tina was a picture of perfect dignity and, had I not already known about Mohit and her struggle with their young child's health, I couldn't have guessed it that day. Tina's father, a retired cavalry general, asked me the professional details of the operation. 'You must square this,' was his solitary suggestion.

It was impossible not to detect the pride in the voice of the families I met. And sitting there, as my eyes welled up, I wondered what makes members of the Army surmount even the most profound grief and accept it as a contribution to a higher cause. How have we been transformed in this way? I think you already know the answer – it is the silent yet immensely powerful impact of the Army's winning culture. But how has it come about?

The innumerable families who treat the untimely death of their young kin while serving in the Army not merely as tragic but as worthy and meaningful is a confounding phenomenon. Many outsiders ascribe this to a 'higher patriotism' among Army families, as if the act of joining this profession magically imbues the civilian family members with a sense of deep love for the country. The families of soldiers are no less or more patriotic than anyone else. After losing their young wards or husbands in active operations, they invariably maintain ties with the Army and even strengthen existing bonds – which tells us that the answer lies elsewhere. The Army thoroughly integrates families into its culture, and they in turn respond by becoming a powerful support system.

The social character of the Indian Army weaves all these different families into one giant family. Unlike in the corporate world, the families of soldiers are an intrinsic part of the organization. Their participation is not official, of course. They informally take part in various activities, social interactions and get-togethers. Equations are built within families and not merely between fellow officers; stag events are few and far between. The involvement of family members adds nuance and value, resulting in extraordinary bonding within the organization.

II

Swati Shedge married Santosh Mahadik, an Army officer, in 2003. They both came from Satara in Maharashtra, where she had grown up and Santosh was a Sainik School cadet. He was the first uniformed man she had ever known, and a decade or more later, her knowledge of the professional end of the Army was still rudimentary. 'Even as the wife of a commanding officer, I couldn't differentiate between a corps and a brigade,' she later told me.

While Colonel Santosh Mahadik, a Special Forces officer, commanded a Rashtriya Rifles battalion in the militancy-ridden Kupwara district, Swati stayed in Udhampur with their two kids. She taught children with special needs, particularly those with autism. Life was peaceful and stable, except for the absence of Santosh.

And then, everything changed forever.

On 17 November 2015, Swati returned from school and broke her customary weekly fast. Usually, she would have watched television, but the neighbours dropped in briefly to check on her. She received a call from Santosh's brigade commander. He gently informed her about her husband's gunshot injury.

Despite all her unfamiliarity with the technicalities of professional Army life, Swati was certainly aware of the significance of the words relayed to her. She had known paratrooper colleagues of her husband who had been wounded and invariably survived. The news rattled her, but her thoughts never gravitated to the worst possibilities. She called up the principal and sought leave to travel to Srinagar.

Within minutes, another teacher – an Army colonel's wife – arrived to take over the responsibilities during her absence. Or so Swati assumed. But once she saw COs of three parachute battalions trooping in, she began to fear the worst. One of them asked her to sit down and gently broke the news. Colonel Mahadik had lost his life in operation.

What thoughts cross the mind of this thirty-seven-year-old widow whose only world, as she knew it, had shattered without notice? She wasn't angry – neither at the militants nor the circumstances that had abbreviated the life of a man she dearly loved. She often teased that he loved his battalion more than he loved her. Those who spoke to her in the days that followed detected no bitterness and certainly not any vengeful thoughts.

'I decided I should join the organization he had served to his last day. The Army was my family. It had given me so much. And if I could wear a uniform, when I see my image in a mirror, perhaps I will see that he was still alive.'

Joining the Army was an impossible enterprise. There was no legal provision to allow a lady her age to even appear for the multiple entrance examinations; that boat had sailed a decade and a half ago. She had no clue about the challenges of filing for such a process, much less the gruelling fate that awaits newly minted cadets in the Officers' Training Academy. She was physically in no shape to cope with even a fraction of the hardship that trainees must endure.

She had previously met only one lady officer in the flesh and had never even heard of another martyr's wife who had joined the Army.

Swati was conscious that her desire stemmed purely from a fount of emotion. But soon she began to see it as a deliberate call, a decision she would follow through on, irrespective of the steep challenge.

The Army has no 'quota' for the wives (or children) of soldiers who have died while in service. Neither is any concession made to the family members of a slain soldier – because the Army cannot afford to recruit someone merely based on compassion; every new entrant must meet exacting standards. A month after Santosh passed away, Swati began applying for an age waiver.

Simultaneously, she started going on long walks and, later, running. Soon after, she added sit-ups and push-ups to her regimen, something she would not have even remotely contemplated doing a few weeks ago. She had known nothing about the Services Selection Board. But now, she was diligently learning about current affairs.

The problem of obtaining a waiver proved particularly intractable. Swati wrote to anyone and everyone she assumed might have the authority – including the defence minister and the prime minister and different departments of the Army. Most had nothing to do with the subject. There was a fair amount of back and forth, but the colleagues of Colonel Santosh did their utmost to help out.

'I even received a reply from a clerk who pointed out that my application was not as per the Minor SD,' she told me with a chuckle. She did not have the slightest idea of what Minor SD was.* Whenever

* Minor Staff Duties is an extensive and rigid protocol followed by the Army for all forms of correspondence; even the slightest violation of the templates and abbreviations is not tolerated.

she tried to apply online and indicated her age, the site would not let her proceed further.

But the near-impossible happened when the Army and the Ministry of Defence came together. Swati received the age waiver. Then came the written examination and the Services Selection Board, where no quarter is given, no matter the candidate's background or circumstances.

She admitted her children, Kartiki and Swaraj, to a boarding school and embarked on her eleven-month gruel at the Officers Training Academy in Chennai. At thirty-seven, Swati was among girl cadets more than a decade younger and inestimably fitter than her.

On most days, especially in the beginning, it became clear to Swati that the expedition was exponentially more formidable than she had ever imagined. In meeting the standards of physical tests, the Army does not proffer concessions based on gender. No allowances were made for her age either. Two weeks into the training, Swati was so deadbeat that she could not even stand by the end of the day. Other girl cadets would gently hold her up to steady her. A few helped her do simple things she would run out of energy for – like parking her bicycle and tying her shoelaces.

Another week later, her legs stopped cooperating with her mind. She wanted out. Swati decided to report sick to take a break. But the Company Havildar Major, a woman instructor with a forbidding exterior and manner, sternly threatened her, 'If you quit, I will punish the whole batch by keeping them awake at night.'

A few things are considered a greater sacrilege in the Army than imperilling one's comrades. This culture strain seeps in early, the osmosis facilitated partly by the privation the groups suffer together. Of all the bonds, this one is the quickest to form. Communal suffering fuses it and makes it break-resistant.

Unwilling to expose her coursemates to additional hardship, Swati soldiered on and rejoined the training. Under her breath, she cursed the CHM. Two days later, the same CHM quietly asked her if she wanted to report sick. Swati refused.

'The CHM had done the most wonderful thing by refusing to let me escape hardship,' she later said. 'The gruelling training became a healing process for me.'

But her limbs were hardly keeping up with her spirit. Even as the cadets rode their cycles to the training area or to academic classes, Swati was invariably in the last squad. 'Once I pushed myself and entered the second squad, and you know what – my coursemates celebrated!'

To advance, a cadet must pass several tests. Another demanding series is the Physical Proficiency Test, a group of activities designed to measure strength, stamina and agility. Swati failed the crucial five-kilometre run by twenty seconds. 'I was delighted when I realized I had successfully pushed myself to within twenty seconds of the qualifying mark. It was a significant achievement, particularly when I had no age-related time concession.'

Two failures later, Swati surmounted the twenty-second lag.

But challenges were hardly in short supply. Next came a twenty-kilometre inter-company competition which involved running with a backpack, equipment and weapon. Their officer instructor Maj Girija ran with the cadets from start to finish, even though she was not required to do so. This inspired Swati. Her company, Zozila, adopted an intelligent strategy. Knowing that the chain's strength is its weakest link, the softer runners were placed in the vanguard. The stronger athletes brought up the rear, pushing and nudging everyone to keep moving. The plan worked; the entire company ended up in the 'excellent timing' category.

That is when Swati discovered that she had a debilitating fear of heights. She couldn't bring herself to go even halfway when it came to the test that required climbing a four-metre vertical rope. Over time, this became a spectacle. Everyone watched the cadet unable to suppress her fear of heaving up to the top of the rope.

'Shedge,' yelled the instructor on one occasion, using her maiden name. 'If you don't go up, I will punish your batch with a *bajri* order.' She was referring to a common punishment wherein cadets are summoned in fatigues and backpacks full of gravel and ordered to stand still indefinitely. The instructor offered another option in her tongue-in-cheek manner: could she be declared successful even though she had failed the test?

Several failed attempts later, one night, in the presence of her entire batch, Swati Shedge Mahadik, thirty-seven and a mother of two, beat her fears and went right to the top of the rope. Her mates cheered her on every inch of the way up.

Things became somewhat more manageable in the second term of the training. Swati even did well in the cross-country run. 'We were not in the "excellent" category,' she told me, her voice palpably quivering with happiness, 'but we stuck together and pushed each other to finish the race well.'

In September 2017, Swati became an Army officer and fulfilled her desire to look at herself in the mirror – and see Santosh.

'If I have another shot at reliving my life, my first choice would be to be Santosh's wife all over again. The Army treats officers' wives like queens. It is such a privileged life. But if that is not possible, my second choice will always be to become an Army officer. Without Santosh, this is the best life I could have asked for. Don't get me wrong – it isn't easy or comfortable to be an officer, housewife, mother and father every day. It just does not get any better than living as part of the Army family. I love standing with the soldiers in everything they do. I never miss a parade or physical training. I am happy and have acquired simple goals from the Army – always to be an asset, never a liability.'

III

Not every fallen soldier's family sends someone to join the Army. But it is remarkable how many follow in their martyred kinfolk's footsteps. That would hardly be the case if the families did not feel a special bond with the organization. It is also a pleasant surprise that most such families stay attached to the units and join causes that inspire others to join the organization. Such a trend must stand in stark contrast to many other professions, where losing a life on the line of duty would be considered too tragic for a family member to want to emulate, let alone display abiding loyalty towards the enterprise. When you look at this phenomenon through the lens of 'culture', the puzzle starts to solve itself.

The border between India and China has been under dispute at multiple locations. In the last four decades alone, there have been more than four dozen meetings to unravel this Gordian knot, yielding few tangible results beyond confidence-building measures. China continues to lay claim over large tracts of Ladakh and the state of Arunachal Pradesh. India has consistently maintained that the delineation inherited from the British must hold good. The twain have shown no signs of converging. The line separating the locations currently held by China and India is called the Line of Actual Control.

Before 2019, the LAC was, by and large, an area of peace and tranquillity. There were sporadic violations, including the infamous 1987 Wangdung incursion that led to a standoff at Sumdurong Chu. China appeared to up the ante in 2019, making over 660 LAC violations and 108 aerial infringements. But there was never an exchange of fire.

In May 2020, the situation took a southward turn. There were fierce melees and physical skirmishes near Pangong Tso in Ladakh. In late May, the Chinese began to protest India's construction of roads in the Galwan Valley, an area the former perceived as disputed territory.

A physical skirmish occurred on 16 June after Indian soldiers noticed that the Chinese had put up temporary structures on the Indian side of the LAC and objected to the intrusion. It involved soldiers of a Bihar Regiment battalion, and the commanding officer, Col B. Santosh Babu, personally led the effort.

That morning, Col Santosh's wife Santoshi received a call from one of his colleagues. He softly broke the news that her husband had been killed in a skirmish with the Chinese the previous night. She could hardly believe what she was hearing.

At least twenty Indian soldiers had perished during the hand-to-hand combat. The Chinese appeared to have prepared for the moment with lethal instruments. They, too, suffered multiple casualties.

Santosh had approached Santoshi for her hand in marriage in 2009 in her hometown of Suryapet. She was in the final year of her undergraduate course. 'I did not accept immediately,' she told me. Her reservation was that he was in the Army, an organization she knew nothing about except that it supposedly deployed its members on the borders. With no one in her family having served in the Army, it seemed to her an unattractively dangerous profession.

But she relented. Over the years, she has considered it the most fortuitous decision she had ever taken. Santoshi moved with Santosh to the NDA, where he was posted as an instructor and, many years later, in Menchuka in the Along area of Arunachal Pradesh, Umroi Cantonment, Shillong and briefly in Delhi Cantonment. Their son Anirudh was born in the intervening years, followed by their daughter Abhiana, while they were at the Defence Services Staff College in Wellington. Santosh had reached the college by clearing the most prestigious entrance examination. By then, Santoshi was already steeped in the Army's culture. 'My daughter's birth is my second sweetest memory for me. My husband clearing the Staff College entrance after tremendous hard work ranks as the first,' she said.

For many years, she had to stay separated from him as he travelled on duty to the Congo and with the Rashtriya Rifles battalion in the anti-militancy role in J&K. Like many Army wives, she utilized her time to complete her BA and became a teacher.

In 2019, Ladakh beckoned Col Santosh, and he was destined never to return.

The country watched Santosh's parents on TV a day after his death, stoically dignified in their heartbreak. His mother Manjula said, 'He needed to do much more for his country. But we are very proud of him. I had only one son, and he is gone now … I am very sad as a mother. But he laid down his life for his country.'

Santoshi spoke to me in a soft, understated tone, but her words held only glowing praise for the organization. She said, 'I deeply respect the Army and will always do.' Compared to the civilian life she had previously experienced, she found dedication to duty in everyone in the Army 'from top to bottom'. 'Ever since Col Santosh passed away, messages, calls and visits from so many in the Army have become the norm. It is like a deluge of support. Wherever I go, people from the Army reach out offering to do just about anything for me. It is so amazing. It is much more than a family.'

IV

Let us stay with the recurring theme of Army families who lose their members in operations but continue to support the organization with even greater fervour afterwards. The contrast with the other organizations could not be starker. Would a parent who loses a child in the line of duty in, say, a bank or government department or in any other vocation encourage others to join the same organization? Would a widow who has suffered an untimely loss of a partner decide to leave her life of relative comfort and follow in his professional footsteps? What inner fire urges individuals to take this unlikely course?

Young Sushmita married Neeraj, an officer from the Corps of Signals, in 2010. Most Army families come from small towns and villages; most are 'pioneers' in their families in joining the Army. Sushmita had been brought up in Gorakhpur, Uttar Pradesh; before hitching her life to Neeraj's, she knew nothing about the Army.

Six years into her marriage, she was in her hometown with her son Rudransh. Neeraj was serving a tour of duty in a field area in the Northeast, where families were not allowed.

In mid-March 2016, Neeraj called and informed her that he was leaving for a critical mission; amid landslides, a specialist communication vehicle had gone off a treacherous piece of the road into a gorge. He would lead the team to recover it. Neeraj sounded focused and eager, but promised to come home later in the month. The Army had posted him to Kerala, and they were to move together in a month.

But two days later, Sushmita was jolted out of her peaceful existence. Her husband had slipped and fallen while striving to make the recovery. The cause of death was exertion and hypertension. He was thirty-two.

Three months into her grief, Sushmita, a computer science graduate, made a decision that many families who have suffered similar losses have come to take – to continue the work of the fallen soldier. She decided to join the Army.

'My son was three years old, and I wanted to extend his association with the Army. I wanted him to hear my stories of this wonderful service and relate to it when I talked about his father. I did not want to be just another widow living in my hometown. The Army had taught me enough to want to raise myself in my own estimation. And to inspire my son.'

She did not have the slightest clue about the process. Her brother helped her submit – and re-submit – the application forms. After the second submission, she received a heartbreaking bureaucratic response: her documents had been misplaced!

Sushmita travelled to Delhi to resume her quest. One evening, while on a walk, she spotted an Army Gypsy with Corps of Signals insignia. That prompted her to engage the driver in an informal conversation. The matter of her missing forms came up. The soldier-driver took her contact information and promptly relayed it to his commanding officer. The next day the CO – a stranger to her and her late husband but joined together by the bond of being Corps of Signals officers – called to inform her that he was tasking a JCO with helping her fill new forms and reapply. The JCO would continue to assist her until the forms were processed.

Sushmita began to prepare for the tests. She weighed seventy-two kilos at the time and was supremely unfit to qualify. 'I received amazing support from my husband's ex-colleagues and even their families – the son of a commanding officer constantly guided me as I practised for my interview. Many others would call on the phone with tips and suggestions. No one ever dissuaded me – on the contrary, everyone seemed eager to see me succeed and serve in the Army.'

In November, a mere eight months after she had lost her husband, Sushmita received a call for the Services Selection Board interview at Bhopal. When Neeraj was alive, she had spent a tenure with him in Bhopal and was most reluctant to return to the city and relive her trauma. But she forced herself to make the trip only to feel moved when several of her husband's colleagues turned up to cheer her on. She made the cut but was temporarily rejected on grounds of obesity.

So Sushmita lost weight and once again appeared for the medical examination. She joined the Officers Training School in March, exactly a year after Neeraj's demise.

The training was arduous, and the Chennai heat hardly made it any easier. But in two months, she had dropped twenty kilos. 'When I returned home for a short break, my parents did not recognize me at the airport,' she said.

During the training, cadets are required to fill in choices of future regiments. Mindful of the pain the memories must cause her, Sushmita's colleagues suggested that she opt for a corps other than Signals. But her company commander had a crisp piece of counsel: 'Listen to your heart'. She did and joined her late husband's regiment.

Many of her husband's colleagues – including an ex-CO – travelled to Chennai to attend her passing-out parade, as did her parents.

Life after the commissioning has not been easy for Sushmita, who is now a captain. No concessions are made to her because of her gender or 'status'. She has regularly joined night patrols, checked pre-dawn stand-to drills of soldiers and, of course, attended all physical training sessions and duties.

'But I wouldn't opt for any other life.'

Sushmita served in Jammu and Kashmir and, by coincidence, was put up in the same accommodation where she had once stayed with her husband. How did that make her feel?

'All I wanted to do was call Neeraj on the phone and tell him about everything that I was achieving.'

V

As a young girl, Riya had grown up near the IMA in Dehradun. She had always admired the thoroughly groomed and well-behaved gentleman cadets in identical muftis when they were allowed to visit the town on a 'liberty pass'. In 1995, she got an opportunity to witness one of the final rehearsals of the passing-out parade. She was awestruck by the orderliness of the campus. So close to the chaos and hustle-bustle of life outside the gates and yet so far removed from it. 'I came away thinking there was a place where people believe in values – and uphold them.' The distinctiveness of the young officer recruits' deportment, even the way they walked, reflected a sense of discipline.

Riya could have hardly forecasted that she would marry one of the would-be officers someday. She met Gentleman Cadet Somesh Shrivastava through common friends; he was visiting her neighbours, with his leg in a cast after an injury. 'When I met him, I instantly realized I had never encountered any young person who conducted himself with such dignity.'

Later, Somesh was commissioned into the Engineers, and the Army posted him to the Northeast. He and Riya started to write to each other. He sounded excited and fascinated. She imagined a life of well-turned-out officers, parties, dances and get-togethers. From his effusive description of the unit and the place he had been sent off to, Riya could have hardly guessed that the location – a remote 'family station' – was a nondescript town in the North 24 Parganas in Bengal.

When Riya finished her graduation, the two decided to get married. By this time, Somesh had moved to Ladakh. Immediately upon arrival, Riya realized that life in the Army was quite different from what she had imagined. They did much more than simply being 'cool' and having fun. The area was remote and desolate. As a couple, Somesh and Riya lived in a snow hut. There was no electricity, and even water was scarce.

In the unit, a handful of ladies had joined their husbands. Riya found that, as in any family, the 'senior' ladies took it upon themselves to protect and guide her. 'I was a complete greenhorn. Once, when Somesh's commander came in, I stood up. He politely told me to sit down and pointed out that ladies are never required to rise to greet a gentleman, no matter how senior the latter.'

On a few occasions, she accompanied Somesh to work. He was in charge of supervising the construction of roads and bridges over inhospitable terrain. 'I found that Army officers were hands-on with their work. They would dress akin to the soldiers and stay in bitterly cold, windy places until the end of the workday. They led tough lives. Once when my husband's vehicle broke down, we walked most of the night to reach the unit.'

In March 2001, Riya left Ladakh to appear for her post-graduation exams. She was in Patna with her in-laws when she received the horrendous intimation that Somesh had died while on duty. During a snow-clearing operation, his vehicle had skidded off the highway in the Manali–Leh sector and into a ravine.

In light of Somesh passing, she received several letters of condolence and encouragement, including one signed by the chief of the Army staff.

'I had realized that my association with the Army had ended in one heartstopping moment. I had briefly seen the Army life – all of it in tough circumstances. Yet when they brought Somesh's mortal remains to Danapur for a funeral with military honours and I saluted him, I was surprised that the emotion inside me was not of anguish – rather of pride,' Riya recounted to me.

During her days in Ladakh, Riya had met only one lady officer. She learnt that the wife of an officer who had died during operations had subsequently joined the Army. That must have planted a seed in her mind because she too began contemplating becoming an Army officer. 'If someone is prepared to even die for his country, why should I not join the service that instils such beliefs?' she thought. She spoke to her father and father-in-law, and both supported the idea. She politely refused offers from her husband's sisters to join them in the US and pursue further education and a conventional career.

As in many cases unique to the Army, Riya decided to plunge into a life of hardship. She qualified for all the tests and joined the Officers Training Academy. She bore the rigours of training and became an officer in September 2002. Captain Riya Nehra served for seven years and now works with a leading information technology company.

As an officer, Riya saw another facet of the Army's culture. The organization is a genuinely close-knit family. 'When I joined the corporate world, I heard leaders and managers talk about "human interaction" and "putting people first" all the time. But I realized that most of those words were mere platitudes. All relationships – or should I say equations – were purely transactional. Now I have found an exception in my present company – which does a commendable job with its "Head and Heart" approach. But in most companies, one hears that such exercises are only superficial.'

Riya believes that the Army's culture is quite different. Army relationships tend to last forever. There is a sense of belonging that goes beyond mere intentions. Leaders forge real connections with the people they command.

Even the families feel they are a part of the effort to maintain morale and motivation. If an officer ticked off Riya during work, she invariably found an invitation from that officer's wife to come home for a meal.

'As a lady officer, I was once summoned by my boss and politely told that it was unsafe to come back too late from the town to the mess. With equal politeness – and a smile – I told him that he wasn't my dad.'

The officer replied, 'Sure. But should you ever get into trouble, please call me.'

Riya feels that the Army is not just a career but a way of life. 'My stint in the Indian Army changed me for good. It made me realize my innate strengths and my ability to persevere in order to stand up to any trying situation in life. My perspective on challenges changed totally – and it has been my superpower ever since I stepped into the Army.'

Her biggest takeaway? The Army's culture silently instils one with a quality that makes them unbeatable – a sense of purpose. The phenomenon of women losing their husbands in operations is not uncommon. In several cases, the impetus to join the Army comes from the parents who have lost their child – even if they were an only child.

When they first met, Nitika had no idea she would marry Major Vibhuti Dhoundiyal one day. Vibhuti on the other hand was so confident about having met his life partner that, much to Nitika's perplexity, he announced at their second meeting that they were bound to get married eventually.

Nitika knew little about him and his profession. No one in her family – Pandit migrants from Jammu and Kashmir – had ever served in the Army; by contrast, Vibhuti came from an Army family, where not donning the olive greens was the exception.

Nitika, with a BTech in Electronics and Communication and an MBA in Marketing and Operations, was focused on her career. Tata Consultancy Services had offered her a job through her campus placements and employed her as a business analyst. Her office was in Noida, near Faridabad where her parents lived. The company and its clients appreciated her work. There was even some talk of moving her to the TCS office in the UK.

But it turned out that Vibhuti's confidence was well-placed. The two married in April 2018. A few months before the wedding, Vibhuti received marching orders from a Rashtriya Rifles battalion in the Valley with units whose sole mandate is counter-terrorist operations.

Nitika could never visit Vibhuti's unit – or any other Army unit – because he was in an operational area. He would come home during his leave but seldom burden her with work details. From his brief accounts, she could perceive an unmistakably glowing respect for the Army. Vibhuti may have been laconic in his verbal communication about the profession, but he always video-called her just before he had to move into an operation. He would call again on his return, no matter how unearthly the hour. Nitika remembers that there were occasions when her husband had called in the middle of the night, and she had intuitively woken up, even though her phone had been on silent mode.

She knew almost nothing about what went on during these forays. 'My only advice to him was to stay safe.'

On Thursday, 14 February 2019, a convoy of vehicles carrying CRPF troops was attacked on the national highway by a vehicle-borne suicide bomber at Lethapora in Kashmir's Pulwama district. Forty soldiers lost their lives. The Army went on high alert and launched operations to search for the perpetrators. Deployed in Pulwama, Maj Vibhuti's battalion was among those in the hunt.

During the ten months of her marriage, Nitika would take a train to Dehradun every weekend to meet her in-laws. In the early hours of 17 February, three days after the Pulwama incident, she received a call from Vibhuti. He was moving for an operation. Nitika recalls having had a restless night but could not place her finger on what was bothering her. 'Maybe it was another intuition,' she said to me.

Maj Vibhuti promised her that he would call after it was all over. He signed off by asking her to care for herself and his parents.

Forty-five minutes after that conversation, Maj Vibhuti was killed.

Nitika had boarded a train back to Delhi and learnt about casualties in her husband's Rashtriya Rifles battalion from the news, which revealed an officer of the rank of Major among the fatalities. She instantly knew that it was Vibhuti.

Nitika Kaul Dhoundiyal, the recently married, twenty-eight-year-old corporate professional with a promising future, is today a commissioned officer in the Indian Army. Why would a young girl whose life has been ripped asunder because her husband made the supreme sacrifice while serving with the Army reorient her entire life, give up a lucrative corporate job and put herself on the same dangerous path? Especially one that involves onerous physical and mental challenges, before she can even earn the right to wear an officer's uniform. Is this based on a romantic notion of the Army since it clearly could not become a primary career option? What motivates a young girl to embrace the very service that took away the love of her life?

Before we come to the answers, let us get a better feel for the tremendous odds. Nitika was nearly thirty when she cleared the competitive exam and Services Selection Board interview to join the Officers Training Academy. You might remember that the Army makes no concessions for any cadet. Nitika was to train and compete with girls much younger than her. She was understandably not in the best physical form on arrival and failed the physical screening test. But having been a sportswoman in her school days, she caught up soon enough. After that, she took on the testing regimen one day at a time, never regretting the decision. 'It was a mental challenge more than a physical one. I did well because I knew that if I ever regretted taking this call, it would become only harder for me.'

But what motivated her to join the Army in the first place?

The first suggestion came from Vibhuti's mother, someone who had just lost her only son. Putting her grief aside, she encouraged Nitika to attempt to get the Army commission. Nitika decided to follow that advice. 'My husband was to serve in the Army for many more years. I decided to join and complete Vibhu's remaining service in the Army,' she said.

The explanation for such heroism has many strands – not the least of which is the character of individuals like Nitika, Vibhuti's parents and the rest of the family. But at the heart of this astoundingly selfless thought process is the Army's culture, which is so powerful that it not only urges a million men into daily action but spreads the passion into the families of the serving soldiers. It colours the entire fabric in its hues. And the results can be quite distinctive – not to mention resplendent.

The above tales are neither occasional blips on the radar nor a new development. Over the years, the procession of women following in their husbands' footsteps has become a relentless phenomenon. In

2020, Dr Ranjana Malik, wife of the Army's ex-COAS Gen Ved Malik, recounted her experience meeting several such shining examples. In 1998, two women, who had recently lost their husbands, walked into the AWWA* office to meet Dr Malik, then president of the NGO. Ravinderjit's husband, Major Sukhwinder Randhawa, had died in action in a counter-insurgency operation. The officer was posthumously awarded the Kirti Chakra. When he laid down his life, Ravinderjit was twenty-five years old, and the couple had a one-and-a-half-year-old child.

Ravinderjit told the COAS' wife that while she understood she would get her husband's full pay as a pension for life, she didn't want that. Instead, she wanted to do something for the organization for which her husband had given his life. Ravinderjit explained that her father-in-law was very encouraging, but essentially, it was a call that came from her heart. Part of her motivation came from knowing that her husband would have liked their daughter to grow up in an Army environment.

The other lady was Sabina Singh, whose husband, a helicopter pilot, had lost his life in a crash in the Northeast. She, too, expressed a similar sentiment.

Dr Malik explained to them the challenges that lay before them. The COAS would approach the government for waivers for the two to appear for the tests. But once that was done, they would have to compete like any other candidate. Nor could the women demand postings of their choice.

Ravinderjit and Sabina completed their training at the Officers Training Academy and became commissioned officers in September 1998.†

---

* Army Wives Welfare Association, an NGO manned entirely by wives of officers and soldiers.

† Writing in *Indian Express* on 21 June 2020, Dr Ranjana Malik had this heartwarming postscript to relate: 'A few days ago, I spoke with Ravinderjit, now a Lt Col in Ambala. In the last 20 years, she has been a mountaineer

In 2021, the thirty-three-year-old Jyoti Nainwal, wife of Naik Deepak Nainwal, who had died fighting terrorists in 2018 at Kulgam, also became a lieutenant of the Indian Army, following an extremely tough eleven-month regimen at the Officers Training academy in Chennai. Her two children, nine and seven years old, wore Army uniforms to attend the passing-out parade. The media quoted a tearful Lt Jyoti as saying, 'I never thought I would ever do a job as a homemaker. Only when my husband was in the hospital did I see how the Army takes care of its soldiers. So, I decided to join the Army, and my husband's Mahar Regiment helped. I want to tell other ladies that we should live so our children don't need to take anyone else as their inspiration.'[1]

But her nine-year-old daughter Lavanya gave an even more powerful glimpse into the Army's culture. 'One day, I will make Mumma more proud than I am of her. I will become an Army doctor. First, I wanted to become a doctor, but after my father, my mother, I decided that I would become an Army doctor.'[2]

VI

Girish Kumar and I joined the NDA simultaneously and in the same squadron. He was my antithesis in many ways: quiet, self-effacing and solid in his work. But we became friends and he taught me a few things, not least an expression in Kannada that would get anybody beaten up if used loosely.

Even though Girish branched out to the Air Force and I joined the Army, our friendship remained intact. When we both attended the Staff College course in Wellington, the friendship that my family shared with his cemented further. Over the years, we met several

---

marathon runner and has participated in motorcycle rallies. She has had postings in Srinagar and Ladakh. Her daughter, Simran, about to finish graduation in Canada, is planning to return to India and like her mother, father and grandfather, she is keen to join the Army.'

times and even holidayed in South Africa and Lesotho, where I had been posted as Head of the Indian Army's training team.

When Girish's son Akshay joined the Army, I found him so bright and mature that I predicted to Girish that the young man would outstrip his father in professional achievements. He was sharp, extremely personable and energetic.

But then came a cruel twist. On 30 November 2016, I woke up in the middle of the night. On my way to the bathroom, I gave in to the Pavlovian impulse to glance at my cell phone. The first piece of news that I read shook me to the core. Akshay had lost his life on 29 November while battling terrorists at Nagrota in Kashmir.

Meghna and the rest of the family had first learnt about the ongoing skirmish from the television. At about 8 a.m., on 29 November, a WhatsApp message had come in from Akshay. He was with his Quick Reaction Team. They had been fired at and were fighting back. There were a few casualties already. As the news channels relayed further updates, they learnt that one of Akshay's colleagues, Maj Kunal, had perished during the operation.

Akshay's wife Sangeeta, and their toddler girl were also in Nagrota but did not receive any additional details until much later. At 6 p.m., the regiment's CO informed Sangeeta that Akshay too had laid down his life.

How did the grieving family respond to this devastating news? It would have been understandable if they had expressed bitterness or rancour over the loss of their only son. But there was not a shred of that when I met them soon after; each one of them – Wing Commander Girish; Akshay's mother Meghna, who had grown up as an Army child; her father, a retired Colonel; and others who spoke at his memorial ten days after the incident – said the most pleasing things about Akshay and the armed forces. The Army veteran's grandfather insisted on seeing Akshay when his mortal remains came home. Looking at his grandson's face, he remarked, 'He has gone a satisfied man. Good. He has done what he wanted to do.'

What creates such stoicism in the parents of Army children – and veterans – that even in the face of grievous loss, they instinctively understand what 'duty' means? Their grief was palpable, of course, and the family's trauma began to lessen only after six months. But there wasn't a trace of resentment.

As the pall of pain began to subside somewhat, Girish, Meghna and Sangeeta began a new conversation. What would Akshay want us to do? He was so wedded to the Army. How should they honour his memory? They even joked that Akshay would have jumped into such a confabulation and said, 'Stop talking, do something.'

A year after that fateful operation, Girish and Meghna set up the Maj Akshay Girish Memorial Trust.

Picture this. Without warning, a family loses their only son while at work. There can be no compensation for the hole it has left, but even in recognition of his sacrifice, there may be precious little in the wake – as was the case for Akshay. In most other professions, it would be hard to imagine that such a bereavement would encourage the grieving parents to promote the very calling and cause that consumed their emotional mainstay. The parents established the Maj Akshay Girish Memorial Trust to motivate, galvanize and mentor others to join the armed forces. They knew their son had been proud to have motivated others from Jain University, his alma mater, to follow in his footsteps. Indeed, his college had been among the first to proudly put up a large hoarding to honour his sacrifice. The trust expanded its work to embrace several government-run colleges and schools in Karnakata. It focussed on children deprived of adequate opportunities to prepare for a career in the services. They held day-long interactive workshops to inform and inspire students. In July 2018, several veterans addressed the sessions. Three of Akshay's NDA coursemates voluntarily travelled from other towns. Maj Pankaj Pathak from the Army, Sqn Ldr Abhinav Rao from the Air Force, and Lt Cdr Akshay Raja of the Navy joined these sessions to bolster the enterprise set up in the name of their fallen comrade. The word spread on social media and others, including a few women officers, volunteered to enlist with the band of mentors and guides who would help less advantaged children prepare to join the armed forces.

The trust has continued its work month after month, propelled by the desire to keep Akshay's flame burning. It has expanded its charter to participation in NCC camps, educating school children on what it takes to be a responsible citizen, improving spoken English through storytelling and even participating in the Swachh Bharat campaign and protecting the environment. On Vijay Diwas, the trust honours veterans and families of soldiers who died during the Kargil War. It works in solidarity with other groups that bring succour to wives and children of battle casualties.

It isn't as if they are satisfied with the award conferred on their son – Mention in Despatches, a modest acknowledgement at best. They fervently believe that Akshay's sacrifice merited a higher recognition. But they have compartmentalized this disappointment and continued their work. 'We have the greatest respect for what the soldiers and the Army do,' Meghna, the daughter of a long-retired Colonel, the wife of a wing commander and the mother of a son who made the supreme sacrifice, told me. 'And no amount of grief and heartbreak will ever dilute it.'*

That is what culture can indelibly tattoo onto your heart.

---

* In chapter 4, in the story of the fateful heliborne operation in Jaffna University complex, the entire platoon except Sepoy Gura Singh had perished. Four decades later, through a dedicated social worker Vikas Manhas (he has made it a mission to visit the families of all martyrs), Girish and Meghna learnt that Gura Singh, now a veteran, had fallen on hard times. A series of family tragedies had brought him under a debt and he was living in a shanty-like house in a village near Ferozepur. Girish and Meghna made several visits to the village, quietly embarked on a mission to collect enough money to repay his loans and by 2023, had built him a new two-storeyed modern house, costing ₹30 lakh. When the house was 'inaugurated' the current subedar major of Gura's battalion, two of his previous COs (now aged veterans) and several retired soldiers from the neighbouring villages were in attendance. Prior to this effort, neither Girish nor Meghna had ever heard of Gura Singh.

VII

How do families and veterans stay dedicated to the organization's success long after all formal ties are severed? A powerful element ensures this – the Army never forgets its people. Irrespective of rank or designation, units never forget their veterans during their lifetime – or even after death. During all significant annual celebrations, units invite veterans and their families, including those who have moved overseas or were part of the Army during the Raj. Widows – called *veer naaris* – are invited too. No one is overlooked.

When my regiment celebrated its golden jubilee, among many veterans and families, it invited Lieutenant General Habibullah Khan Khattak, a former chief of general staff of the Pakistan Army who had served in the Bihar Regiment before the partition. At the point of the celebrations, the relations between India and Pakistan were not exactly cordial – but Habibullah Khattak had enough heft to push his government to let him travel to India. He arrived with his wife. Being the seniormost veteran of the regiment in our contemporary history, Lt Gen Khattak, a tall, devout Muslim in his seventies with a sparkling sense of humour, was the guest of honour for all the events during the four-day celebrations. From every dais, his was the first name announced while acknowledging the presence of dignitaries. He made a stirring speech to the troops at the Sainik Sammelan. 'I wanted to come for years,' he said, 'but our governments are full of thoughtless people – they don't let us meet. If you think this Pakistani general is saying sweet things just because he is in India, let me tell you this: my son was born in Bhagalpur, Bihar. He is now the GOC* of an armoured division in Pakistan. But when he makes a mistake, I reprimand him with, "You silly Bihari!" That is how much I miss you all.'

* General Officer Commanding, or Major General

While boarding his flight back to Pakistan, he remarked that returning to the regiment had added at least five years to his life.

All regiments systematically try to stay in touch with their veterans and families. These efforts transcend invitations to annual celebrations. Units reach out to families in need, often with financial help through contributions by the serving officers. The veterans reciprocate in whatever form and shape they can. When invited to annual functions, the veterans pay for their travel, of course, but collect funds to present trophies to their units. Increasingly, there is a trend wherein officer veterans insist on paying for their lodging in hotels and messes, even though the regiments can easily afford to put them up gratis. In the past few years, I have attended such functions where officer veterans took the call to ease the financial burden of the unit they had once served.

VIII

Many norms and traditions help integrate Army families into the broad stream of its culture. Some of these are followed more strongly by units of the 'fighting arms' like the Infantry, Artillery, Armoured Corps and Engineers than the 'services', but the overall spirit that guides it is identical.

Officers socially call on one another, accompanied by their families. Indeed, the quaint British practice of calling on someone meant that an officer wished to formally meet the family of another, often a senior officer. That practice has become somewhat less straitjacketed, but the original spirit of the family-to-family interaction has continued to flourish. Over the years, an officer's family develops close relations with several others – and the strength and quality of many of these equations are indistinguishable from the bonds within any close-knit extended family. They support one another, and the unit infrastructure looks after them, especially when the officers are away for months on training exercises or operations. Such norms – too many to list here – have created a robust ecosystem that collectively adds to the organization's performance.

When a family moves into a new station, unit officers take turns providing meals until the newcomers have settled down. Families are invited to attend most parties hosted by officers' messes and clubs. Indeed, absence from such get-togethers is an exception, not a norm. When the unit tastes significant success, the celebration includes families – unlike the corporate practice, there are no 'team drinks' or 'offsites' that leave out families.

Army cantonments have facilities exclusively for soldiers' families and children. One of the reasons cited for the exceptional success of Army daughters is the confidence they develop due to their exposure to activities often unavailable to their middle-class civilian counterparts.

Then there is the NGO, the Army Wives Welfare Association, which as its name suggests is run almost entirely by the wives of Army officers and soldiers. It is an association that works for the welfare of spouses, children and Army personnel dependents. Strictly speaking, AWWA is not a part of the Army. On occasions, critics of AWWA have raised the issue of resource utilization and the quality of its results. But the fact is that it works effectively to look after the welfare of families, often eliciting feedback for improvement that would not otherwise be possible.

IX

The Army's culture permeates beyond those who serve in it. The families of soldiers are embraced and included to such a degree that it is impossible to imagine the Army performing at such high levels without their support. Integrating families into the its culture adds pillars to the organizational structure. The conscious participation of the families reinforces the spirit of those who wear the uniform. It certainly makes the Army a large family, and most personnel, veterans and their families come to regard it as such.

It does not bear repeating that the environment in which the Army functions is unlike the one in which companies transact business. But could it be that the business world is missing a massive trick by completely divorcing families from the organization? Is there a case for moving beyond token gestures – inviting a few families for occasional functions – and pushing for much closer interaction? Could such a culture help team members more amicable, give subordinates a peek into their leaders' personal, 'human' side and create an additional subliminal reward for employees to stay on with their companies? The premise may sound out-of-the-box, but these are questions worth reflecting upon.

There is nothing to lose here and perhaps much to gain.

7

NAAM, NAMAK, NISHAN: THE CEMENT THAT BINDS

'The Gorkhas, the Rajputs, the Sikhs, the Dogras, the Bengalis, the Mussalmans of the Grenadiers, the Ahirs, the South Indian Signallers and all the others from the four corners of India had nothing to sustain them but their regimental pride and traditions. They had done what they had done because they were soldiers. For no man can do more than give his life for his country.'

– BRIG J. P. DALVI, commander of the brigade that bore the main onslaught of the 1962 Chinese attack

I

IF THERE ARE THREE words that an outsider can expect to hear most frequently from the soldiers of the Indian Army, they are '*naam, namak, nishan*'. Together these words constitute a powerful theme song – indeed, the most potent of ideas that runs like a silent stream through the Army's culture. It is a construct unique to the Indian Army, an unwritten yet clearly understood set of ideals that guide and motivate the conduct of soldiers during war and peace.

Naam means name; for the adherents of this culture, it denotes reputation and esteem. Namak is salt, and the connotation here is unflinching loyalty. Nishan, or sign, signifies the flag with all its symbolism for each regiment. Naam, namak and nishan are not nebulous concepts adorning a vision statement on the walls. They represent ideals that are sharply etched into a soldier's psyche. Officers and soldiers associate these words with their respective battalions and regiments, while collectively, the dividends are passed on to the Army as an organization.

One of the secrets of fostering high levels of motivation at all levels is this: every individual must know the tangible contribution they make to the organization's success. Every team member must be acutely conscious of their larger role underlying the dry bones of the job description. An essential responsibility of the leadership is to spread that awareness so that each employee comes to believe that they are in the service of something far more significant than a pay cheque. It gives individuals powerful stake in the system and a sense of ownership, if you will.

The ethos of naam, namak, nishan accords every soldier with a sense of duty – they are the upholders and custodians of the most cherished values of the Army, even though no one has formally appointed these tasks to them. They would rather die than let down their regiments, if the need arises.

But what sustains this 'potion' in a million-strong Army, a vast and diverse pool of human beings drawn from every country's demographic? The answer is traditions. Adherence to norms. Deference to the ethos under all circumstances. Decades of emotional investment in the ideas underlying this spirit has fused them into the collective memory of the Army. And even though it is vulnerable to the influence of the, sometimes sharply contrasting, civil society culture, it has mostly stayed intact.

II

In 1962, the Indian Army lost a war against China. It was a battle fought against the backdrop of delusional foreign policy, political fecklessness and abysmal logistics. Soldiers of the Army, ill-equipped and sometimes not suitably clothed for the extreme weather conditions, fought to the last man. In his seminal account, the commander of the 7 Infantry Brigade John Dalvi described the situation thus: 'Without basic winter clothing; with only three days rations on the man; no reserves; without mortars and ammunition; without rocket launchers and ammunition; without defence stores and with only personal items of kit.'[1]

Despite the heavily loaded dice against the Indian troops, it was not a one-sided match. The Army lost after putting up a stupendous fight. Indian sources put its fatalities at nearly 3,000; the exponentially better-equipped Chinese, who had attacked from dominating heights with far greater strength, admitted to losing 722 of their soldiers.

A pivotal part of the war was fought along the Namka Chu river that separates the Thag La and the Hathung La-Tsanghar mountain passes. The river emanates from a lake at 14,000 feet and is a catchment area for these two massifs. Following political diktats that 'not an inch of the territory' was to be lost, Indian deployment stretched along the river, entirely dominated by the Chinese on Thag La. Militarily, the only suitable tactical positions were further back, on the Tsangdhar plateau and the Hathung La ridge. But politically, it was considered unthinkable to give up two miles of Indian land and abandon posts like Dhola along the Namka Chu, which is fordable at most places throughout the year and presented no military obstacle.

One of the many constraints on the Indian side was the tenuous logistical support. There were no proper tracks, and the high-altitude terrain considerably diminished the human capability to haul loads; the troops had to rely on a trickle of mule convoys.

Some 4,000 yards south of Thag La, the feature of Tsangdhar presented the first location where guns could be deployed to support a battle. It was also the only patch of ground where an aircraft could attempt to drop supplies. It had a flat top, 120 x 60 yards at its widest, and if used by a Dakota aircraft as a dropping zone for delivering ammunition, equipment and supplies, the troops would be saved seven days of backbreaking effort from the nearest official airdrop point at Lumpo. In all its wisdom, the hierarchy chose to use both Dakotas and C-119 Fairchild Packets in a frantic effort to drop as much as possible in the few days before hostilities broke out. The resultant drops often missed the target, and a large percentage of the load drifted into ravines or got caught on the rhododendron-covered slopes, making retrieval a task of immense privation and complexity. Among the weapons thus lost due to misdirection were a few 75mm Howitzers – prized artillery pieces.

But let me travel back to 1959 for a moment. That year, a battalion of Gorkhas, the 1/9 GR, had been inducted in this area. After serving its tour of duty, the unit moved out in August 1962 and was on its way to Yol Cantonment for a well-earned 'peace' tenure, which opened with Dussehra festivities. A battalion of Grenadiers had taken over and while on their way out, the Gorkhas had reached Misamari in Assam, where they awaited transportation by rail.

Once the war clouds began to gather, the 1/9 GR and a unit of Rajputs in a similar situation were ordered to return to the Namka Chu area. The two battalions had to march back, a gruelling exercise over several days. The soldiers were now bereft of winter clothing, stripped off on the way to the 'peace' station, and abysmally short of ammunition for even a minor skirmish – each man had only about fifty rounds of small arms ammunition. And there was just three days of ration. On arrival into the battle zone, at a height of 15,000 feet, the troops spent the initial nights in summer uniform and one blanket each.

On 20 October 1962, the Chinese launched a massive attack. Aware of the Indian troops' deprived state, the Chinese did not even attempt to hide their intent. In fact, they showed utter disdain while attacking the tactically indefensible positions downhill. But the Indian soldiers fought back with what they had. A peek into the attrition by the overwhelmingly superior Chinese numbers tells us a part of the story. On the morning of the attack, the 513-strong Rajput battalion lost 282 soldiers, including four officers. Eighty-one were wounded and captured. Only sixty survived the onslaught. A similar fate befell 1/9 GR. The battalion's casualties totalled 226. Of these, eighty had perished, forty-four were wounded and 102 were captured.

For decades after the war, the Indian Army was not in the area adjoining the Namka Chu. In the early 1980s, it was decided to post a small team of civilian intelligence officials around Sumdurong Chu, close to the location of the 1962 battles. The team was deployed during summer and pulled back in winter when inclement weather prevailed. In 1986, this team discovered that the Chinese, too, had moved up troops to establish a permanent post in the same area. This triggered a build-up of the Indian formations to occupy the heights of Hathung La, facing the Thag La ridge. But now, the deployment was mainly along the heights and following tactical common sense.

In 1989, 1/9 GR, who that had heroically fought in the 1962 war, were reinducted into Arunachal Pradesh in an area that was a two-day march away from the battleground where they had lost a sizeable number of its soldiers twenty-seven years ago. A battalion of the Jat regiment now occupied the site of the previous battle.

Leaving soldiers on the battlefield, whether alive, wounded or dead, is unthinkable in the Army. This mandate is one of the many that provide flesh and blood to the naam, namak and nishan ethos. Several of the Gurkha soldiers who had perished never received an honourable farewell. This tragic thought had dogged the battalion's collective conscience for the past three decades. Even though the officers and soldiers who were a part of 1/9 GR in 1962 were long gone, the memory of the unfinished task remained undimmed. The naam of the battalion needed salvaging.

In 1990, the Gorkhas requested the Jat regiment for assistance in locating its soldiers' mortal remains. It tasked its officer, Sunil Nautiyal, then a 2nd lieutenant, to lead a team of hardy Gorkhas back to Namka Chu.

I have had the good fortune of serving in that area and know how difficult it is to patrol, let alone undertake digging expeditions. Oxygen is rare; even after acclimatization, just being present there can be enervating. But for the participants, these hazards were not consequential. 'I was very lucky that I was allowed to be a part of this effort,' the now retired Col Sunil Nautiyal told me.

The 1/9 GR team, assisted by the Jat troops, systematically dug up the area, often under the observation of the Chinese on the Thag La. I wonder if the activity would have bemused or perplexed the enemy troops, but they did not interfere from across the icy Namka Chu.

After days of effort, the mortal remains of nearly fifty Gorkha soldiers were found. The vagaries of the climate and the ravages of time had reduced the bodies to mere skeletons, but an astonishing piece of identification had survived. Each soldier wears an oval metallic identification disc around the wrist during the battle. It carries specific details, including the service number and blood group. This made it possible to confirm that the remains indeed belonged to soldiers of the 1/9 GR.

Each soldier was given befitting final rites. Photographs were taken for their kin. All the bayonets, helmets and water bottles were collected and stored under a hut made out of a giant parachute. It is now called a 'mandir'.

And what was the overriding emotion at the discovery of these fallen soldiers? Col Nautiyal said, 'My chest swelled with pride when I saw that each of them had taken a bullet in their foreheads. There were holes on the helmets.'

Nearly three decades after the battle, a newly minted battalion officer felt honoured that he belonged to this outfit and found solace in knowing his compatriots had done what they had been asked – which was to fight the enemy without turning away. The dead had upheld the battalion's nishan, given ample proof of their fidelity to the idea of naam and namak.

Can the business world create a value system that puts reputation, loyalty and symbolism on a similarly high pedestal? That is questionable because the dynamics vis-à-vis the army are starkly different. To begin with, compared with the corporate, there is minuscule attrition in the Army because most of its rank and file sign up for life. Thus, a modicum of permanence facilitates the perpetuity of naam, namak, nishan. A chalk-and-cheese difference also exists in how the Army and the corporate view 'profit' and thus 'efficiency'. These are only examples, and many other motivations separate the two. Therefore, the idea here is not to suggest that anyone should try to clone the Army's value system (though some elements can be advantageously replicated to a degree) but to point out that value systems do matter. A thoughtfully created value system and a bouquet of traditions can only strengthen corporate culture. They are worth the leadership's close attention and sustained effort.

III

It is not only the wounded or fallen compatriots that the Army's culture encourages its men to evacuate from the battlefield. The namak here extends to another component – the nishan, or the flag.

The flag is a prime symbol reflecting a regiment's pride and heritage. Historically, amid the smoke and din of battle, the flag's sight was a rallying point for the troops. It marked the commander's location, a reassuring thought for those jousting on the battlefield.

Losing the flag to the enemy meant only one thing – defeat, indistinguishable from ultimate disgrace.

What does a flag (or 'colours') signify? It is a colourful piece of cloth, emblazoned with insignia and the marks of famous battles won by the regiment, mounted on a staff. But it is also far more than just military symbolism. It has a mystical import and sway on the minds of soldiers. On all ceremonial occasions, whenever the official colours are paraded, armed guards march astride as escorts, soldiers and officers pay compliments to it.

In India, infantry battalions and armoured corps regiments are awarded colours. These represent the history of the unit's being – the sacrifices made and the memory of the martyrs. As in many other traditions, the unshakeable reverence for the colours unites soldiers to a higher cause, which may entail sacrificing their lives at a moment's notice.

The artillery, however, does not have a flag for its colours. While it carries a burgundy red and navy blue President's banner, gunners treat their guns as their 'colours' and accord the weapons the same sanctity as a traditional flag and mast colours.

In 1962, in the run-up to the Sino-Indian War, a few – perhaps only two – artillery 75mm Pack Howitzers, each weighing over 600 kilograms, and 450 rounds of ammunition were para-dropped by a Dakota aircraft onto the Tsangdhar dropping zone. A few of these parachutes missed the stamp-sized target, drifted off into ravines.

The 17 Para Field is an artillery regiment raised in 1941 as a Rajput unit and later converted to a parachute regiment. It went on to fight in every war since then, notably winning battle honours at Zojila in 1947–48 and Poongli Bridge during the 1971 war. When the 1962 hostilities broke out, an officer from the regiment, Captain (later Major General) Harjeet Singh Talwar was moved forward to control the fire of its guns. He arrived at Namka Chu after an arduous days-long march. But once the regiment had joined the battle, only two of their guns participated in any action; the other two were lost into the ravines forever. The guns fired their last salvo on 20 October 1962, and were silenced only when their ammunition was exhausted. The Chinese assaulted the position with naked bayonets, killing eight soldiers and capturing others who had refused to abandon the guns.

These two guns lay in the open during the subsequent three decades when neither the Indians nor the Chinese visited the area, presumably to maintain a degree of de-escalation. One of these guns was completely enveloped by the rhododendrons that paved the area and was no longer visible.

In 1986, triggered by the Chinese move into the Sumdurong Chu area (described earlier), units of the Indian Army too moved into this sector and occupied heights dominating the Namka Chu river. A young regiment officer, Capt Ashok Kumar G., posted near the area on deputation as a staff officer, wrote to the then commanding officer of 17 Para Field and suggested that an effort to retrieve the guns be made. The CO, Colonel A. K. Chowdhary, concurred that notwithstanding the herculean nature of the task, the two guns – the regiment's colours – must be brought back. After all, the Army's culture demanded that the nishan could not be abandoned on the battlefield.

'For anyone else, these guns would have been souvenirs. These were our colours, our pride – a part of our history. I felt that these symbols would motivate the generations to come, and the effort was not only well worth it. It was a matter of our izzat to make that effort,' Col Chowdhary later ruminated.

In April 1991, an attempt was made to locate and retrieve the two guns. From first-hand experience, I know how formidable that task would have been. Tracks, other than winding narrow trails through boulders, are non-existent. Both ascent and descent can be thoroughly draining.

This team marched for days for over a hundred kilometres, from the monastery town of Tawang to the hamlet of Zimithang, up the slopes to Lumpo and then made its bid to reach the desolate

Tsangdhar plateau. There were no roads or tracks, and a helicopter lift was improbable. 'Helicopter or not, we can't fail,' was Captain (now Major General) Sanjay Singh's resolve. But that attempt had to eventually be abandoned when a severe cyclone lashed Bangladesh; the weather in the area of the guns too worsened beyond all estimation.

In August 1991, the team led by Capt Sanjay Singh and Lt Sameer Ul Islam returned for another expedition. Sanjay was twenty-seven years old, and Sameer a couple of years younger. I met them at Lumpo at the brigade headquarters and was struck by the steel of their determination. Sanjay said that many had pointed out the impossibility of the mission, but that had spurred them on even more to restore the regiment's colours to the rightful mantle.

The thirty-man team packed everything it needed for weeks and began its expedition. After days of painstaking marching – suffering leeches, heavy rains and numerous other challenges – twenty-four men eventually reached the area of operations, the remaining six having developed severe hypertension. Then began the search for the guns.

The team located them both. Barrels had to be winched up using ropes. One of the guns briefly captured by the Chinese lay dismantled. They had presumably found it too burdensome to haul and left it in situ. Each piece weighed a hundred kilograms, if not more, even stripped to its parts. The other was unused, oil still fully preserved in its recuperator, lying among the prickly rhododendrons. The team hacked its way through the plants to get to it.

'How did you even know where to look?' I asked Sanjay.

'We had approached the Army headquarters and managed to dig out several details, including the alignment along which the dropping aircraft had flown. Once we had that information, we sought sanction to conduct a reconnaissance of the routes and the old dropping zone. We even managed to get copies of the old maps of the area. That is how we got there.'

Once the guns were found, the men began dismantling them into carriable loads, each piece managed by several soldiers. For this, Sanjay set up an ad-hoc workshop.* Rivets were removed, components carefully disassembled, oil and grease wiped off and makeshift harnesses were created to fit each part. Eventually, nothing could be reduced to less than sixty-five to eighty kilograms. Weight wasn't the only criterion either – the parts had to be wieldy and fit for carriage by men and mules. The team decided to cut up the barrels into four pieces each and weld them back after the evacuation was over and the colours had reached back home.

More than a month later, the 'pilgrims' made their progress back, one painful step at a time, over a route that one of them later described as 'killing'. After several days, still short of the start point of Lumpo, they were greeted by a convoy of mules sent by the brigade headquarters to ease matters. I know from personal experience how the stoic determination of this team of paratroopers had enthused us all. Every day, their progress had been at the heart of our conversations.

The team arrived at Lumpo, bone-weary and victorious. Beyond this point, Mi-17 helicopter sorties were organized to fly the colours home. Today, the guns occupy pride of place, one at the Artillery Museum and the other at the Quarter Guard of the 17 Para Field unit.

'Everyone supported our boys,' Colonel Chowdhary recounted. 'The Para brigade contributed soldiers as a part of the team. The 77 Mountain Brigade [Chindits] under Brigadier V. C. "Dimpy" Khanna supported the team with tremendous commitment, even though there was nothing in it for them. Everyone knew what we were trying to do – restoring our nishan to its rightful place.'

Sanjay told me, 'We felt that it had to be done. How can you leave your colours on the battlefield? Incidentally, while it was a 17 Para

* This is to stretch the word 'workshop' beyond all acceptable definitions; it was a table made of stones.

Field expedition, many troops from other units had joined it, units that had nothing to do with our colours.'*

Nishan and naam are central to the Army's value system. Translated for the corporate, both these values mean 'reputation'. Shouldn't reputation as a value be intrinsic to every company's culture that wants to keep winning? In one stroke, focus on reputation brings the cornucopia of quality, the standard of service, brand, customer-centricity and after-sales service into focus. It would be worth every moment of thought and effort to create norms and traditions that put the company's naam at the centre of its value systems. What traditions or symbolism will support this cultural push would be a matter for the corporate leadership's vision and imagination to craft. But one takeaway stands out – every significant action that builds the company's naam must be celebrated and rewarded. That is how such values will eventually become abiding traditions.

IV

Tradition is one of the strongest threads woven into the Army's culture. It fuels action that goes beyond cold logic and justifications. Organizations – armies, corporations, families – that recognize the value of tradition embrace it and make it inviolable. This binds everyone to a common cause and makes endless analysis redundant. When cultivated with purpose, this aspect of a culture asserts, 'We cannot fail.'

Traditions sustain and continually fuel formidable ideas that often defy logic from an outsider's perspective. But they are not the same as the mindless pursuit of the past. Traditions are guideposts that serve a powerful purpose of perpetuating a culture's underlying themes.

---

* On 3 July 2001, Major Sameer Ul Islam, the youngster who had been Sanjay's deputy during the mission, made the ultimate sacrifice in an operation in Haflong in Assam. He was posthumously awarded the Shaurya Chakra.

One of the Indian Army's traditions is that the leader does not care for himself more than those he commands. This element of the Army's ethos comes from the Chetwode credo, engraved on the entrance to the Indian Military Academy's entrance hall – these are words that most officers know by heart:

"The safety, honour, and welfare of your country come first, always and every time. The honour, welfare, and comfort of the men you command come next. Your own ease, comfort and safety come last, always and every time."*

The Chetwode motto is not a mere treacle. Over the decades, it has been etched into the Army's collective memory. It manifests itself in countless ways – officers literally leading from the front to protect soldiers being the most visible of them.

At other times it plays out more unpredictably.

In June 1999, during the Kargil War, one of the critical posts that the Army needed to occupy was Point 5770 (at a height of nearly 19,000 feet). The Army had anticipated that unless its units moved expeditiously, the Pakistanis – who had not reached it until then – would indeed move in to capture it.

The task was daunting. The oxygen-depleted atmosphere would have made it hard to undertake any strenuous physical mission, even if the terrain had been undulating and flat. In this case, the direction chosen for the stealthy approach was a one-kilometre vertical ascent, negotiable only by fixing ropes and climbing straight up. The troops would have to make this effort only at night, under the enemy's nose, with winds howling and unrelenting temperatures dropping

* The origin of the motto is itself rooted in history. Its authorship is ascribed to Field Marshal Philip Walhouse Chetwode (1869–1950), a British general who saw action during the Second Boer War, the First Battle of Ypres, and then in the Sinai and Palestine campaigns. After the war, he held a series of senior military appointments, including two in India – Chief of the General Staff in 1928 and Commander in Chief in 1930. Chetwode was among the pioneers of the Army's modernization and 'Indianization'. The motto was a part of his address in 1932 during the inauguration of the Academy.

below -40°C. The then CO of the 27 Rajput Regiment, Colonel (later Lieutenant General) Konsam Himalay Singh told me with a chuckle that things were 'far comfortable' during the day when the mercury 'rose' to a high of 4°C.

Fixing the ropes took three nights of an almost unendurably painful effort. Then suddenly a shot was heard, evoking apprehensions that the surprise may already have been lost.

The climb for the assault began in the early hours of 27 June. It was meant to be what the Army calls a 'silent attack' – no protective artillery bombardment to cover the assaulting troops' move so that, hopefully, the attackers could scramble up without being detected by the enemy. The Army manuals note that silent attacks may eventually turn 'noisy'. Sooner or later, the enemy is bound to spot the approaching forces and once it opens up a volley of fire, there is no further benefit in muzzling one's artillery fire. Two-sided mayhem may then ensue.

On this day, however, the attacking troops completed their arduous climb with the enemy being none the wiser. In his definitive account of the war, *Kargil: From Surprise to Victory*, General V. P. Malik describes the scene as recounted later by the survivors: '.... they reached the top, but to their horror, found that eleven Pakistani Army personnel had already reached there from their post, Pimple. The Pakistanis were unaware that the Indian task force had stealthily crept up from an unexpected direction. Some were busy constructing a sangar (a small cave-like inhabitation made of stones), two were writing letters, and some were resting in a makeshift fibreglass hut nearby.'[2]

The Indian party, led by Maj Navdeep Singh Cheema, attacked swiftly and killed all the Pakistanis. This action provoked intense artillery fire on the victors but fortunately, they did not incur casualties. Point 5770, which the Pakistanis called Bilal Top, was re-christened Navdeep Top in honour of Maj Cheema's leadership.

After it had consolidated its foothold on Point 5770, the Indian unit did what its culture of 'honour' instils in its rank and file – they undertook backbreaking efforts to bury all the enemy soldiers with dignity and military protocol. 'We did not know the proper religious rites other than that the men had to be buried. Our battalion *panditji* was therefore tasked to find out about the basic rituals so that the remains could be given a proper send-off.'

The dead carried identity cards on them. Among the Pakistani fatalities was Captain Taimur Malik of the Special Service Group (Pakistan Army commandos, also known as Maroon Berets). He was on loan to the 3rd Northern Light Infantry, one of the units that had surreptitiously intruded into the Kargil area. The twenty-three-year-old had completed three years of commissioned service on the day he perished.

After the war, India received a strange request through the defence attaché in London. Taimur's grandfather, a Pakistani ex-judge, had approached the Indian embassy with a poignant request. Would it be possible to locate Taimur's mortal remains and return them to his country? For most of the period during and after this war, Pakistanis, even at the highest levels, had persisted with the canard that this was a purely mujahideen operation. The refrain went that the Pakistan Army had no involvement.

The request reached the chief of the Army staff, General Ved Malik, who asked the concerned formation to explore possibilities. It involved another exhausting attempt in an area where even walking can be laborious. The CO accepted the challenge but had a counter suggestion: 'Why just the body of an officer? Several Pakistani soldiers, too, had been killed and buried there. Going by our ethos, it would only be proper if we accorded the same privilege to the soldiers as we will do to the officer. After all, we never leave our soldiers behind on the battlefield. We will apply the same norm to the Pakistanis.' To that end, he was willing to increase the gruelling effort by multiple times. The chief of the Army staff gave his approval.

Finally, after a punishing effort involving nearly forty soldiers working for two days, the bodies of Capt Taimur and several other Pakistani soldiers were exhumed and flown to Kargil on a Mi-17 helicopter, and returned to the Pakistan Army with full military honours.

This is, of course, a story of large-heartedness and valour. But it also holds up a mirror to a powerful element of the Army's culture. You do not abandon your comrades, whether they are dead or alive. It is unthinkable and indistinguishable from honour. And you even extend the same honour to the enemy.

It is not hard to imagine how this must play out in the minds of the rank and file when they know that they will never be left unsung and unattended. The Army conflates this sense of camaraderie with its deeply cherished value of izzat – that it will leave no one behind on the battlefield. As is evident from this story, this is a critical part of the culture that seeps through to Army families as well. It ties them to the Army with an invisible but imperishable umbilical cord.

While this chapter closed, Lt Gen Konsam Himalaya Singh, whose battalion 27 Rajput Regiment had performed heroically during the Kargil War, had a lingering regret in his heart for seventeen years. He had felt that his battalion had not received appropriate recognition for its contribution during the war.

An integral part of the Army's culture is that awards – known to soldiers as 'decorations' – are inestimably valued. It isn't about the monetary benefits; only a fraction of awards carry pecuniary advantages, and even these are more symbolic than substantial. It is all about the honour – the izzat – that is conflated with such recognition. Individuals are awarded either for extraordinary feats of gallantry in operations or distinguished service rendered beyond the stipulations of the mandate. Units receive 'battle honours' for wartime heroics and achievements or commendations from the chief of the Army staff and Army commanders leading the six regional commands.

These awards are then suffixed to the name of the individual and the unit. The permanence of the award ensures that the flame of pride burns forever. Their mention finds its way into war diaries maintained not only to retain factual perspective and historical accuracy but to instil respect and reverence in the generations that follow. The concept of izzat is thus permanently woven into the Army's fabric. It is a shining hill of its culture.

It is equally their culture not to protest if awards do not come the way of the hopeful. No one complains beyond a few mutterings about the lack of recognition, just as, on another level, no one begins an inquisition of any sort after casualties in an operation. The unwritten honour system, cemented by folklore, practice and longevity, is a cultural bulwark; people adhere to it even in the most trying circumstances.

So, seventeen years after the war, when Lt Gen Konsam Himalaya Singh hosted Gen Malik, the Kargil War became a part of the evening's tête-à-tête, and the 27 Rajput regiment's exploits came up in conversation. Lt Gen Singh politely expressed his abiding disquiet over the fact that his battalion had received less than its share of the credit; while gallantry medals (arguably of lower denomination than was warranted) had been awarded, the unit did not receive the battle honour it deserved.

General Malik graciously admitted that it was possible that all the gallant actions did not come to light at the right time. He was fulsome in his praise for the battalion's assault on Point 5770. Lt Gen Singh had a suggestion.

'I know it will be unfair on my part to even ask for the issue to be reopened. But can you do something that will restore our pride to a substantial degree?'

'What is it?' General Malik asked.

'Can I reduce the true account the collective gallant effort of the battalion during the war to writing and send it to you? All I need is the acknowledgement of our wartime chief for the battalion's war diary.'

General Malik accepted the suggestion.

'The only reason I did that,' Lt Gen Singh later told me, 'is for the sake of honour. I knew that it would bolster the morale of generations to come. We may not have got the official recognition we felt we deserved, but we now had it on record that we had done our duty. Our izzat was preserved.'

There are many moments in our lives when we are confronted with challenges and questions that have never before been posed to us. On several occasions, business leaders have to make tough decisions where ethics and profit collide. In such situations, a value system can be of inestimable help to reach the right conclusion – as it was for Lt Gen Singh. Thus, when the naam of the company is likely to be bruised or worse, no value-based leadership will ever prevaricate over which road to take.

V

Over the past seventy-six years, the Indian Army has experienced a quiet internal revolution. The rank and file have become more aspirational. Accordingly, the officer leadership's approach has also discarded some of the stiff formality of the British days and become more egalitarian. The soldier is far better educated, financially secure and ambitious to scale the ladder of social mobility. The percentage of cadets in the National Defence Academy whose parents are JCOs, NCOs or soldiers has risen exponentially. With the general dissolution of feudalism in our country, there is also an attendant rise in equality between officers and soldiers – though that does not imply that there was ever a vast chasm between the Indian Army officer and those whom he led.

Some things, of course, never change – and should not change. The officer–soldier bond, built on leading by example and from the front and deep-seated regimental mores, has always been intrinsic to the Army's culture.

Notwithstanding the changes that have shaped the post-Independence Army, it has preserved its core traditions and values. From the distinctiveness of regimental uniforms, salutations, war cries, officers' mess norms, marching styles and speeds, festivals, to religious functions – regiments implicitly follow their unique traditions. Even in minor matters, there is a strong inclination to preserve tradition – as a visit to my parent battalion, in which I was commissioned more than four decades ago, reminded me.

I was in Trivandrum in 2016 to attend the Raising Day celebrations of in which I was commissioned more than four decades ago – 4th Battalion, the Bihar Regiment. During one of the events, I walked up to the battalion's jazz band to applaud the skills of its members. That is when I noticed misspellings on all the pennants around the stage. Instead of 'Jazz Band', stitched on each of the pennants were the words 'Jorz Band'. I pointed out the error to one of the veterans.

As it turned out, it wasn't quite a misspelling. One of the ex-commanding officers explained the 'error' with a nugget from recent history. In 1990 or so – by which time I had already left the battalion– the CO had decided to put together a jazz band. The subedar major – an Adivasi from Jharkhand who was an iconic hockey player but largely unfamiliar with English – always referred to it as Jorz Band. Maybe he suspected this ensemble was merely another tradition inherited from the British, named after some unknown 'George'. Every day, as part of his evening report, he would inform the CO of the progress the Jorz Band was making.

The CO corrected him on several occasions, but Subedar Major Marshal Minz could not wrap his soldierly mind around this alien entity known as 'jazz'. Once the band had reached a level of proficiency and was formally launched, the CO ordered that henceforth, to honour Marshal Minz, the seniormost from the rank and file, the band would always be called Jorz Band.

Only once during the preceding three decades did one CO contemplate correcting it to 'Jazz'. But the veterans protested, and Jorz it remains to date.

Such adherence to traditions brings stability to organizations on matters where daily cynicism and critical thinking are not required. It binds the followers in a common thread and instils a sense of belonging and pride. The Army lives and dies by its traditions. In turn, these same traditions strengthen the fabric of its culture.

VI

The Army inherited some fine traditions from the British and continued to tweak and build on them to suit the Indian context. Two that have served it and the country very well are the Army's apolitical and secular nature. Its refusal to meddle in politics and its steadfast secularism have flourished even as the sub-continental environment has militated against both; it indicates the resilience of the Indian Army's long-standing traditions.*

Take the Army's unique approach towards religion. In the Army, each officer of the 'arms' (Infantry, Armoured Corps, Mechanized Infantry, Artillery, Engineers) identifies with the religion of the troops he commands. In regiments where the soldiers are from more than one religion, the officers – and indeed all jawans – attend the weekly religious prayers of all faiths. A Hindu or Christian Malayali officer commissioned in a Sikh battalion would always

* Some outsiders have begun to question if the Army's culture will forever withstand the changing environment. It is hard to crystal-gaze on this matter – but the strength of the Army's culture indicates that it will continue to be an island where various religious practices will flourish in a secular environment.

wear a pagri during major festivals and even participate in all the rituals. A Bengali Brahmin commissioned in a Gurkha regiment would participate in the animal sacrifice on Dussehra. Muslim officers attend 'mandir parades' in the unit, and Hindu officers in Muslim battalions are known to have observed *rozas*. My battalion had a mix of Hindus and Christians. I can't count the number of times I have trooped out of the battalion mandir only to enter the battalion church next door.

The composition of the J&K Light Infantry regiment is an equal mix of Dogras and Muslims from Kashmir. These troops are mixed into every sub-unit down to sections (ten soldiers). They dine in the same kitchen where the menu carefully takes into account the diners' religious sensibilities. One of the regiment's senior veterans, Lt Gen S. K. Dua, recounts that officers like him – many of them agnostic towards rituals – observed fasts during navratras as well as Ramzan. On Eid, Hindu soldiers would take on the bulk of the duties so that their Muslim colleagues could be free to celebrate; the reverse invariably happened during Diwali.

A few years ago, praying to the gods became even simpler; the Army decided that instead of separate mandirs, masjids, gurudwaras and churches, all faiths would share premises for prayer. Now *sarva dharma sthals* (common prayer rooms) are the norm across the Army. It is not uncommon to see soldiers from different religions praying simultaneously in the four corners of these rooms. Indeed, there are places where a fifth 'corner' has been created for Buddhists. For officers like me, who in their young days had to go to two different 'sacred places' to conform to the composition of the battalion, it saves that walk!

Perhaps it is because the Army genuinely believes in two central truths – the oneness of god and victory in operations. Both are so sacred that we cannot nitpick and question the basics. Sometimes the Army even mixes up the two. On a visit to the holy cave in Amarnath a few years ago, I saw a plaque mounted on the side of the hill by a battalion that had once guarded the annual yatra. It said, 'Best wishes from X battalion. Deployed for Operation Amarnath.'

In another instance, I remember a commanding officer ordering the battalion maulavi to conduct the proceedings of Janamashtami prayers because the pandit was on leave on compassionate grounds. No one found it unusual. It was the most rousing and well-prepared sermon in praise of Lord Krishna that the battalion can recall.

In the Rajauri sector, a company of Khemkhani Muslim soldiers replaced a Dogra battalion on the Line of Control. Over the next few days, Pakistanis shelled the post heavily, and there were a few non-fatal casualties. One day, the junior commissioned officer of the company, Subedar Sarwar Khan, walked up to the company commander Major Sharma* and said, 'Sahib, ever since the Dogras left, the mandir has been shut. Why don't you open it once every evening and perform aarti? Why are we displeasing the gods?' Major Sharma shamefacedly confessed that he did not know all the words to the aarti. That night, Subedar Sarwar huddled over the radio set under the weak light from a lantern and painstakingly took down the words of the aarti from the post of another battalion.

Indian Army troops stationed along the entire border shared with Pakistan, abstain from alcohol and non-vegetarian food every Thursday, as it is *Pir* day – a day of religious significance for the local Muslims.

In 1984, after Operation Bluestar, there was anguish within the Sikh community over the desecration of their holiest shrines. Some of this anger and hurt was visible in the Army too. I remember the first Gurpurab festival that fell just a few days after the operation – the number of Army personnel of every religious denomination that thronged the regimental gurudwara of the nearest Sikh battalion was the largest I had ever seen. I distinctly remember how each officer and soldier who put his forehead to the ground to pay obeisance

* Both names changed.

appeared to linger just a wee bit longer than usual. Empathy and fellow feeling were implicit in the gesture which appeared to say, 'You are hurt, and we all understand.'

We were deployed on the Line of Control in those days. Soon after the news of disaffection among a small section of the Sikh troops was broadcast on the BBC, Pakistani troops positioned opposite the Sikh battalion in Poonch yelled across to express their 'solidarity' with the Sikhs, suggesting that they defect or hand over the post in protest of the 'violation' of their faith. The Sikh havildar shouted back that the Pakistanis had better not harbour any wrong notions. 'Don't worry about our internal issues. We will mow you down if you dare move towards this post.'

A day before Christmas in the year 1986, two boys of a Sikh battalion were overheard discussing the following:

'Why do we have a holiday tomorrow?' asked Sepoy Singh.

'It is Christmas,' Naik Singh replied.

'But what is Christmas?'

'Christmas,' Naik Singh said, with his eyes half shut in reverence and hands in a spontaneous prayer clasp, 'is the Gurpurab of the Christians.'

The Army's simultaneous respect for the religiosity of the soldiers (who primarily come from backgrounds where religion is an intrinsic part of life) and true secularism has held it in good stead. The latter has led to mutual respect and trust, values that are indispensable for an organization where team spirit can quite literally be a matter of life and death.

But this is not a prescription for companies in the business world. The seminal point behind these stories is that when you create a value system-based culture, your company can be a haven of excellence, insulated from the malevolent strains that may infect others. A robust culture will ensure that in a cacophonous world of contradictory noises, you have your own drumbeat to follow as you march towards victories.

VII

It isn't necessary that other organizations should try to replicate the honour-driven culture of the Army. Instead, the implicit suggestion is that they could invest in ideas that will instil a value system unique to their setup. The first step towards kindling such a powerful undercurrent can be taken only if the leadership believes in it and consistently sets an example. The value system that the idea represents must be articulated – and repeated often and widely.

More than the framework of data, stories help build desired behaviours. Well-told stories, with sufficient emotional content, light up those neurological regions of the brain that help the listener put themselves in the characters' shoes. Stories of courage, loyalty and utter selflessness move people and silently motivate an individual to replicate these behaviours in their own lives.

Some of these stories are 'living organisms' and may even appear quirky to the listeners. The protagonist of one such tale is Rifleman Jaswant Singh, who was conferred the Mahavir Chakra for extraordinary valour during the 1962 war with China. Legend has it that this soldier of the 4th Battalion of the Garhwal Rifles had held the Chinese at bay for three days. The Chinese had, therefore, supposedly cut off Jaswant Singh's head and taken it to China, but a Chinese commander, impressed by his bravery, returned Singh's head along with a brass bust of the martyr. The statue, presumably created in China, is now installed at the site of the battle. A shrine has come up at a site where all passing vehicles stop to pay homage. Jaswant is also treated as if he is alive: his boots are shined, and his uniform is maintained by his regimental personnel posted at the shrine. He has even received all his promotions in time!

A similar shrine that celebrates another folklore exists near Nathu La and Gangtok. Baba Harbhajan's temple has its genesis in the story of a sepoy by the same name who served with the 23rd Battalion of the Punjab regiment. Harbhajan went missing four decades ago and, as per the legend, was instrumental in his recovery. Soldiers believe that his spirit protects all those who serve in the area. He, too, was treated as 'alive' and given all promotions until his 'retirement' in 2016.

The Army is a vast reservoir of inspiring stories, though it must be said that the bulk of these are true tales of courage and sacrifice and lack the peculiarity of the legends of Jaswant and Harbhajan. These narratives are preserved in war diaries, logs, regimental histories, folklore, war museums, memorials and, of course, through veterans. Such stories feed the Army's culture. They continually stoke human emotions by celebrating the highest ideals upheld by 'ordinary people like us'. They encourage one to identify with specific values and success.

Does the corporate world tell enough stories? Is there even a mechanism within companies to collect extraordinary case studies? Is there a structure to circulate these tales and ensure they get etched in the minds of its team members? Can a company develop its folklore based on values of honour and loyalty that will resonate with its employees forever? Why wouldn't an organization spend time developing a system that instils pride in its people – at no cost?

How does an idea like naam, namak, nishan sustain itself? It is driven by history, of course. It is created by thoughtful and reflective leadership and preserved by the sheer momentum of traditions and norms. When the customs are followed year after year, they add to our collective identities. That is what makes a soldier identify with his battalion or unit or regiment – and collectively, that is how everyone identifies with the Army. This group identity, a sense of honour that ripples just beneath the surface, motivating a soldier to readily endure privations and make sacrifices, often eludes the corporate sector.

Even as employees come and go, creating a reservoir of stories will provide a the company a continuity of traditions – and a certain pride. Let the stories of the sacrifices made by team members to uphold the company's reputation be repeated at annual conferences, founders' day celebrations and all such major events and celebrations, highlighted in company journals and become the subject of internal case studies.

Ideas similar in nobility to naam, namak, nishan can be instilled in organizations and, indeed, great enterprises are cognizant of it. For example, many companies focus on diversity or quality or ethics, even when these might dent their bottom lines. But a caveat bears mentioning: you cannot create a value-based culture by merely making proclamations from pulpits or splashing it on colourful posters on the walls. When the rubber meets the road, values must be unfailingly adhered to. The talk has to be walked.*

* As I wrote this, it struck me that in my four decades in the Army, no one had ever preached about naam, namak, nishan from a dais to me. Nor had I ever seen a poster that announced its existence. It was simply followed.

8

HOW TO TRANSFORM CORPORATE CULTURE

> 'The sowers may mistake and sow his peas crookedly; the peas make no mistake but come up and show their line.'
>
> – RALPH WALDO EMERSON

I

A THOUGHTFULLY DEVELOPED CULTURE has the beauty of a manicured lawn. Remove the thoughtfulness, and you are left with wild grass and weeds. In either case, the grass will inevitably grow. And once a culture has come into being, it is hard to transform. Indeed, just like an individual's 'personality', it is an obdurate animal that can't be wrestled to the ground in one deft move and made to relent. It takes technique, patience and perseverance to change. Culture is 'not to be flung out of the window by any man but coaxed downstairs one step at a time.'* So, what will move the cultural needle for an organization? Where do we start as we embark on what will always be a steep haul up the slope?

* Mark Twain said this about habits, but the context equally applies here.

Or, maybe, we can first dive into what creates a culture in the first place. For in its evolution lies the kernel of truths to guide us along the transformation of the culture of our organizations. This final chapter is a primer for leaders who wish to review, refine and recreate parts of their company's culture. We can only renovate that edifice after we understand its building blocks.

Whenever a company comes into being, it tends to do so purposefully. Without exception, that purpose is the deeply cherished brainchild of the founder or, to use a more generic term, its owner.* It is this founder who is the fount of the new company's culture. And while the employees, environment and circumstances contribute to its shape and development, the most profound imprint comes from the person at the top – the most potent prime mover.

It is the founder who injects the initial entrepreneurial spirit. He articulates his vision of the path to success, legislates rules and norms and, most vitally, by his conduct, sets the tone of interpersonal dynamics within the company. The founder's deeply held beliefs are reflected in recruitment, team-building, conflicts and the aspects that make the employees feel safe and wanted.

The strengths and infirmities of his personality inevitably cast a shadow on the evolving culture. Strangely, even as they moan about the debilitating weaknesses of the company's culture, many founders are oblivious to their inadvertently baleful influence, leading to the undesirable situation they abhor. Only the most reflective and introspective founders eventually 'get it' and surmount this problem.

When a 'strong' founder exits the scene, the culture often destabilizes in the aftermath. The sacking of Steve Jobs from Apple Inc. in 1985, the subsequent cultural turmoil under the leadership of the three CEOs that followed and the calming and positive effect of

* The term founder or owner may be used in the singular or plural. But the fact is that even where there is more than one founder or owner, there is always a dominant one whose ideas prevail more than those of the other(s). Not surprisingly, it is this person who controls the purse strings.

his return in 1997, are notable examples of how culture flows to the dictates of gravity. But Apple is not the only example. The history of businesses worldwide is littered with instances where one man's departure caused similar upheaval.

The owner's ultimate responsibility in creating and sustaining culture can be both fruitful and damaging. The locus of control for change lies primarily within themselves – hence cultural change can only be triggered from just beneath their chests. Conversely, if founders keep searching for external scapegoats, nothing will change. This is a harsh but fundamental truth.

Over time, as the owner steers the ship, the team members settle into a behavioural or cultural pattern. At the core, all individuals work for their self-interest – a large assembly of disparate psychological and material needs, often inaccurately dumbed down merely to 'money'. The team members follow what appears to work – to make the company successful, of course, but also what advances their personal goals, lowers existential anxieties and shrouds them in an imaginary cloak of safety.

In larger companies, formed by corporate groups, the founder's influence may recede once the reins have been handed over to a CEO or a senior executive. The bottomline is that culture will flow from whosoever holds the all-powerful pen in his hand and can make decisions that will impact the employees materially and psychologically.

No founder will admit to encouraging gossip, bias and arbitrariness (the root cause of all company politics), indifference to the team members' needs and to unethical practices. Yet many wink and nod at actions that will secure a quick win but could be detrimental to the organization's long-term well-being.* Some founders also find

* One of the fundamental tragedies of human nature is that, for most of us, short-term gratification scores over long-term advantage. What lies in the distance is hard to value. And, yet, the formula for success in all decision-making is just that – what is good for the long-term may seem hard to do but is the right call to make.

it expedient to let inter-departmental and interpersonal conflicts simmer, so long as they do not have to personally dive into the uncomfortable business of resolving matters. A managing director I know often pointed out senior managers resorting to 'petty' power games, not sharing complete information in order to show each other down and resorting to tittle-tattle . His response? 'I have no time for such rubbish. I am here to grow the company.' Alas, ignoring that 'rubbish' not only led to chaos and unnecessary conflict but also encouraged the growth of the tendencies he was ostrich-like in wanting to avoid.

Thus, it is not only what a founder espouses that matters. It is what he does that sets the cultural narrative.

II

The starting point of cultural development, change or transformation is that the administration must have absolute clarity of what needs to go and what should replace it. How does the management acquire that understanding, especially when it may itself be part of the challenge? Any leadership worth its salt would indeed know the key issues that require attention. But could the 'real' infirmities lie elsewhere?

Titan, the world's sixth-largest watch company, wasn't always perched on that pedestal. Its initial journey began in 1984 following a partnership between the Tata Group and the Tamil Nadu Industrial Development Corporation (TIDCO) – incidentally still the dominant shareholder – which was not always smooth. The company's mainstay was its Hosur plant that manufactured watches. But over the years, it diversified into a collection of several portfolios. The corporate headquarters was in Bangalore, away from the Mumbai group head office, which would prove to be fortuitous. Titan's is a story of an established company always searching for a better culture, whose leadership was alive to its weaknesses and set about the transformation thoughtfully.

It could – or should – be the story of every company. No organization can claim to have reached the sweet spot of a perfect culture. And while one routinely hears MDs and CEOs lament the imperfections in the culture of their companies, there appears to be an enervating lack of understanding as to how one can repair the cracks. Cultural changes are not amenable to simplistic cliches like 'the use of the rod', 'everyone works for money' and 'there is no work ethic among this generation'. One needs a more reflective approach to begin the climb. Titan understood that.

At the outset, the company had a couple of advantages. During its inception, all of Titan's division heads came from other Tata companies and thus shared a broad consensus on cultural orientation. Its founder and managing director, Xerxes Desai was a clear-headed leader, determined to chart an independent course. This period coincided with the imminent departure of JRD Tata and the induction of his successor, Ratan Tata. The geographical separation from the group headquarters eliminated the yoke of daily interference, enabling Titan to independently create a culture that its founders had envisaged. We know that culture in a family-owned business stems from the owners and from the collective leadership in other corporate entities. In either case, a degree of day-to-day freedom from the 'headquarters' is beneficial. Such latitude was available to Xerxes Desai.

Over time, the company branched out to several other areas, though not always with sterling success. The strategic direction was to enter relatively disorganized, underpenetrated and underserved customer segments. Titan aimed to introduce high-quality products wrapped in aspirational brands, focusing on design, to dominate the market. It owned the entire value chain, right up to retail distribution – forays into jewellery were followed by eyewear, perfumes, saris, accessories and even aerospace components.

At any point, the company had a spectrum of businesses – mature on one end and nascent on the other. And through this diversification, the leadership wanted to keep the entrepreneurial spirit alive.

By the time Xerxes Desai came up for superannuation, several other stalwarts were on the threshold of retirement or departure. The company had foreseen it and, in the preceding five-to-six-year window, put a talent assessment and leadership development process in place to identify future leaders from within – an instructive clue on how to sustain culture.

Titan decided to take the qualitative-analysis route, marked with extensive interviews with all stakeholders – employees, vendors and franchisees – to get a deeper understanding of its cultural landscape. Carefully selected focus groups of ten–fifteen employees with varying lengths of experience were selected for interactions. Veterans, greenhorns, as well as those who had once left and returned to the Titan fold, had their say. It provided a granular understanding of how all employees perceived the organization's culture. The management debated the findings in a series of workshops – which elements to retain, discard, modify or introduce for a better future. Instead of succumbing to the temptation of drawing up an unwieldy laundry list of multiple conclusions, it finalized a tighter list of seven focus areas.

After the exercise, the management felt reassured that the company's culture was on a sound footing on three counts: people orientation, customer centricity and social consciousness. But, more importantly, four areas needed to be remodelled or strengthened: innovation that must firmly have the future in its sight, ownership and accountability in some pockets, ability to foresee, adapt or pivot and greater agility in decision-making and execution.

Based on these conclusions, Titan formed cross-functional teams that worked on the perceived weaknesses. Notably, the groups were led by business heads and not the head of HR. This is a vital pointer for anyone striving to address a company's culture. HR facilitates the shift, but Operations must draw from their ground experience to give it the required shape.

The teams then worked quietly to develop programmes that would drive the transition. 'People have to feel the change,' the then CHRO Raj Narayan said, 'and when you form groups specifically addressing culture, the word spirals and spreads.'

The redesigning of culture was born out of intense and regular conversations. Goal setting and review processes – aligned with the desired culture – were created without making them cumbersome. One example of the many programmes that resulted from this endeavour was the Titan Ignitor programmes. Introduced in 2012–13, Ignitor was aimed at encouraging new ideas from anyone in the company. Its first effort harvested over 750 innovative ideas that arrived as short write-ups and a PowerPoint presentation. The shortlisted 'winners' presented their ideas to an external jury. The final three teams were given the freedom and resources to develop those ideas to boost Titan's business. Not only did this exercise bolster the culture of innovation as a by-product, it also strengthened ownership, a belief that team members were co-creators of the company's future.

Titan's example reminds us of a self-evident truth. One must first understand what needs to be changed in order to make a change. How do we go about such a transformation?

It is true that perspicacious employees best understand the real depth and nuance of a company's culture. But should the leadership turn to a consultant to zero in on the heart of the matter? An outsider, or consultant, can also be valuable, provided the management implicitly meets a few requirements.

First, the leadership must accord the consultant complete authority to collect data. Second, the consultant must have adequate support – including the target group selection – to design and execute the process of understanding the prevailing culture. Lastly, it is incumbent that the consultant wins the trust of the individuals brought forward based on the principles of confidentiality and openness.

There are, of course, two tools for eliciting the required data – quantitative and qualitative. A well-designed survey may provide some insights into the company's culture, but the rub lies in the words 'well-designed'. Many managements favour the quantitative approach because it gives them the psychological comfort of the presumed reliability of empirical data. But the truth is that such surveys can often produce a deeply flawed picture as averaged numbers may not indicate the magnitude of the problem or even point in the right direction. After all, the outcomes will primarily be driven by the weightage accorded to each question, not to mention the type of queries included in the form.

There is every indication that one-on-one, or group interviews, are far more practical. The initial questionnaire should be structured, but the subsequent discussion can be freewheeling. The consultant would have interacted with the management before such an exercise; he would know the direction to take in the line of questioning. The interaction would aim at team members' underlying assumptions and emotions about various facets of the company.

A Bangalore-based services company with its headquarters in the US was in the process of acquiring an Indian family-owned business. The underlying premise was to expand the parent company's market (Company A) by acquiring Company B. But as is the case with most mergers and acquisitions, the marriage hit turbulence soon after the relationship began. The reason? While the two companies had assiduously crossed the t's, dotted the i's and thought through the emergent structure, they had paid scant attention to the fact that their cultures were extremely divergent. How often does this happen?

Companies undertaking an alliance often consider cultural differences as the last point on the merger checklist. It is hard to assess the impact of culture on revenues and profit, growth and expansion, failure and success. And yet, the smartest leaders understand that without a sound and cohesive culture, the best-laid plans may falter.

While interviewing the leadership and top managers of the two companies – A and B – the consultant had four initial questions. These had been made available to the participants. The answers were to be covered by the principles of non-attribution and anonymity and, to foster trust, were not electronically recorded.

The consultant asked:

What are the main strengths of your parent company?

What are its weaknesses?

Where do you perceive the most significant challenges when the two corporate cultures merge?

What is that one thing that will allow the merged Company A to reach the next level of success?

This, of course, is only one set of questions that gives us a flavour of how to approach qualitative analysis. The interactions that followed were insightful and revealing. Even in the follow up discussions, the consultant rarely used the word 'culture'; instead, the focus was on behaviours, processes, challenges and feelings. Whatever the modus operandi of concluding the changes required in the company's culture, this is the beginning of the process. Whenever a successful cultural shift has happened, the clarity of the leadership's vision is at the very core.

The instructive tale of Arvind Fashions points to the leadership's role in such a change – and has many other lessons for all of us.

III

K. E. Venkatachalapathy joined Arvind Fashions Ltd as its CFO in 1995; he had held a similar position in other companies, notably Asian Paints and TVS.

Arvind Fashions had a dozen Mega Mart outlets for selling its premium brands at a discount – Arrow, Newport, Wrangler, Lee and others. The HR head doubled up as the business head for these stores. Once the HR head resigned, the mandate devolved upon Venkat, who now had to don two hats.

In late 2005, when J. Suresh took over as MD and CEO, some brands were struggling. Arvind Fashions was no newcomer to the market, but in the early 2000s, it was facing debilitating headwinds. Eventually, to infuse cash into the system, its successful brands, Lee and Wrangler, had to be sold to the original owners. Under Suresh, the management decided to expand the operation of Mega Mart by injecting exclusive brands like Ruggers and Excalibur and tightening inventory management. It opened larger stores to build a formidable chain. Under Suresh's direction – and that of Venkat, who subsequently resigned as CFO to focus entirely on the retail chain – Mega Mart showed impressive growth. Over a decade, the eighteen-crore turnover shot up to nearly 700 crores. The number of stores grew to 120.

Venkat attributes success to one key factor – cultural change. He lays the credit at the door of J. Suresh and his clear-eyed vision as the topmost leader. It is a fundamental law that culture flows from the top. But it takes a great deal to build that culture. Once it is in place, it manifests as teamwork – and great numbers on the spreadsheet.

When J. Suresh began his fifteen-year journey at Arvind Fashions, he realized that a few significant strands of the company's culture needed to be replaced. For one, the collective behaviour reflected a lack of proactiveness. He noticed that people took too long to respond and do things internally. Culture changes only when the last man absorbs it, he knew. Since the fount, invariably, is the top, the leadership must believe in the change and walk the talk.

'A crucial component of my success was that the Group Chairman implicitly supported me. I had complete freedom to instil the culture I thought would work best for the company. I even routinely told Chairman Sanjay Lalbhai about the practices of my previous company HUL, and how Arvind may replicate these; he never objected. And the fact that we were located in Bangalore, far away from the Group at Ahmedabad, helped enormously. There was no daily control over the change.'

Freedom for the leaders to act! In story after successful story, this stands out as part of the recipe for effective cultural change. And yet it is so hard for many a management to embrace. The trust deficit induces wearying bureaucracy and an environment of endless approvals and feedback. It takes courage to allow leaders to act without perpetually staring into the rearview mirror.

Suresh identified the cultural challenge and decided to focus on a few issues, particularly one element of that transformation – conscious cultivation and nurturing of the 'will do' spirit into the fabric of the company. He realized that the culture must impel every leader to step up, feel accountable and be wedded to the company's success.

For cultural change to gather momentum, it needs to be articulated in terms that everyone who is part of the rank and file understands. The directness of words matters. Like other successful leaders, Suresh's message was encapsulated in simple terms; he defined the desired culture as 'will do'. What such a culture would look like was made the subject of perpetual interactions – in groups, one on one, at the headquarters led by the MD, and in regions by functional heads. These conversations focused on the aspects of behaviour that needed a change to support the proposed philosophy.

On his frequent visits to the stores, Suresh would ask groups of employees, 'What are we trying to achieve as a company?' 'Profitability' was the most common answer. And then a conversation on 'How will we do that?' ensued. At a subliminal level, the idea was to build a sense of ownership by eliciting ideas.

He devised a simple slogan – 1K*10*11 – that expanded to 'achieving Rs 1000 crores of sales with a 10 per cent operating margin by the year 2011'. He missed no opportunity to repeat it. Repeating a message is an effective way in which leaders can establish the seriousness of their intent. When leaders convey cultural change objectives through simple communication and repeat them at every forum, the message resonates and begins to inhabit the collective mindspace. It is an essential step in building culture, for how could one bring about change if team members don't even remember the need for it?

You cannot build a robust culture on the back of employees whose morale is low. Suresh decided that for the change to succeed, every employee must know that the management cared for them. It is a no-brainer that we respond best to those who are *genuinely* interested in our well-being.

Suresh felt that the seeds of a better culture could not be sowed in a land rendered fallow by a lack of genuine caring. He prompted all leaders to ask their followers, 'What is troubling you?' Unsurprisingly, the answer was almost invariably 'poor administration'. That is what needed to be fixed. And experience tells us that the explanation for a culture that triggers poor employee retention often lies in indifferent administration, even though HR analysis goes on touting better remunerative opportunities as the leading cause for outmigration. It isn't always about money, but who in the corporate world believes that?

At the same time, slogans alone do not shift the dunes of culture. Arvind Fashions instituted a completely quantified appraisal system to encourage merit to rise. Training programmes were introduced to look after areas of culture that needed redressal. The Finance department was known to be a ponderously moving train; its name was changed to Customer Service, a clear signal of expectation to the department and the rest of the company.

Also instituted was the SMILE programme, reflecting a focus transcending mere tokenism. SMILE was an acronym that stood for several incentives. One, the employees would always receive salaries right on time. Two, medical facilities well beyond the statutory Employee State Insurance (ESI) – any employee who had served for more than a year was automatically eligible for ₹50,000 in medical support for their family. Three, an automated system that provided career progression and performance details at the click of a button. Four, the company's commitment to employees' learning through scholarships for higher education and making the work environment enjoyable.

A significant component of that enterprise's success came from the unfettered freedom given to each leader. Business heads were to drive the business as they thought fit, mindful that the credit or otherwise of the ultimate delivery would be laid entirely at their doorstep.

There was near-zero interference from above. Suresh sought clarifications and made suggestions only during the monthly meetings. Managers were free to act as they wished, so long as it conformed to the 'will do' mantra. The atmosphere of trust and independence of action blew like fresh air through the company, wafting its dividends to the entire rank and file.

Venkat recalls what that change heralded by Suresh looked like in a few months.

The days leading to Diwali are always a big season for sales. In the run-up to Diwali, Arvind Fashions traditionally redefined the month's targets. Incentives like gold coins were offered to the employees. In this period, Mega Mart stores consistently increased sales by as much as two and a half times.

In 2008, the annual sales of Mega Mart hit Rs 100 crores. In 2010, buoyed by the evolving culture of dynamism and 'will do', the management decided to aim for the moon – achieve 100 crores in a month. It wasn't just a diktat; targets for each store were revised only after a buy-in from the teams.

As the CEO, Venkatachalapathy knew that the numbers were near-impossible to achieve. How do you climb a mountain in one month that had previously always taken a year's back-breaking effort? He toyed with the idea of scaling things down. But the 'will do' spirit had kicked in, and he decided to take counsel of his wildest hopes. With store managers on board, suggestions poured in on tweaking the approach to 'freebies' and the infusion of new stores.

But the beginning was hardly encouraging. In the first four days, stores reported about 60 per cent of the daily average sales target. By the time Dussehra arrived, the stores had pushed themselves to their limits to reach 82 per cent of the running target – 28 against 34 crores. There was still a long way to go. The CEO continued to tell the teams 'to gun for 100 crores'.

'On 30 October, magic happened. We began to exceed the daily targets. Cumulatively we were still lagging, of course. There was a tremendous catch-up ahead of us.'

On 4 November, with one day to go, Mega Mart stores had raked in 90 crores, an impressive feat by any standards. And that is when the teams set about doing the impossible.

In the preceding days, the stores were routinely kept open until 11 p.m., by which time the premises invariably bore the look of having been ransacked by mobs. On the penultimate day, with a shortfall of 10 crores to be met in just a few business hours, the teams worked until 4 a.m. to clear up the aisles. They stocked up fully and prepared the display for the last day. Everyone napped for four hours or less and returned to their battle stations.

Fired up to achieve the unachievable, the team made frenetic efforts to sell. Regular customers were drawn to the store with personal calls, regardless of whether Diwali was likely to be their major festival. Sale figures were relayed every fifteen minutes. By 6 p.m., the score was nudging 96 crores.

At this point, exhausted to the bone, the store teams decided to keep the business open until midnight. When the date turned, Mega Mart had achieved a sale of 100.1 crores for the month.

'We celebrated by taking everyone to Goa. It was clear that something big had shifted inside Mega Mart,' said Venkat.

What had shifted were elements of culture. And there was even a topline to prove it.

IV

The Arvind Fashions story gives us several valuable insights into bringing about cultural change. Let us draw up a summary. Transformation can only start from the very apex of a comprehensible understanding of what must be reformed. The enterprise only succeeds when the harbingers of the cultural shift, i.e. the seniormost bosses, have the blank cheque of authority to prosecute change as per their vision. That is not always easy because it takes courage to allow leaders the unfettered freedom to carry out such an ambitious exercise. And upgrades do not feed on slogans – though its simple articulation helps immensely, as does a regular expression of the objectives by the leadership. Finally, cultural metamorphosis occurs the most in an atmosphere where employees feel wanted and safe.

Going beyond the Arvind Fashions case study, other paradigms need attention. The theme song of successful change is this: it will occur so long as movers and shakers accord genuine importance and attention to critical elements of the desired culture. The key here is the word 'genuine' – or 'authentic' if you prefer. Too many managements confuse slogans with action, vision statements with vision and cliches with inspiration. Remember, people do what works for them. Mere intentions and words will not cut. So, what will?

Cultural transformation will be achieved when all the SOPs, procedures, processes, norms and traditions are aligned with that change. And the rewards and punishments reflect fidelity to the aspects central to the proposed culture. Any glaring contradiction between the desired culture and the above would sound the death knell for the proposed shift.

The last paragraph is so vital I encourage you to reread it.

The Indian Army, aware of the shadow that rewards and punishments cast on its culture, treats some offences as more equal than others. Abandoning a wounded colleague, cowardice and issues of financial probity invariably attract not just expeditious action but harsher outcomes than, say, making an error of judgement on the battlefield. The first set of violations is considered more seriously as they militate against some of the most cherished aspects of the Army's culture. Offences against women are also in the category – of errors of intent – that evoke stringent punishments. But mistakes of judgement on the battlefield or while at work are treated with far more empathy and gentleness. The idea is to fortify the culture of initiative and making decisions in difficult situations.

Since discipline is the bedrock on which the Army readies itself for war, commanding officers have immense powers to punish disciplinary infringements. A CO is empowered to accord weeks of rigorous imprisonment and penal deductions.

The same goes for daily norms. An officer broaching the subject of politics, religion or women in the officers' mess will, in all probability, be instantly stopped in his tracks by others. An open dalliance with these subjects would be considered against the Army's apolitical, secular and 'gentlemanly' culture. Respect for hierarchy and obedience to orders on the battlefield is critical; hence the principle of 'seniority' is strictly followed.* An officer who graduated

* If two Army officers are strolling, the one who is senior would always be on the right. If an Army man walks into another's office, he would never sit in the incumbent's seat, irrespective of seniority. Similarly, the person who is entering an office will invariably salute, no matter what the difference of rank. Some of these examples may appear trivial and sometimes evoke bemusement among civilians, but the fact is that unless all the norms strengthen the culture, there is likely to be dissonance.

from the Academy with greater accolades will forever be considered senior to his colleagues in the same rank.

The seeds of the culture of teamwork – and, indeed, every other critical attribute – are sowed during this initial training. Violation of punctuality, even by a minute, would invite reprimand and more. As a cadet in the National Defence Academy, I remember that week after week, the entire auditorium full of cadets and officers would wait for the arrival of the commandant for an event by silently staring at the giant clock next to the dais. On every single occasion during those three years, the voice that announced, 'Gentlemen, the Commandant', immediately making us rise to our feet, would boom at the designated time, accurate to the last *second*! There was not even one exception.

Similarly, several unwritten norms in training academies are held more sacred than any religious edict. These include never ratting on a colleague (cadets go to extraordinary lengths of enduring physical pain to protect team members) and helping struggling teammates during gruelling long-distance runs, often by carrying their weapons and personal loads.

The conclusions here should be obvious. Rules, regulations, norms must be aligned with the culture you want. And achieving that takes time and thoughtful effort.

V

Concurrently with the effort to align processes, procedures, rewards, punishments, norms, traditions and symbolic gestures, another stratagem needs attention – messaging. What is the organization trying to reinforce, shed or change? This must be conveyed to the rank and file at every opportunity and through various mediums. Wise leaders often begin their addresses by mentioning the cultural elements that are being promoted. In 1983, when Bob Galvin set up the first-ever Competitive Intelligence Group within Motorola, he realized that the enterprise might sputter along at best without a supportive culture. He began to publicly endorse this group, telling whoever was listening that its mandate was to be 'sufficiently annoying' in search of facts 'beyond the headlights'.[1]

The messaging must also be concise and memorable. Clunky statements that attempt to be all things to all employees can never secure attention, much less recall.

Rajeev Bakshi, a former MD of Cadbury, believes that businesses – indeed all organizations, including the armed forces and political parties – undergo continual change. This happens because business imperatives demand or the leadership pivots to a different thought process and strategy. To enjoy even a modicum of success, the culture – the collective behaviour of the system, how individuals and teams react to a particular stimulus – must be aligned to that change. Or mediocrity – even failure – will surely be written in the stars.

Rajeev joined Cadbury in 1992 as a director. He had been inducted after a successful stint at Lakmé. These were the years when the winds of liberalization began to break the Licence Raj's cobwebs. In the preceding years, Cadbury had struggled. Its products – biscuits, ice creams and chocolates – were punching below their weight. Part of the reason was the company's culture that flowed from the mindset of the management. Cadbury's leadership had been forced to adopt a defensive business strategy; the lack of freedom to import machines to improve production and its parent organization's apathy to field financial resources in a closed economy were examples of what fuelled that thinking. 'I was wet behind the ears, even a bit immature,' Rajeev told me. 'But I had been mandated to bring about a major change of direction, especially in marketing. We needed a giant leap.'

In devising a strategy for that leap, Rajeev discovered a facet central to creating the culture: the management's perception regarding the heart of the business. He found that at Cadbury, the belief that permeated across the board was that 'manufacturing' was the crux. You could hardly blame them for it – the core competency of most top-rung leaders was manufacturing. That wasn't exclusive to Cadbury. Securing a licence and manufacturing were the only mountains to climb during the closed economy. Marketing was but a blip on most radars.

As you may well know by now, cultural change needs two catalysts – an unambiguous shift in the mindset of the leadership and a few initial successes. The rank and file must see it working for the company and its future self-interests before the nascent culture embeds itself.

'This is what separates boys from men. Leaders have to be at the forefront of change. Only then will the boys follow,' Rajeev believes. For culture to sink into the fabric, leaders must display a consistency of actions – a lesson we have repeatedly seen in the Army.

The narrative needs powerful messaging. Not the rambling and jargon-filled bullet points that adorn the walls of many a company – and, I daresay, are seldom even glanced at – but a sharp, easy-to-comprehend message that rings bells of motivation in the employees' minds. It is often a slogan but is pregnant with the crux of the company's business purpose.

When Rajeev became the MD, his slogan to everyone was 'a Cadbury in every pocket'. It wasn't a marketing tagline meant for the rest of the world. It was a clarion call to the rank and file to bring about a shift in their mindsets – and culture. Its five-word simplicity created a visual image: ' We must become the leader, we must grow, we must be universally desired.'

Slogans. Names. Symbols. The results can be dramatic when these are crafted with care to cloak a powerful message with overt simplicity. Shireesh Sahai learnt this lesson in the early part of his fifteen years with GE Healthcare. 'When you have a goal, rather than laying down revenue targets or profit or cost reduction and so on, give it a name that evokes an image of what is to be achieved.'

Giving an endeavour a name or concise slogan burns it into the team's memory; an inspiring phrase can spur people to put in a more significant effort.

That is what 'a Cadbury in every pocket' did. It told the company that the goal was not manufacturing but creating a huge market. The chocolate it made was not merely to be produced or manufactured but desired, a simple message that strove to shift the cultural focus from manufacturing to marketing and business development.

Over the ages, the Army has mastered the stratagem of simple messages that have created a powerful cultural imprint. An expression that has entered the DNA of every soldier is '*ek goli, ek dushman*' (one bullet, one enemy) – it underscores the culture of weapon proficiency and training. There's also 'one leg on the ground', a tactical edict that stipulates teams never to throw themselves into imbalance and that a part of the team should be stable while the other manoeuvres. 'The more you train in peace, the less you will bleed in war' is also popular. They rule the collective memory of soldiers like commandments.

Messaging matters. And reinforcing it from every platform matters equally.

But a culture nudged into shape by messaging can only be sustained when two other requirements are met: the consistency of the example set by leaders and training aligned with those messages.

We have already spoken about how leaders set personal examples in the Army. Cadets aspiring to be officers are trained far harder than other soldiers. During drills, they themselves go through every hardship a soldier is expected to endure. They must set far higher professional proficiency, conduct and behaviour standards than the men they command. Units wherein there is dissonance between what the leaders profess and what they are seen doing invariably perform poorly in both war and peace.

Then, of course, the Army's unique focus on training does not stop after recruitment and pre-commissioning regimens; it gathers momentum. There are the daily physical drills, individual training exercise 'cycles', firing on the range, specialist courses in training establishments, cadres designed to prepare soldiers for promotions, an exercise called battle inoculation to put soldiers through 'live' firing, collective'battle exercises', sand model discussions, wargames to validate plans and a great deal of academic instruction as well.*

Intensive training certainly spurs professional competence. But when the curriculum is thoughtfully designed, it also strengthens the prevalent culture.

We see this manifested in IndiGo's on-time performance.

VI

'I was born in IndiGo,' Pratik Sen, a trainer at the airline's IFly Training Academy, told me. I asked him to explain.

Raised in an affluent Bengali family of academically brilliant members – a clutch of IIT and IIM alums, some with gold medals – he wanted to chart a different course for himself. Becoming a doctor or engineer didn't excite him. These were the early days of the new millennium. Aviation, as an industry was beginning to explode onto the scene. He gravitated towards it, seeking a life of glamour and, hopefully, without any more academic grind.

After passing through the portals of the Air Hostess Academy at Kolkata, he briefly flirted with hospitality jobs in Dubai. That didn't hold his fascination for long, so he returned, this time as an aspirant for a new airline company named IndiGo. His first lesson in leadership came early – the co-founder Rahul Bhatia

* Officers and soldiers undertake long courses, sometimes in civilian institutions, to earn under- or postgraduate degrees. Many are sent abroad for training. Others, like me, who joined the Army after graduating from school, finally ended up with a bachelor's, an MSc and an MPhil degree, besides learning at think tanks overseas.

himself interviewed the prospective candidate for one of the most junior positions in the company. He became acutely aware during the conversation that there was a palpable sensitivity towards punctuality – schedules were respected, and so was others' time.

When I met him, Pratik was a trainer, the youngest ever to take up that role. 'From day one, two things were drummed into me – always smile at your customers and ensure they reach their destination on time.' In his eyes, the company's culture validates that instruction. Everybody from the uppermost echelons in the management directed downwards has an acute sense of time. In his thirteen-year stint, Pratik does not remember a single month when there was a delay in salaries; everyone got their pay cheque on either the last day of the month or the previous Friday. That sends a powerful subliminal message about the implicit adherence to schedules. 'We are creatures of self-interest,' he said with a chuckle. 'And when the company's culture converges the self-interest of its employees with a fundamental tenet of its culture, it strengthens the latter.'

The reporting time for training classes, scheduled for 8 a.m., is set at 7:40 a.m. The stratagem ensures that people are set up for success in punctuality. Trainees are taught to manage disruptions ('Irregular Operations' or 'iOps'). If the company cab doesn't reach your home by the cut-off time, take an Uber, and the company will reimburse you. But be on time.

Based on their experience, most domestic travellers settle into a preference for one airline over others. Everyone has their personal criteria for making this choice, but most travellers will likely rank punctuality as a significant attribute. Then there are other factors, including hygiene, the crew's friendliness, the quality and variety of fare served on board and leg space. But 'being on time' is what ultimately counts the most. On this attribute, what is the differentiator that creates the gap between the leaders and the laggards?

There are many factors and, clearly, training is prime among them. But all the other efforts of the airline also help solidify its culture. Indeed, it can be argued that the ongoing practices generate a focus on grounding and other 'factors', thus driving a self-fuelling engine that silently and powerfully shapes the airline's culture. This hypothesis is valid for all organizations.

IndiGo has repeatedly been rated India's best domestic airline. In 2019, when I visited the IFly Academy, its market share stood at a staggering 49.9 per cent. At that point, it needed no rearview mirror because, at 13.9 per cent, Air India, still the national carrier, was several bends behind, followed by SpiceJet at 13.1 per cent. Others were trailing these leaders, but two names that would have starred in such a compilation even a decade ago – Jet Airways and Kingfisher – are not even on the scoreboard today.*

That was not always the case. In 2010, Jet Airways was the leader with 26 per cent, followed closely by Kingfisher at 23 per cent.

What brought about such a reversal? To be sure, the quality of decision-making would have played a critical role. But the intervention of the leadership and the environment it creates is integral to the organizational culture of any setup, and airlines are not immune to this rule.

IndiGo came into being in 2006 and surprised aviation watchers by ignoring high-profile routes for its inaugural flight. Instead, it chose Delhi–Guwahati–Imphal and back as its first flight, reflecting its management's innovative mindset and courage to depart from the beaten path.

Those who have been associated with the airline from its inception will tell you that IndiGo chose people with rich experience to lay a solid foundation. For example, it brought in Shakti Loomba, who had years of experience with Air India and its subsidiaries as Vice President (Operations).

---

* Quoting data released by the DGCA, CNBCTV18 reported IndiGo's April 2023 market share at a 'dominant' 57.5 per cent, Tata-owned Vistara's market share at 8.7 per cent, SpiceJet at 5.8 per cent, GoFirst at around 6.4 per cent, Air India at 8.6 per cent and Air Asia at 7.6 per cent.

The airline wanted to embed itself as one with a difference and chose on-time operations as a critical attribute. In those days, a delightfully elastic sense of time defined the culture of many airlines. IndiGo set about changing that. Its pioneer pilots were required to train at its Operational Control Centre in Gurgaon, where every nuance of 'being on time' was discussed. 'On-Time Performance' conferences three times a week are still an assiduously followed norm. Timelines are regularly reviewed backwards to define the time for each activity, such as closing the counters before a plane is airborne without losing its original slot. The DGCA recognized the intrinsic value of these norms and legislated it for the entire ecosystem.

A visit to the IFly Academy brings the focus on punctuality in sharp relief. A giant glass board that carries the name of each team member of the academy and their punctuality status for that day greets you as you stroll through the office. I spent several hours attending various activities and returned after a few days to watch a graduation ceremony, during which too there was not a minute's deviation from the programme schedule.

Training and other sets of processes, standard operating procedures, checklists, rewards and punishment systems have resulted in a distinctive culture of punctuality that is visible even to the most indifferent observer. At every stage, from approach to counters to boarding the buses to getting seated in the aircraft, you receive the polite but firm nudge from each employee to ensure no delays. Every employee seems to be time-sensitive and keen to keep the wheels turning, something that can only be explained by one word – culture.

How has such a culture come about? Capt Rakesh Srivastava, who served for twenty-two years with the Indian Air Force as a fighter pilot and two stints with private companies, joined IndiGo in 2010. He provides some sharp insights.

The company's values, pasted everywhere for all to see, are:

- On-time performance
- Low fares
- A courteous and hassle-free experience

Notice that every employee can influence two of the values at the heart of punctuality. And the secret of IndiGo's culture is that the leadership has made every team member aware that they have a personal stake in upholding those values. The ultimate secret of culture-building is sensitizing each individual to the role they are required to play. Unless that happens, the glossy posters proclaiming values are just decorations on the wall.

The leadership recognized that to create an 'On-time performance' culture, it must focus on each element of the vast chain engaged in a complex operation supporting each flight. Every cog in the wheel is vital, from loaders that are not even IndiGo employees to engineers involved in maintenance and rectification to cabin crew, ground staff and, of course, the pilots. Every moving part must act in unison to ensure that the flight can be 'turned around' for the next sortie within the stipulated timeframe, often as short as a twenty-seven-minute pit stop.

'Everyone is involved. I remember watching ground staff racing across the tarmac to complete all documentation relating to fuel, etc., so that we could take off on time. The question is, how has IndiGo welded nearly 16,000 people to that central theme?' Srivastava asked before sharing the answer.

At IndiGo, instilling a culture aligned with values begins with an extensively structured onboarding. Many companies squander this opportunity. For them, onboarding is an HR-led lip service couched in bureaucratic tokenism. For example, in some airlines, the onboarding process takes two months. At IndiGo, this takes seven months, a high-cost strategy that the airline willingly exercises to sustain its practices and culture.

Leadership at all levels makes great effort to relay expectations from each employee. Annually, when KRAs are drawn up, on-time performance forms an integral part of the list and applies down the hierarchy to the last technician or employee. Adherence to the values is ensured by building an environment of responsibility and loyalty, recognition and constant evaluation. Take the engineers, for example. The top leadership visits each station monthly to review processes and challenges, giving every single employee the chance to regularly to meet the higher-ups.

IndiGo has a robust system of acknowledging high performance. The CEO and other senior leaders attend reward and recognition celebrations. Along with the team members, even retirees are on the guest list. Commendations are given to the best-performing employees, down to the baggage loaders. There are various ways an achiever may be recognized: appreciation, gratitude, commendation and certificates of excellence. Or they may get virtual (online) applause for, say, treating a customer well, ensuring the speeding up of activities to ensure punctuality and so on. The company's internal portal prominently features such high performers.

IndiGo also follows an institutionalized system of feedback. The employees being onboarded are asked if each part of the training was useful, and the management uses their responses to tweak the system.

The leadership holds meetings to review performance thrice a week.* The COO chairs these sessions. Every flight that was delayed for any reason is discussed to dissect the underlying causes. During these review meeting, the station managers, the engineering head and the Chief Pilot Line Operations (who looks after cultural issues, including punctuality) are available on the call for their input. 'Even if the doors of a flight closed slightly later than the stipulated time,

---

* Capt Srivastva said that if the airline slips below the top position in On Time Performance record of all domestic carriers, it sends enormous alarm bells within the top-hierarchy.

it would be analysed threadbare. Was the boarding gate closed late? Did the buses ferrying the passengers take more time than planned? Was the cabin not ready in time? During the interaction, everything is mapped. Whatever the reason for delays – the team aims to fix it for the future.*

You would think every airline should be able to replicate this, but that is not the case. Culture cannot be bent to your will with slogans or money. It is challenging because even the best-laid plans and strategies cannot succeed without building a culture that supports them. To shift the hurdle called culture, organizations need a leadership full of tremendous energy and focus, capable of crafting thoughtful processes, training and rewards. Not to mention supply inspiration through an enabling work environment and personal example.

It is evident that IndiGo gets it.†

---

* I recently got more first-hand evidence. Waiting for our flight (by a small ATR aircraft) to be announced, I saw an IndiGo staff member walking about looking at the size of handbags of the waiting passengers. Wherever he felt that the bag was large and might cause space issues and, therefore, delay, he would ask the passenger if he was flying by the IndiGo flight and offer to check-in the handbag without any charge. The entire proactive exercise was aimed at obviating a delay.

† It is not to say that the entire success is attributable to the culture of punctuality – though the 'always on time' perception must fuel demand for the airline's tickets. IndiGo also introduced simple, common-sense strategies like ensuring that 'all surplus capacity is used for carrying cargo'. This proposition brings far more revenue than passengers and certainly much more than letting the surplus go to waste! It decided to offer no free food on board, rejected the idea of installing even low-cost food warmers on aircraft to obviate wastage and accidents, chose to provide no freebies whatsoever, and introduced corporate accounts with great reluctance. Many other low-cost airlines have not achieved such spectacular results because revenue generation and its first cousin cost-cutting are not esoteric goals but have to be intrinsic to the company's culture.

VII

A culture change is not an academic exercise that produces somewhat intangible results. As chapter after chapter of case studies from the Army tell us, culture transforms individuals to a point where they start producing extraordinary results. The joint effort of J. Suresh and Venkatachalapathy to revamp the culture of Arvind Fashions and Mega Mart stores resulted in many wins.

Whenever Venkat visited the Mega Mart stores, he would invariably gather the employees and ask: 'Who pays your salary?' Each time, the spontaneous chorus from the smiling bunch was 'the customer', he told me a decade later. When this sentiment rises above cliched sloganeering, as was the case with Mega Mart and Arvind Fashions, magic happens. The story of Govind Raj shows us a slice of that magic.

Govindraj was the thirtysomething manager of a small Mega Mart store – no more than 1500 square feet – in Kukatpally, Hyderabad. He had downed the shutters for the night and was approaching home to rest his weary frame. It was past 10 p.m., and a downpour seemed imminent.

For its size, the Kukatpally store was considered successful in 2012; every month it returned figures of 15–18 lakhs worth of sales. Govindraj's proactive approach to staying connected with customers was no meagre reason for its success in the changing culture of ownership and independence of action.

As Govindraj neared his house, his phone rang. On the other end was a harried customer calling from Panjagutta, some twelve kilometres away. The man, a senior IT professional, was due to take an early morning flight to London, where was supposed to make a high-stakes presentation to a prospective client. He had spent the last few days completely immersed in preparing for the big moment. And he had been so preoccupied that he had missed out on a major detail; since his wedding a year ago, he had put on considerable weight and now, at the very last minute, discovered that none of his business suits fitted him by inches. He could not present himself for the all-important sales pitch to his British client unless he had a proper suit to wear. Since all the stores were closed and he only had Govindraj's mobile number, he was calling the manager for help.

'Of course,' said Govindraj. 'Just give me the details of size, colour preferences and your address.' He turned his scooter around and picked up a customer sales assistant from his home. As the duo, riding a two-wheeler, returned to open the store – no doubt in violation of the laid down norms – it began to rain heavily.

Govindraj picked five suits which, in his judgement, fitted the requirement. He then dug out large polybags and loaded them. As midnight approached, Govindraj and the assistant drove through the downpour for forty-five minutes to the customer's house for a trial and selection. He tried all the suits, made his pick and expressed hearfelt gratitude.

The postscript of the story is this: the now dapper customer did secure a significant order in London. When he returned, he headed straight for the Kukatpally store and made a large purchase.

Are there other Govindrajs who display uncommon initiatives that, over time, reap great dividends for their companies? Certainly there are. But such feats are no doubt an exception, not the rule. Often, we all come across a manager or employee who cites a rule or timing to decline making a sale or helping out with a service. When that happens, you can instantly see the wheels of hesitant thought turning in the service provider's mind: 'This is beyond the stipulated timeframes or outside my remit, I might be upbraided. I will surely not be appreciated. Anyway, I am not the boss, so what the hell!'

A spontaneous initiative can certainly not be widespread in any organization unless there is an implicit buy-in, a culture-driven perception that each employee makes a difference, and a wide berth is available to operate with freedom. Evidently, these boxes ticked for Govindraj, despite his salary of ₹25,000 a month.

VIII

I could have easily called this concluding section 'The Checklist'. But to avoid reducing the eight chapters to dry bullet points, I decided to do what the Army does at the end of each battle exercise. It distils the lessons and throws up ideas for further exploration.

What, then, is the summary of the steps you need to take to transform your organization's culture? What might be the caveats? And which elements of the Army's culture that we delved into might apply to a corporate entity?

The Army and the corporate worlds are acutely dissimilar in many facets. It is not my case that anyone should make a headlong plunge into copying the Army's culture. The theme here has been to underscore the value of having a culture that is robust and thoughtfully crafted.

But notwithstanding the stark differences between the Army and corporate bodies, a few attributes can most certainly be replicated, albeit in forms that are applicable to each respective organization. That is partly so because the concepts of leadership – and culture – have a certain universality. We can all share the base recipe.

The following framework is merely a summary. It should be read with the previous chapters:

Firstly, culture comes into being and will eventually change only from the very top. The highest rungs of leadership must possess a lucid understanding of what needs to be discarded, embraced or tweaked.

Second, the changemakers must be clear that the dunes of culture do not shift if one blows words at them. Articulation is important too, but the transformation will always demand a great deal of coordinated action and time.

Third, if there is a lack of clarity about the existing cultural infirmities, the management should undertake a formal diagnosis. A thoughtfully designed qualitative analysis, stemming from interviews with a broad cross-section of team members, is likely to yield the most optimum understanding. This may be validated through quantitative analysis, though one must be cautioned that the weightage accorded to attributes and questions will heavily influence the results.

Fourth, once the leadership is clear about the cultural deficiencies, it needs to review all existing processes, norms, traditions, rewards, punishments and rules to ensure that nothing contradicts the desired attributes of the proposed culture. For instance, if improving accountability is the goal, the rewards-and-recognition policy must be geared to celebrate those who outstandingly display this aspect. The penalties for the converse should also be in the statute book. Similarly, the KRAs and KPIs must include 'accountability', and HR should design a measurable yardstick. The CEO or the MD should refer to their focus on accountability from every forum. There should be no tacit or inadvertent encouragement for violating the principle of accountability. The revising of all policies and procedures will be time-consuming. It must be handled by a thoughtful and experienced set of individuals who have the management's trust – and access to information.

Fifth, the leadership should select a group of high-performance employees to carry out workshops to explain the proposed changes and the underlying rationale. This exercise will motivate some employees to buy in, who can then become the management's 'ambassadors' to promote change, among others. These workshops can gradually have other editions for the remaining employees.

Sixth, the management should discuss the proposed changes in small groups with as many employees as possible.

Seventh, the leadership must be acutely aware of its role in catalyzing change through personal example. If a culture of austerity is the goal, the top rung must start with itself – and for all to see. If punctuality is on the proposed menu, the movers and shakers have to set the tone by being on or ahead of time. Leading by example is non-negotiable.

Eighth, an environment of genuine employee care is the fertile soil needed to let a new culture flourish. No spontaneous change can ever occur in a toxic workplace marked by bias and opacity. The rank and file must also be able to see that the changes benefit the company and them equally. When an organization extends the line of sight of its benign attention beyond the employee to their families, the dividends may be disproportionate to the effort.

Lastly, the leadership must persist. Cultural change is not an easy enterprise. It is a needle that moves slowly but surely, if the project is implemented in the right way. Once a policy has been put into place, there must be no deviation for anyone. A strong whiff of favouritism is enough to stymie the efforts towards change. Simultaneously, the leadership must stay tuned to the response – by structured and candid feedback from all the stakeholders.

The selection of areas for change would be particular to each organization. Everyone can, however, benefit from some of the strongest suits of the Indian Army.

At the very apex is the lesson of leading by example and always from the front. It is hard to imagine a company, club, NGO or family that would not benefit from this powerful leadership facet.

Next comes the valuable strategy of making everyone aware of their contribution to the organization's success. Each team member needs to be crystal clear about what is expected of them – and what they can expect from the organization. We have a role, not merely a job description.

All equations within the company – especially between the leadership and the rank and file – should be relational and not transactional. Selfishness and inauthenticity can hardly be the ingredients for a great workplace – and its culture.

Encourage storytelling and recounting history to sow the seeds of latent pride in the company.

Train. Training not only makes you competent, but it also increases your luck quotient.

Last but not least, if you want a culture of initiative and proactive risk-taking, learn to foster a climate wherein errors of judgement are treated with gentle empathy, errors of omission are corrected and mistakes of intent are dealt with an iron hand. This critical differentiation can teach leaders how to correct the course of an erring follower without destroying initiative.

Many leaders talk about culture but do little to create a winning one. Perhaps deep inside, they do not believe that culture shows up in the company's revenue or its bottom line. Maybe some even believe that it is a peripheral aspect that does not move the needle of success. Nothing could be more erroneous and potentially self-defeating.

A peek into the Indian Army's culture – and that of many companies – will provide a serious professional with the evidence that culture is the greatest competitive advantage a leader can create for his outfit. It is in fact the main ingredient in the secret sauce of victories.

A thoughtfully created culture equals robustness and expediency. It can only lead to wins.

NOTES

Introduction

1. 'Kashmir: How I Started A War', *Time*, 12 July 1999. Available: https://content.time.com/time/subscriber/article/0,33009,991457,00.html.

Chapter 1

1. Stephen Conmy, 'What Does Culture Eats Strategy for Breakfast Mean?' The Corporate Governance Institute, 4 May 2022. Available: https://www.thecorporategovernanceinstitute.com/insights/lexicon/what-does-culture-eats-strategy-for-breakfast-mean/.
2. Nasim Zehra, *From Kargil to the Coup: Events That Shook Pakistan* (Lahore: Sang-e-Meel Publications, 2018).
3. Ayaz Amir, 'The Ghost That Won't Go Away', *Dawn*. 23 July 2004. Available: https://www.dawn.com/news/1072909.
4. General V. P. Malik, *Kargil from Surprise to Victory* (New Delhi: HarperCollins Publishers India, 2010), 243.
5. Ibid, 305.
6. Imran, 'Kargil - Tales & Bodies ...' *Mani Junction*. 7 August 2021. Available: https://www.meemainseen.com/2021/08/kargil-3/.
7. Rone Tempest, 'Sri Lanka Guerrilla Chief Accepts Peace Plan : Tamil Tigers to Avoid Showdown With Indian Troops, Surrender Weapons', *Los Angeles Times*, 5 August 1987. Available: https://www.latimes.com/archives/la-xpm-1987-08-05-mn-820-story.html.

Chapter 2

1. Ashraf Wani, 'J&K: Army Major among 4 soldiers killed in Pulwama encounter today', *India Today*, 18 February 2019. Available: https://www.indiatoday.in/india/story/jammu-and-kashmir-pulwama-encounter-1458498-2019-02-17.
2. 'Army Major killed, another officer and two jawans injured in Kashmir encounter', *India Today*, 17 June 2019. Available: https://www.indiatoday.in/india/story/army-major-killed-another-officer-and-2-jawans-injured-in-kashmir-encounter-1550513-2019-06-17
3. 'Sohan Singh - By Field Marshal Sam Manekshaw', *StoryWorks*, 28 December 2018. Available: https://www.youtube.com/watch?v=zbc9Motmbgo.
4. Neeraj Bali, 'Of all the strengths of the Indian Army, its culture is the foremost', *Financial Express*, 10 January 2023. Available: https://www.google.com/search?q=Edmond+Chandler%2C+who%2C+writing+in+1919+in+the+Sepoy%2C+said+that+%E2%80%98%27the+Gurkha+does+not+love+his+officer+because+he+is+a+Sahib%2C+but+because+he+is+his+Sahib%2C+and+the+officer+has+to+prove+that+he+is+his+Sahib.

Chapter 3

1. Ralph Waldo Emerson Quotes and Sayings. Available: https://lovequotes.symphonyoflove.net/ralph-waldo-emerson-love-quotes-and-famous-sayings.html
2. Stephen P. Cohen, *The Indian Army: Its Contribution to the Development of a Nation*, (New Delhi: Oxford India Paperbacks, 1990), 51.
3. John A. Nagl, 'Preface', *Learning to Eat Soup with a Knife: Counterinsurgency Lessons from Malaya and Vietnam* (Chicago: University of Chicago Press, 2000). Available: https://press.uchicago.edu/Misc/Chicago/567702.html.
4. Lt Gen H S Panag(R), Twitter. Available: https://twitter.com/rwac48/status/853103586028302336.

Chapter 4

1. Norman F. Dixon, *On The Psychology of Military Incompetence* (New York: Basic Books, 1976).
2. As recounted by General V. P. Malik in his book *Kargil – From Surprise to Victory* (New Delhi: HarperCollins India, 2010), 160.

Chapter 6

1. 'Wife of soldier martyred in 2018, Jyoti Nainwal becomes Indian Army officer', *India Today*, 21 November 2021. Available: https://www.indiatoday.in/india/story/wife-soldier-kulgam-martyr-2018-indian-army-officer-jyoti-nainwal-1879134-2021-11-21.
2. '"Will become Army Doctor," says 11-yr old daughter of Late Major Deepak Nainwal', *DNA India*, 20 November 2021. Available: https://www.dnaindia.com/india/report-will-become-army-doctor-says-11-yr-old-daughter-of-late-major-deepak-nainwal-2920484.

Chapter 7

1. Brig J. P. Dalvi, *Himalayan Blunder - The Curtain Raiser to the Sino-Indian War of 1962* (New Delhi: Natraj Publishers, 1969), 253.
2. Malik, *Kargil*, 207.
3. Cohen, *The Indian Army*, 52.

Chapter 8

1. Jenny Fisher, 'Competitive Intelligence A Case Study of Motorola's Corporate Competitive Intelligence Group, 1983–2009', *The Intelligencer Journal of U.S. Intelligence Studies* 20, no. 3 (Spring/Summer 2014): 1. Available at: https://www.afio.com/publications/FISHER_BusIntel_CaseStudy_Motorola_FINAL_2014July14.pdf.

LIST OF ABBREVIATIONS

AGL: Automatic Grenade Launcher
ANPRC: Army Navy Personal Radio Communication
ASC: Army Service Corps
ATR: Avions de transport régional (Regional Transport Airplanes)
AWWA: Army Wives Welfare Association
Brig: Brigadier
BSF: Border Security Force
Capt: Captain
Cdr: Commander
CHM: Company Havildar Major
CHRO: Chief Human Resources Officer
CO: Commanding Officer
COAS: Chief of Army Staff
Col: Colonel
COO: Chief Operating Officer
CRPF: Central Reserve Police Force
DG: Director General
DGCA: Directorate General of Civil Aviation
DGMO: Director General of Military Operations
DHA: Defence Housing Authority
Div: Division
DRDO: Defence Research and Development Organisation

EME: Electrical and Mechanical Engineers
ESI: Employee State Insurance
Gen: General
GOC: General Officer Commanding
GR: Gorkha Rifles
GTO: Ground Test Officer
Hav: Havildar
HMG: Heavy Machine Gun
HUL: Hindustan Unilever Limited
IAF: Indian Air Force
IED: Improvised Explosive Device
IIM: Indian Institute of Management
IIT: Indian Institute of Technology
ISI: Inter-Services Intelligence
ITBP: Indo-Tibetan Border Police
JCO: Junior Commissioned Officer
KPI: Key Performance Indicator
KRA: Key Result Area/ Key Responsibility Area
LAC: Line of Actual Control
LMG: Light Machine Gun
LoC: Line of Control
Lt: Lieutenant
Lt Cdr: Lieutenant Commander
Lt Col: Lieutenant Colonel
Lt Gen: Lieutenant General
LTTE: Liberation Tigers of Tamil Eelam
Maj: Major
Maj Gen: Major General
MMG: Medium Machine Gun
MVC: Maha Vir Chakra
NCC: National Cadet Corps
NCO: Non-Commissioned Officer
NDA: National Defence Academy

NEFA: Northeast Frontier Agency
NLI: Northern Light Infantry Regiment
NSCN: National Socialist Council of Nagaland
OR: Other Ranks
QRT: Quick Reaction Team
R&AW: Research and Analysis Wing
RAJRF/ RAJ RIF: Rajputana Rifles
RAP: Regimental Aid Post
SASO: Senior Air Staff Officer
SD: Staff Duties
SF: Special Forces
SIKH LI: Sikh Light Infantry
SMILE: Support for Marginalized Individuals for Livelihood and Enterprise
SOP: Standing Operating Procedure
Sqn Ldr: Squadron Leader
SS: Short Service
TCS: TATA Consultancy Services
TIDCO: Tamil Nadu Industrial Development Corporation
ULFA: United Liberation Front of Asom
VCO: Viceroy's Commissioned Officer
VrC: Vir Chakra
WAC: Western Air Command

ACKNOWLEDGEMENTS

This book is based on conversations with several exceptional, brave and selfless people who stirred a million emotions in me as they recounted the stories that form the fount for the lessons this book offers. Their names are listed below, but I sincerely apologize in advance if I inadvertently made any omissions.

Gen V. P. Malik, one of the most respected soldiers of my time; Lt Gen Praveen Bakshi, my lifelong idol; Lt Gen Nirbhay Sharma, who taught me several leadership lessons through his conduct; the inimitably courageous Jubin Matthews; my forever friend Surinder Chhikara; Lt Gen (now Governor) K. T. Parnaik and other quintessential soldier–leaders Mohit Saxena, Binoy Poonnen, Alin Saha, S. S. Sahota, Sanjay Bhide, T. S. Gill, Pradeep Rathee, Avin Uthaiya and Lt Col R. S. Sethi – they were all generous with their time.

As indeed were B. S. Raju, Anil Sengar, K. H. Singh, Prakash Menon, Rajiv Shirwalkar, Sunil Nautiyal, Devika Gupta, Nilaav Surendra, Mahesh Bhure, Sanjay Singh, Sai Sankar, Sundaresan, Rajeev Athreye, S. K. Dua, Paul Vinay Kumar and the master wordsmith Maj Gen Raj Mehta.

An important chapter in this book is about the contribution of families – particularly women – to strengthening the Indian Army's cultural fibre. A glimpse into this phenomenon came from interactions with Sushmita Pandey, Swati Mahadik, Nitika Kaul, Riya Nehra and Santoshi Babu.

I have drawn inspiration and support from several friends. Girish and Meghna exemplify grace and courage; the account of their selfless endeavours (after their son Maj Akshay made the supreme sacrifice) is recounted in two chapters. Author Chander Suta Dogra has been a valuable sounding board and cheerleader for me. I owe a debt of gratitude to two people who have always expressed greater faith in my abilities than I ever had – Brig V. C. 'Dimpy' Khanna and my friend Shekhar Naidu.

I received some excellent support from leaders in the corporate sector. Capt Rakesh Srivastava; Summi Sharma and Pratik (all from IndiGo); my brother Nittin Dutt; ex-MD of Arvind Fashions Ltd. J. Suresh; Venkatachalapathy, previously of Mega Mart; Shireesh Sahai; Raj Narayan and Rajeev Bakshi gave me their time and inputs magnanimously.

My gratitude to Shreya Gupta of Pan Macmillan India, who did the last round of editing; she surprised me with her exceptional eye for detail and style – and the consequent revelations of the imperfections of my effort! Finally, the amazingly meticulous Teesta Guha Sarkar, who edited the book and shored up my confidence with compliments while simultaneously murmuring that my work pushed her to do 'heavy lifting', is why the book may read well. The flaws that still linger on its pages are attributable to me.